*FOOD WASTE,
FOOD INSECURITY,
AND THE
GLOBALIZATION
OF FOOD BANKS*

FOOD WASTE, FOOD INSECURITY, AND THE GLOBALIZATION OF FOOD BANKS

Daniel N. Warshawsky

UNIVERSITY OF IOWA PRESS, IOWA CITY

University of Iowa Press, Iowa City 52242
Copyright © 2023 by Daniel N. Warshawsky
uipress.uiowa.edu

ISBN 978-1-60938-933-8 (pbk)
ISBN 978-1-60938-934-5 (ebk)

Printed in the United States of America

Design by April Leidig

No part of this book may be reproduced or used in any form or by any means without permission in writing from the publisher. All reasonable steps have been taken to contact copyright holders of material used in this book. The publisher would be pleased to make suitable arrangements with any whom it has not been possible to reach.

Printed on acid-free paper

Cataloging-in-Publication data is on file at the Library of Congress.

Photo used on pages ii–iii: Capital Area Food Bank in NE, Washington, D.C., in 2018. USDA photo by Preston Keres.

To my parents

CONTENTS

Acknowledgments ix

Preface xiii

Introduction 1

1 The Rise of the Food Bank 9

2 Food Banking in the United States 31

3 Food Banking in Israel and Southwestern Asia 53

4 Food Banking in Germany and Denmark 65

5 Food Banking in Italy and Hungary 79

6 Food Banks in India and South Africa 91

Conclusion: Putting Food Banks in Their Place 117

Notes 131

Bibliography 163

Index 201

ACKNOWLEDGMENTS

I want to thank the many people who inspired me to write this book. To start, I would like to thank my academic advisor, Jennifer Wolch, for her guidance and support during my time as a graduate student and junior faculty member at the University of Southern California and beyond. She has been instrumental in every step of my academic career, guiding me through my dissertation, job search, and early career. Jennifer has provided me with critical feedback on my writing, advice on how and where to publish, and guidance on how to build a successful academic career. Her comments and suggestions on my book proposal were critical in the development of this book. In addition, I would like to thank John Wilson at the University of Southern California for offering me my first academic position and showing me how to be a successful member of the academy. Without their combined mentorship, I would not be where I am today. They have been important role models for me as I started my academic career.

Also, I would like to thank my colleagues in the School of Social Sciences and International Studies at Wright State University. To start, I am especially grateful to Myron Levine for reading drafts of this book. His comments, friendship, and encouragement were invaluable as I edited this book. Also, Jerri Killian, December Green, and Laura Luehrmann have been important leaders in the department and encouraged my professional growth as a faculty member. Other faculty and staff within the department formerly known as the School of Public and International Affairs who deserve thanks are Liam Anderson, Shirley Barber, Enam Choudhury, Carlos Costa, John Feldmeier, Edward Fitzgerald, Lee Hannah, Rashida Hussain, Pramod Kantha, Margie McLellan, Vaughn Shannon, Tracy Snipe, Jen Subban, Mary Wenning, and Sean Wilson. I have been very fortunate to have had such support and camaraderie from faculty colleagues at Wright State.

I also want to thank my previous mentors and colleagues across the academy, including Michael Dear, William Worger, Jamie Peck, David Wilson, Geoffrey DeVerteuil, Jonathan Crush, Bruce Frayne, Jane Battersby-Lennard, Susan Kamei, Robert Vos, Darren Ruddell, Yao-Yi Chiang, and Lisa Sedano. Thanks to you for your guidance and continued professional support and friendship over these years.

The University of Iowa Press has proved to be an excellent fit for this book. Approximately ten years ago, I had a conversation with Catherine Cocks, who was an acquisitions editor at Iowa at that time. She encouraged me to submit a book proposal on my work on food banks. At that point, I was still in the field researching and writing; however, my conversation with her sparked my interest in writing a book. In addition, my positive discussions with her propelled me to think of Iowa many years later, once I was ready to submit a book proposal and subsequent manuscript.

Led by director Jim McCoy, the staff at the University of Iowa Press have guided this book from draft to publication. It has been a pleasure to work with everyone at Iowa. In particular, I want to thank Jim McCoy, managing editor Susan Hill Newton, design and production manager Karen Copp, and all of the other staff members who have ensured that this book was published in line with the editorial vision and rigor that Iowa is known for across the country. I also owe a special thanks to Liz DeWolf, who painstakingly read through this entire manuscript and offered invaluable editorial advice on the book's content, themes, organization, and writing style. This book is much stronger due to her editorial guidance.

In addition, I am particularly grateful to the many people I spoke with across the world during my research over the last decade. Thanks are due to the farmers, street vendors, fieldworkers, government administrators, corporate managers, civil society organization staff, and other community stakeholders for discussing their opinions with me. I would like to thank the funders of this research, including the University of Wisconsin,

University of Southern California, Wright State University, and the American Association of Geographers. Without your support, this research would not have been possible. I would like to thank Ummey Tabassum for her research assistance with some food bank interviews, transcriptions, and figures. All errors and omissions are the sole responsibility of the author.

Most importantly, I want to thank my family and close friends for being a consistent source of inspiration and support. To my parents, Susan and David, your tenacious curiosity and commitment to academic pursuits and social justice gave me the inspiration to study important topics such as poverty and social inequality. Mom, you have supported me throughout every stage of my life, patiently listened to all of my endless ramblings, provided a needed sense of humor, and always encouraged me to follow my interest in geography. Even though my dad is not with us to see this book published, I know that he would be proud that I could continue the Warshawsky tradition to publish a book (as both he and his father did). His spirit and those of Joe, Lillian, Dov, Ann, Wally, and Judy are all part of the intellectual and moral force that motivated my work.

To my older sister and Bengals superfan Lisa and her Dan, Carson, and Carolyn, your energy and commitment to family helped me put my work in perspective. Debbie, with our unique bond toward all things Cincinnati, urban studies, and family, you have provided me with my north star over these many years. To my inspiring and dedicated brother-in-law Alula and nieces Jorie, Remi, Mila, and Ellie, you have made Cincinnati a more meaningful place to live. To my incredibly supportive in-laws, Mark and Robyn, and my extended family of Greg, Michelle, Charlie, and Felix; Justin, Diana, Ethan, Henry, and Lydia; Ben and Sarah, Hanna and John; Asfaw and Lemlem; Beruk; Robert; and my relatives across Australia and Africa, thank you for giving me the large family I always wanted. During all the times when I have been disillusioned with the world as it is, you give me hope that something greater is possible. To my lifelong friends Brian and Paul, you have been a great source of support and friendship throughout the years. I am especially indebted to Brian for his advice about the book publishing process.

To my two young beacons of hope and energy, Maya and Abby. You have changed our lives and given us a new sense of purpose. We hope that you will become engaged citizens of the world and be inspired to make the world a better place as you have done for us.

And, to my wife, Kim, with your constant support and connection to your place of birth, you are the reason I conducted research in South Africa. You were not only a sounding board for ideas but also ensured that my research focused on topics that truly mattered. I also want to thank Kim's extended family in South Africa for so graciously hosting me while I stayed in Johannesburg for those many months. In particular, I owe a deep debt of gratitude to Lea, Judy, Hymie, Jennifer, Alan, Ryan, Jodi, Linzi, Wendy, Damon, and Alice: you ensured that my stay in Johannesburg was both comfortable and enjoyable.

PREFACE

My interest and experiences with food banks and local food organizations began in the 1980s and 1990s during my childhood years in Cincinnati, Ohio. My monthly trips down to what was then known as the Over-the-Rhine Soup Kitchen introduced me to the extreme spatial inequality of the city. Hunger became real and personal as I interacted with homeless and food-insecure people living in the downtown Cincinnati area. I was shocked by the extensive lines of people at the soup kitchen during what was supposed to be one of the longest-lasting periods of economic growth in the 1990s in the richest country in the world. Through my volunteer work at the soup kitchen, I began to see how food insecurity, hunger, and the emergency food assistance system had become institutionalized in the United States. Living without food had become normalized, and the nonprofit sector's network of food programs seemed to be a permanent fixture in the city. While these experiences reflected my personal perspectives as a child, they set the foundation for me to explore the deeper reasons for the existence of the emergency food system in the United States.

During my college years, I continued to study urban inequality and the food system through my studies in geography at the University of Illinois. There, I learned how food insecurity and social inequality could be reproduced and perpetuated through structural inequalities in cities. Upon graduation in 2003, I found a one-year AmeriCorps position with the Eastern Illinois Foodbank using geographic information systems (GIS) to conduct spatial analysis on the food bank's geographical service area to identify gaps in coverage. This work involved meeting with hungry people, often in small, remote rural towns. Given that most of my previous life experiences were in cities and suburbs, my time with the Eastern Illinois Foodbank provided me with the opportunity to see the extent of rural poverty in the United States and the critical role that the food bank played for many people in that context. This time also introduced me to the power of GIS and mixed methods to collect data, analyze it, and understand food systems.

Following completion of this one-year AmeriCorps research position, I enrolled in a master's degree program at the University of Wisconsin–Madison in geography, where I studied the evolution of the Chicago food bank system and its network of beneficiary organizations. It was an important period for me to understand how the experiences of the food insecure intersected with the structural limitations of the social safety net and the food banking enterprise. While most of my previous work was descriptive and based on personal volunteer work, my research in Chicago allowed me to understand how spatial patterns on the ground in cities were connected to broader structural inequality as theorized by political economists.

After traveling to cities in Africa and Asia during my early years as a PhD student in geography at the University of Southern California, I decided to focus my attention on local food organizations within cities of the Global South. Primarily, this was due to the immense scale of food insecurity and the complex nature of food systems in the Global South. I became increasingly interested in exploring the relationships between the state and civil society. These dynamics were intellectually challenging but also rapidly changing as the urbanization of food insecurity and poverty created a set of varied governance challenges that seemed to be especially pressing to understand and overcome.

This newfound interest took me to South Africa and the highly unequal urban food systems that existed in Johannesburg. I found Johannesburg to be challenging, both intellectually and personally, as the city is a sprawling, extreme, and sometimes a daunting and intimidating, urban environment.

My timing in South Africa also coincided with the introduction of what was then known as FoodBank South Africa in 2007. This was fortuitous, as I was not planning on studying food banks in South Africa. However, after learning about FoodBank South Africa and its role in the broader food system, I developed a strong interest in the Global FoodBanking Network and the globalization of food banks in cities of the Global South.

Since 2007, I have continued to explore the food banking enterprise across the globe in cities throughout Europe, Africa, Asia, and Australia. During the writing of this book, the COVID-19 pandemic produced widespread collapse of economic systems and informal livelihoods and sharp increases in food insecurity and disruptions in food system operations. While food banks gained increased visibility as important food relief mechanisms because of the pandemic, the crisis also exposed their structural weaknesses and the fragility of the broader charity-based food relief system. In my estimation, this further underscored the need to understand the structure, operations, and impacts of global food banks across the world's regions. While my examinations of food banks are not meant be comprehensive, this book explores my experiences with these rapidly growing and important institutions.

*FOOD WASTE,
FOOD INSECURITY,
AND THE
GLOBALIZATION
OF FOOD BANKS*

INTRODUCTION

We are in the midst of a long-standing global food security crisis. According to the Food and Agriculture Organization (FAO), approximately 2 billion people—27.6 percent of the world's population—are food insecure or lack regular access to enough nutritious food.[1] Numbers are particularly elevated in parts of Sub-Saharan Africa, South Asia, Central America, and South America, with some areas more than 50 percent food insecure. Globally, food insecurity rates are higher in rural areas; however, the rapid urbanization of the planet has significantly increased hunger in cities.

Food insecurity is largely driven by low incomes, unemployment or underemployment, and the lack of sufficient food or income support programs in a particular region.[2] In rural areas, residents engage in a range of livelihood strategies, with small-scale farming the most important means to earn an income and access food. Declining rural economies, urban migration, and challenges to small-scale farming have combined to decimate living standards in rural areas.[3] In cities, urban residents purchase food in the cash economy; however, they are confronted with a range of obstacles that make them vulnerable to food insecurity. Although city dwellers access food through the range of supermarkets, grocery stores, corner stores, small shops, farmers markets, restaurants, and other formal and informal food vendors, food can be more expensive, unavailable, or unhealthy.[4] Even though rural and urban pathways to food are connected, there are different obstacles to food security in cities than rural areas.[5]

Meanwhile, as an increasing number of people lack access to sufficient food, more than one-third of the global food supply is lost in production, postharvest, processing, and distribution, or wasted during the market sale and consumption of food.[6] Recent figures indicate that approximately 900 million tons of food are wasted in the retail, food service, and household levels.[7] Various studies have explained the reasons why food loss and food waste occur in the food system, as weather, markets, labor costs, quality controls, food prices, logistical limitations, consumer expectations, and lack of information or time among consumers all contribute to wasted food in places for different reasons.[8] Moreover, financial speculation and inequality in the global food system, patterns of excess, weak waste governance structures, and consumer patterns of throwing away packaging for single-serving food items all contribute to food waste.[9]

As food insecurity and food waste have become greater concerns, international organizations like the United Nations (UN) have formulated specific policy goals to address these challenges and bring more attention to them. In Goal 2 of its Sustainable Development Goals (SDG), the UN aims to reduce hunger, malnutrition, and promote food security in member countries, especially in Sub-Saharan Africa, Central, South, and Southwest Asia, and Latin America.[10] Goal 12—Responsible Production and Consumption subcomponent on Food Loss and Waste[11]—has contributed to increased attention to the global food waste crisis across sectors, scales, and global contexts.[12]

In North America and Europe, the Food Recovery Hierarchy has emerged as a common framework for corporations, governments, and some community organizations to prioritize how to redirect food waste sources. In this model, which originated with the U.S. Environmental Protection Agency and the European Union, institutions are encouraged to choose the most preferred method of food recovery from the following: source reduction, feed hungry people, feed animals, industrial uses, composting, and landfill and incineration as a last option.[13] Importantly, leading business coalitions such as the Food Waste Reduction Alliance utilize the Food Recovery Hierarchy in their operations to promote companies as sustainable brand leaders in the industry.[14] While this framework has been critiqued by some scholars for its simplicity, it has provided many institutions with a common framework to implement food waste reduction schemes.

As the urbanization of poverty increases globally, food insecurity and food waste may become more difficult to manage over the next one hundred years.[15] Institutions operating at household, community, metropolitan, provincial, national, and global scales in the private, public, and nonprofit sectors are on the front lines in the effort to govern small, medium, and large cities across the planet.[16] However, they are often limited by extreme urban governance challenges associated with the legacies of colonialism and extreme sociospatial inequality; structural unemployment, persistent poverty, and growth of informal housing; and limited government capacity due to institutional ineffectiveness, corruption, or global economic pressures.[17] Challenges associated with the availability, access, utilization, stability, agency, and sustainability of food systems threaten the livability of cities and the future of those who reside in metropolitan regions.[18] This is especially true for those living in lower-income regions in the Global South where the urbanization of poverty and rapid population growth are expected to continue throughout the twenty-first century.[19]

In cities, food access is strongly associated with income and the capacity to buy food in the cash economy. Yet, on a global scale, urban residents confront a range of challenges associated with unstable food costs, irregular food options, lack of nutrition, health and safety concerns, and other high fixed costs in cities. Although city residents may receive support from government or nonprofit programs, this support network may be insufficient to reduce food insecurity adequately in cities.[20]

Food waste is also a challenge in cities as the volumes of food are extreme and the sources of food are diverse. Cities rarely have the infrastructure necessary to process food waste quickly or efficiently at a low cost. In addition, although some municipalities have developed policies to reduce food waste, they are typically not legally binding. Thus, most cities take an ad hoc approach toward food waste management with a range of government, business, civil society, and households acting independently for food waste reduction.[21]

Food banks—civil society institutions that collect, systematize, and redistribute excess food—have expanded into one of the largest systems

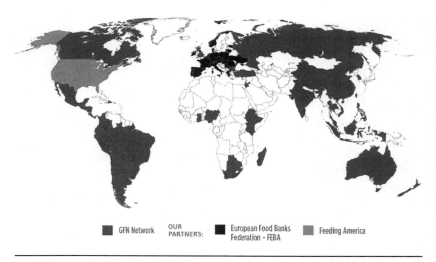

FIGURE 1. The globalization of food banks (courtesy of Global Food Banking Network, 2021).

for reducing food waste in the world's cities. From their origins in North America in the 1960s, food banks now provide food to communities in approximately one hundred countries on six continents, including many countries across the Global South (see figure 1).[22]

The food bank is often promoted by corporate, state, and nongovernmental partners as a community-driven, independently funded, efficient hunger and food waste reduction mechanism. In many cases, the food bank's mission is to overcome the triple bottom line associated with the global food waste crisis, including food insecurity and poverty, economic inefficiency and increased costs, and environmental degradation and climate change.[23] Key drivers of the expansion of food banks across the globe are major food charities such as Feeding America, the Global FoodBanking Network (GFN), the European Food Banks Federation, and the Food Banking Regional Network.[24]

Many scholars have argued that the supposed successes of food banks are not supported by facts on the ground in many contexts.[25] As noted by food researchers Rachel Loopstra and Valerie Tarasuk, although food banks often highlight record amounts of food delivered or numbers of persons served, it is not clear that these numbers indicate lower food insecurity.[26] When it comes to food waste, it is equally difficult to show a direct correlation between food bank development and lower food waste levels; statistics from 2018 state that food banks may reduce as little as 1 to 3 percent of food waste across the world's regions.[27] Importantly, food waste is hard to quantify given that food waste data are not readily available from the food industry and there are no universally agreed-upon methods to define food loss, food waste, and food surplus.[28] This has given profit, government, nonprofit, and household institutions an opportunity to apply the concept of food waste as they see fit.[29]

Additionally, the number of other social variables associated with the political economy of poverty and food insecurity, such as changing expenses associated with housing, health care, and food, as well as political instability and other extreme social crises, make it difficult to isolate the role of the food bank in terms of its impact. Food banks also struggle to operate in areas with the highest levels of food insecurity such as informal economies, rural areas, and the Global South, since food banks are typically designed for urban areas with well-developed infrastructure and food corporations.[30] In short, there are many reasons why we need to question the impact of food banks.[31]

If food banks are not effective in ordinary circumstances, the onset of the COVID-19 pandemic in 2020 illustrated that food banks are certainly not set up to address sudden and severe societal crises. With the pandemic came the widespread collapse of economic systems and disruptions in food systems, immediately driving up the number of food-insecure people.[32] Estimates from the Food and Agriculture Organization indicate that, during the initial months of the pandemic, the number of food-insecure people may have doubled to over 1.6 billion globally.[33] It is estimated that food insecurity will remain elevated in many communities for the coming decade.[34]

In the first half of 2020, as the world scrambled to adjust to the pandemic, food banks faced unforeseen structural challenges, such as rapid increases in demand, unmet need, reduced food stocks, disruptions in food donations, higher operational costs, uneven funding support, insufficient operational resources, decreases in volunteers and personnel, lack of personal health and safety equipment for frontline workers, and closure of some charities.[35]

6 Introduction

The COVID pandemic also contributed to significant amounts of food loss and waste as disruptions in food systems, challenges in transportation, and extreme fluctuations in demand from food retailers, restaurants, and households contributed to large volumes of food being left on farm fields, plowed over, or simply wasted.[36] The disconnect between those who need food and the large volumes of wasted food highlight the contradictions, excesses, and warped incentives that determine how food is produced, sold, transported, and consumed by various institutions in the food system.[37] Although some government legislation was passed to mitigate this wastage through increased delivery of edible food to the food relief network, most of the work to rescue food was completed through a somewhat disorganized ad hoc process whereby groups of people or individuals rescued food, cooked food, or developed other creative methods to reduce waste.[38]

The specific challenges brought on by COVID have only further underscored the fact that food bank systems are more of a patchwork of charities than a systematic network to reduce food insecurity and waste on a significant scale. It is notable, then, that even during 2020–2021, food banks were still heralded as the answer to food crises. Food banks also successfully increased their partnerships with governments across the world during the pandemic as their work became key to humanitarian relief efforts in many contexts. As noted by an administrator at GFN, food banks placed themselves in the center of the emergency food aid network during the COVID-19 crisis.

> Food banks have been and continue [working] on the front lines of local response. As noted by the FAO's chief economist, in conjunction with government action, the mobilization of food banks worldwide is of crucial importance in addressing urgent food security needs in the COVID global emergency now and toward more resilient communities and food systems in the future recovery.[39]

Without question, the COVID pandemic's food insecurity crisis increased the visibility of the GFN and its programs. For this reason, the GFN and its partner food bank networks used the opportunity to position food banks as key institutions in the battle against food insecurity and to raise money for its programs. As stated by an administrator with the GFN, food banks found the COVID pandemic to be a critical time to fundraise from public, private, and individual stakeholders in order to support their mission.

> We are calling on our private sector supporters, corporations, foundations, and agri-food donor partners to stand with us in solidarity at this critical time.... We are likewise calling upon multilateral institutions and governments to support the work of food banks as an indispensable response of civil society to address rising food insecurity accompanying this pandemic. Significant resources must be committed from all societal stakeholders and urgently made available to support the people we serve.[40]

To this end, food banks achieved record fundraising goals during COVID as governments, corporations, and individuals supported food banking. Critical to this messaging is the emphasis that governmental strategies should embrace and fund food banks as part of their food relief.[41]

This book seeks to shed light on a central question: Why are food banks promoted by governments, companies, and the public despite the lack of evidence that they reduce food insecurity or waste on a significant scale? Utilizing approximately fifteen years of in-depth fieldwork on four continents in cities across North America, Europe, Asia, and Africa, this book analyzes how and why food banks have developed across the world. I argue that food banks proliferate globally because they help to manage the symptoms of poverty and excess—namely, hunger and food waste. However, rather than addressing the root causes of food insecurity and waste, governments and corporations promote food banks as a way to deflect attention from their own institutional shortcomings. In this way, food corporations and governments may be benefiting more from food banks than the food insecure. These central arguments drive the rest of the book.

CHAPTER 1

THE RISE OF THE FOOD BANK

The food bank—a civil society organization that collects, systematizes, and redistributes unused food from corporations and other donors—has emerged as a solution to the enduring crises of food insecurity and food waste. Through its triple-bottom-line approach to reduce food insecurity, economic inefficiency, and environmental degradation, the food bank has positioned itself to confront the world's greatest challenges associated with sustainability.[1] Food banks are strongly promoted by government, corporations, and other stakeholders across the world, despite the fact that insufficient evidence exists to show that they can effectively reduce food insecurity and waste.[2]

Initially developed as an ad hoc solution in one U.S. city over fifty years ago, the first food bank, Feeding America, has become the country's largest charity.[3] This chapter examines how global networks such as the Global FoodBanking Network and the European Food Banks Federation have developed across the world, and presents a critical analysis of the role that food banks play in contemporary food systems.

FEEDING AMERICA

The first food bank was founded in Arizona in 1967, when a retired Phoenix businessman named John van Hengel stored food in a warehouse to give to the hungry. In the 1960s, van Hengel volunteered at a local soup kitchen, where he met a woman who told him that she fed her family from food discarded in grocery store dumpsters. She suggested that it would be easier to access food if it were stored at a centralized location, similar to how people access money at banks. This is how the idea of food banking started, as van Hengel transformed this vision into the first food bank.[4]

Within its first year of operations, van Hengel's St. Mary's Food Bank distributed 275,000 pounds of food to the food insecure in the Phoenix region. As the food bank continued to grow in size and recognition, van Hengel helped to develop food banks across the United States. By 1977, eighteen food banks existed across the country in cities such as Cincinnati, Detroit, Los Angeles, San Jose, Salt Lake City, and Oakland. Two years later, Second Harvest, a national food banking network, was formed and operations expanded into most large cities across the United States. In the years thereafter, Second Harvest's name changed to America's Second Harvest and then to Feeding America, which it retains today.[5]

Although nonprofits and the voluntary sector have always played a key role in food relief, U.S. food banks have emerged as key institutions over the last fifty years.[6] Food banks first proliferated in the United States as a temporary institutional support mechanism during the deep economic recession of the 1970s and transformative welfare state hollowing-out that began during the Reagan administration in the 1980s.[7] Also, in the 1970s, the U.S. Department of Agriculture launched its Emergency Food Assistance Program to stabilize agricultural markets, which led to an excess in food commodities and set the stage for food banks to manage that excess. Given that the program was started as a market control mechanism, the type, quality, quantity, and timing of foods delivered was driven by the market and not by community needs.[8] With welfare state restructuring in the 1980s and 1990s, nongovernmental organizations (NGOs), including food banks, became elevated to a more prominent role in U.S. society.[9] Then, with the passage of welfare reform in the 1990s during the Clinton administration, it became clear that food banks were likely here to stay, as welfare retrenchment took on a bipartisan approach.[10] Equally important, the Good Samaritan Food Donation Act of 1996 created legal protection for food donors, a key ingredient to convince food corporations that Feeding America was legitimate and worth supporting.[11]

Feeding America has grown significantly over the past few decades. As of

2022, its revenue was measured at $4.2 billion, serving 6.6 billion meals per year.[12] It is the most important nonprofit food bank network in the United States, given that it is by far the largest and most institutionalized in terms of connections to government and private industry and public consciousness across the country. Its mission is to "feed America's hungry through a nationwide network of member food banks and engage our country in the fight to end hunger."[13] Feeding America's network of food banks is vast, covering all fifty states and reaching more than 53 million people annually through its more than two hundred network food banks and more than 60,000 local beneficiary organizations, including food pantries, school feeding programs known as feeding schemes, soup kitchens, and community gardens; care centers for the young, aged, disabled, sick, or homeless; schools, day care facilities, and centers for vulnerable children; and development centers for educational, skills, or occupations training (see figure 2).[14]

In part, Feeding America has grown so rapidly because it has been able to promote its mission in somewhat apolitical terms. As noted by an administrator at Feeding America, food banks focus on marketing the stories behind food insecurity rather than the structural causes of poverty:

> We are here to end hunger. We want anyone who wants to make that happen to join us. . . . One of the ways we want to do that is to build empathy on the issue and tell the stories of the everyday Americans that we serve to build a movement [to change how people think about hunger and the food insecure].[15]

However, within the last ten years, Feeding America has taken a more active role in federal food advocacy.[16] As stated by a national council member with Feeding America, many food banks engage in broader policy discussions related to food policy.

> Over the last [few] years, Feeding America and many Feeding America food banks have also begun to embrace policy [and advocacy] as part of our work. And I think it is one of the more important shifts happening within food banking. I think it is seismic. I think it has shifted how we work, who we work with, and frankly what our end goal is.[17]

Not only does Feeding America have a Washington, DC, office specifically focused on food policy, it also utilizes its broad base of institutional

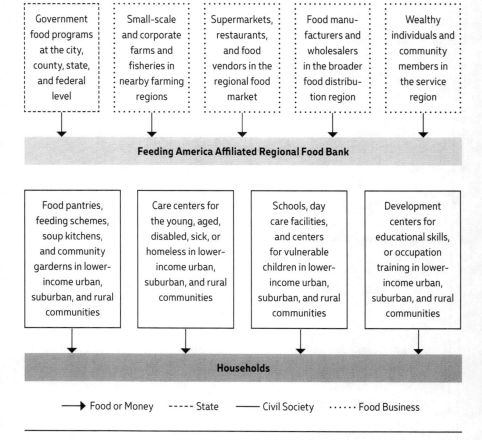

FIGURE 2. The Feeding America food banking model (courtesy of Warshawsky, 2020).

support to rally support for key food programs, including the Supplemental Nutrition Assistance Program (SNAP); Emergency Food Assistance Program; Commodity Supplemental Food Program; Child and Adult Care Food Program; National School Lunch Program; School Breakfast Program; Summer Food Service Program; Women, Infants, and Children; Farm Bill; Child Nutrition Reauthorization Act; and tax policy that helps nonprofit food organizations and hunger relief programs more broadly.[18]

While Feeding America often lets its local food banks advocate for their own policies, it also takes clear positions to support federal food policy, as seen in various efforts to secure additional funding during the acute phase of COVID and numerous political attacks by the Trump administration on various food programs.[19] Given its USDA contracts for the Emergency Food Assistance Program and the Commodity Supplemental Program, Feeding America has carefully navigated the political arena where government contracts can easily be politicized.

As a nonprofit organization, Feeding America can legally advocate for clear positions that promote its mission; however, the IRS's language for legal nonprofit lobbying is narrow in scope, as nonprofits can only participate in lobbying if it is a small part of their activities. This vagueness of the rules contributes to fear among some nonprofits that excessive lobbying could jeopardize their nonprofit status. The IRS defines lobbying as a specific subcomponent of advocacy that includes the influence of elected officials to vote in a particular way on legislation.[20]

In addition, with its strong ties to food corporations, there are limits to the types of initiatives and depth of advocacy that U.S. food banks employ. Minimum wage campaigns and support for corporate tax increases are often viewed negatively by the food industry, as they hinder corporate profitability. For this reason, food banks tend to avoid advocating for policies that conflict with the interests of the food industry, given that food corporations are the primary supporter of food banks.[21]

THE GLOBALIZATION OF FOOD BANKING

As food banking expanded in size and influence in the United States, demand for international food banking led to the development of a spinoff organization called the Global FoodBanking Network (GFN), based in Chicago, Illinois, the same city where Feeding America is headquartered. Founded in 2006 in conjunction with leaders from U.S., Canadian, Argentinean, and Mexican food banks, the GFN is a nonprofit organization financed primarily by large corporations, especially in the food industry.[22] Some of the largest funders include the Bank of America Charitable Foundation, Enterprise Holdings Foundation, General Mills, Kellogg Company, PepsiCo Foundation, PIMCO Foundation, Cargill Incorporated, Griffith Foods, H-E-B, and Unilever, as well as the Tracy Family Foundation, Thankful Heart Fund Community Foundation, and numerous small

14 CHAPTER 1

FIGURE 3. The Global Food Banking Network model (courtesy of Global Food Banking Network, 2021).

individual donors.[23] As of 2022, the GFN operates food banks in forty-seven countries.[24] It feeds approximately 39 million people and delivers 692 million kilos of food to 59,296 local beneficiary organizations (see figure 3).[25]

The broader network of food banks includes more than forty core GFN network member countries and approximately sixty additional member countries through the European Food Banks Federation (FEBA) and the Food Banking Regional Network (FBRN), who work primarily in Europe and Africa and Southwestern Asia respectively (see table 1).[26]

TABLE 1. The Location and Affiliation of Food Banks by Region

Region	Number of Countries	Countries with Food Banks (%)	Countries with GFN-Affiliated Food Banks	Countries with FBRN-Affiliated Food Banks	Countries with FEBA-Affiliated Food Banks
Africa	54	27 (50.00)	9	22	0
Asia	48	28 (58.33)	15	14	0
Europe	44	30 (68.18)	2	1	30
North America	23	10 (43.48)	10	0	0
Oceania	14	2 (14.29)	2	0	0
South America	12	9 (75.00)	9	0	0

Since 2006, while on site in each country, the GFN has provided leadership support, technical training, and financial and human resources in consultation with local needs. The GFN promotes Feeding America's U.S.-based system of food banking as a best-practice model in local contexts.[27] This includes GFN programs that enhance the impact of regional food banks, such as partnering with new food banks, training and knowledge exchange, building capacity, partnering with global food companies to leverage scale and international relationships, and certifying safety and legal compliance.[28]

In fiscal year 2022, the Global FoodBanking Network's expenses were $14.8 million. Sources of financial support included 88.3 percent from corporations and foundations, 11.4 percent from individuals, and less than 1 percent from other sources.[29] The size of GFN's operating budget has grown dramatically, from $2.7 million in 2015 to $17.5 million in 2022 because of increased fundraising and capacity to showcase what the GFN can do.[30]

Since its founding in 2006, the GFN has developed a process to certify national food bank systems as members of their broader network. Certification requirements include efficient financial and organizational management, and food safety procedures and training, as well as cooperation with corporate, government, and nonprofit food system partners. GFN certification provides its members legitimacy and access to new funding and in-kind donation networks, and it grows the GFN's reach and influence over food banking expansion globally.[31] As of 2022, there were forty-seven certified member food banks on six continents.[32] National member food banks such as Foodbank Australia, FoodForward South Africa, and India FoodBanking Network each operate their own food bank system within their respective country and determine how beneficiary charities will receive food from the national food bank warehouse.

The GFN has been very active in marketing their ideas in other contexts across the world, as well as to other key stakeholders in the food donation system, such as food corporations. Most notably, since 2007, the GFN has operated the Food Bank Leadership Institute (FBLI) to inform food bank managers, food corporations, government leaders, and other key stakeholders across the world how to learn about best practices in the field of food banking.[33] In 2019, more than two hundred people attended the FBLI in London from fifty-four countries. This included more than thirty representatives from corporations.[34] The FBLI positions the GFN as the purveyor of knowledge and creates buy-in from the corporate sector, government sector, and food bank administrators across the globe. Importantly, the FBLI has played a key role globally to reinforce food banking as a legitimate, effective, and efficient solution to the crises of food insecurity and food waste.[35]

In addition to the FBLI, in collaboration with Harvard Law School Food Law and Policy and the Walmart Foundation, the GFN has also published *The Global Food Donation Policy Atlas* to showcase how food banks work in locations across the world. The focus of the atlas is to identify and work to overcome key legal and operational obstacles to food bank development. Rather than highlighting the structural causes of food insecurity or food waste or the broader political, economic, or social context in which residents live, the atlas focuses rather narrowly on the specific government policies needed to facilitate food bank growth.

Since its founding in 2006, the GFN has sharpened its operations and increased its support for member food banks, broadening its role from certifier of new food banks to supporter for ongoing food bank development.

A key part of this process has been to increase the GFN's knowledge of the political, cultural, and other social factors that facilitate or limit food bank development.[36]

While food banks aim to positively impact the sustainability triple bottom line associated with hunger and food insecurity, economic inefficiency, and environmental degradation through food waste, administrators at the GFN have stated that the primary purpose of the food bank is to provide the necessary logistical support to reduce corporate food waste.[37] As noted in the GFN's 2019 report called *Waste Not, Want Not: Towards Zero Hunger*, the GFN articulates the purpose of food banks:

> The food bank model is uniquely positioned to address the paradox of global hunger and food loss and waste. Food banks are truly the "green" hunger relief solution.... Food banks represent a "triple win" in the communities where they operate, reducing food wastage and protecting the environment, providing food assistance to hungry and vulnerable people, and strengthening civil society through support of local humanitarian charities.[38]

Building on this logistics theme, food banks are designed to fit within markets and the demands of their corporate partners, as stated by Jeff Klein, the GFN's previous CEO:

> I am a big believer in markets.... We know that in the marketplace nobody forces a transaction to take place, since all participants work to seek value for what they want to buy or sell.... I get very excited when I see the number of relationships GFN has developed with companies and NGOs.... They partner with GFN because they believe in the mission. It aligns with their own values and philanthropic objectives.... They determine that GFN provides a valuable product, service, or experience.[39]

The market for food banks is also distinctly geographical, as food bank systems have been designed to operate in large, wealthy urban areas, with well-developed corporate food businesses, where food waste is a part of the business. This is emphasized by CEO Klein:

> [The GFN model] tends to be successful in urban areas. It usually tends to be in places where there are large grocery stores and large manufacturers

that give rise to higher waste. The grocery communities will input capital at risk because they think there is enough demand and because so much comes off the shelf before expiration. What we have found is that if you go to rural areas where there is only agricultural abundance, you are going to have trouble [developing a food bank].[40]

Not surprisingly, this has resulted in the development of food banks where food companies are most profitable, namely North America, Europe, and Australia, as well as Latin America and to some extent Asia. However, parts of South and Southeast Asia and Sub-Saharan Africa are key gaps in the food bank map, in part because of their underdeveloped corporate food sector and nonurban population distribution.[41]

Although initially hesitant, administrators at the GFN are actively pursuing food bank expansion in Sub-Saharan Africa and Southeast Asia. In fact, of the nineteen food banks added to the GFN roster since 2019, seven are in Sub-Saharan Africa, including Ethiopia, Ghana, Guinea-Bissau, Kenya, Madagascar, Mozambique, and Nigeria, and seven in South and Southeast Asia, including India, Indonesia, Malaysia, Philippines, Sri Lanka, Thailand, and Vietnam.[42]

The GFN is positioning itself to be on the front lines of global conversations around food insecurity and food waste. As noted in its own publications, the GFN is deliberating building its mission to achieve the two relevant SDGs as defined by the UN.[43] First, food security is a key part of the most recent version of the UN's SDG in Goal 2: Zero Hunger, which aims to reduce hunger and malnutrition, and promote food security in member countries, especially in Sub-Saharan Africa, Central, South, and Southwest Asia, and Latin America.[44] In addition, UN SDG Goal 12: Responsible Production and Consumption, subcomponent on Food Loss and Waste (SDG 12.3), highlights the visibility of the food waste crisis.[45] In line with their ambitious strategic plans moving forward, the GFN aims to reach more than 50 million people worldwide by 2030 through their food bank networks.[46] As stated by an administrator at the GFN, the GFN hopes to connect with the UN, G7, G20, and other leading global institutions:

> We are aligning ourselves very intentionally and very publicly with the United Nations Sustainable Development Goals. [We would like

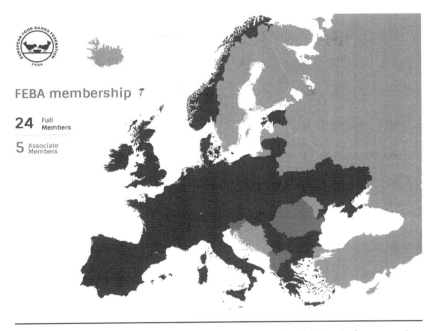

FIGURE 4. The European Food Banks Federation and its member food banks (courtesy of European Food Banks Federation, 2021).

to become] a real player at gatherings like the G20 and even the G7 and be able to represent the voice of food banking with the dual focus of mitigating food waste as well as feeding hungry people in those forums where influencers are gathered and who could have significant impact on the scaling of food banking on the mitigation of those two parallel problems.[47]

These efforts have been successful in raising GFN's profile within the UN, as the FAO has showcased food banking as a key means to reduce food insecurity and food waste globally.[48]

The European Food Banks Federation (FEBA) is a partner of the GFN and one of the most extensive regional food bank networks in the world. As of 2022, it operates in thirty countries.[49] In 2022, FEBA redistributed 907,280 tons of surplus food to 11.8 million people through its 45,810 partner charities in 341 food banks across the European continent (see figure 4).[50]

FEBA was founded in 1986, two years after Sister Cécile Bigot communicated with the founder of the Edmonton Food Bank in Canada. To confront persistent food insecurity in Paris, Bigot worked with Bernand Dandrel at the Catholic Relief charity to partner with Emmaüs and local Salvation Army charities to develop the first food bank in Europe. Soon thereafter, a food bank was developed in Belgium and a European-scale umbrella food bank network was established.[51]

Food banks grew quickly across Europe following this initial start-up phase. Between 1988 and 1992, food banks expanded quickly across the continent, opening in Spain, Italy, and Ireland. Between 1994 and 2001, food banks opened in Greece, Luxembourg, Portugal, and Poland. Since 2004, new food banks have opened in more than fifteen countries. After almost forty years, FEBA is strong and continuing to grow, as new food banks are developed and existing ones such as Germany are added to the FEBA network.[52]

The mission of FEBA is "to contribute to reducing hunger and malnutrition in Europe, through the fight against food waste and the call for solidarity, by supporting and developing food banks in countries where they are most needed."[53] To fulfill this mission, the food bank collects food from the European Union, producers, retailers, and individuals, sorts and stores this food in warehouses, and then distributes food to charities across the continent (see figure 5). Each country manages its own food bank system.

FEBA focuses on three main activities. First, FEBA strengthens the network of food banks through training and knowledge exchange, transfer of best practices, global reach of food bank partnerships, and compliance with the network's rules and regulations. Second, FEBA develops food banks through consulting services, facilitation of food and fund sourcing, support for new emerging food banks, and development of food bank projects and programs. Third, FEBA promotes advocacy and awareness raising of poverty, malnutrition, and food waste, highlights the role of food banks in society, markets EU food aid programs, and facilitates maximum participation and institutional flows of food donations to people in need.[54] FEBA utilizes the amount of food redistributed to measure its impact on food insecurity and food waste. According to FEBA, their work provides value for end beneficiaries, partner charities, companies, and communities.[55]

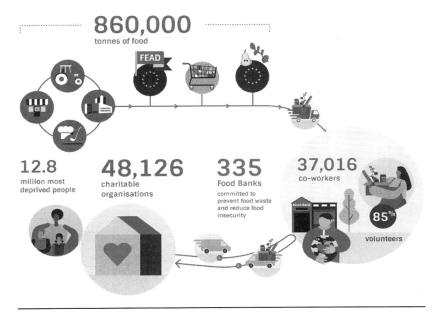

FIGURE 5. The European Food Banks Federation food donation system (courtesy of European Food Banks Federation, 2022).

Although each of these institutional objectives plays out differently across the continent, northern Europe tends to emphasize the environmental aspect of food waste prevention while southern Europe prioritizes the social aspect of poverty reduction. This has occurred in part because southern Europe has higher poverty rates and older, more established food banks with strong antipoverty reputations, whereas northern Europe has lower poverty rates, newer food banks, and stronger environmental movements.[56]

While originally located in Paris, FEBA has moved to Brussels to be closer to the European Union government headquarters offices. FEBA's operating budget was €1.7 million in 2020, approximately double that of 2019 due to sharp increases in funding to confront the fallout from the COVID pandemic. The sources of funding were 80.0 percent from corporate and foundation donations, 14.0 percent from European Union subsidies, 5.1 percent from membership fees, 0.9 percent from individual donations, and less than 1 percent from other revenues.[57] As noted by a FEBA administrator, FEBA actively collaborates with the EU on a number of food bank–related issues: "We [work with the] EU Commission and Parliament because some food that food banks receives comes from the EU food program. We also work with the EU to lift obstacles to food donation in member states. Sometimes, there are regulatory issues or bureaucratic rules, so they can help us to make [food donations] a simpler process."[58]

Although a relatively well-developed food bank network, FEBA has faced some challenges. First, the network itself is unevenly developed. The strongest food banks are in western Europe primarily, and the ones with the greatest need are in eastern Europe, which reflects the economic disparity of the continent in general. Thus, the places with the greatest food insecurity challenges are also those with the weakest and least developed food bank network, where food aid is needed the most. This is an area of focus that FEBA is keen on improving in the near future.[59]

In addition, FEBA members face challenges associated with limited human and financial resources, as food bank staff in many countries are volunteers, and funding varies by year. These dynamics were exacerbated during the COVID crisis, as countries such as the Netherlands, which is staffed 100 percent by volunteers, and Greece, which has uneven donor support, experienced severe instability during 2020 and beyond.[60] In addition, lack of government support is often a significant problem in post-Soviet eastern European countries where the state is suspicious of outside initiatives, especially ones originating in western Europe or the United States.[61]

FEBA is also working where countries have relatively well-developed social safety nets, so FEBA administrators are not interested in reducing or replacing the welfare state. However, as noted by an administrator, FEBA is often in a defensive position, as it must explain the value and efficiency of food banks in European society:

> On one side is the surplus, and on the other side there are poor people. How can we avoid throwing food away and help needy people? You could say, "You don't really deal with the source of poverty," and this is correct. We provide the services. Yes, we would like the state to do more. Yes, we would like the government to recognize that we are fulfilling a social mission and for [the government] to help us. But

the reality is that [the food bank] is a terribly efficient model. "Give us one Euro and we provide 10 to 29 euros of food to people." It's terribly efficient. And sometimes people do not like that.[62]

In line with global attitude shifts toward food waste, FEBA has tried to balance cross-sectoral interest in food waste reduction as an environmental cause and food relief as a core mission of the organization.[63] To this point, the EU has actively worked with its member states to develop and promote food waste reduction plans.[64]

Yet, despite the levels of investment food banking has received across the globe, insufficient evidence exists to show that food banks reduce food insecurity and food waste on a significant scale. The next section takes a more critical look at the relationship between food banks and their partnerships with government, food corporations, and civil society to interrogate why and how food banks are so widely promoted across the globe.

A CRITICAL EXAMINATION OF THE ROLE OF THE FOOD BANK

Welfare state retrenchment and economic stagnation in the 1970s and 1980s and the neoliberal devolution, decentralization, and privatization of government income support and food programs since the 1990s has led to growth in civil society organizations (CSOs) and corporate philanthropy as way to promote local initiatives and reduce the size of state spending in many parts of North America and Europe.[65] In this context, neoliberalism is defined as the state movement toward market-oriented reforms that deregulate markets, increase privatization of services, and engage in austerity to reduce the size of the welfare state.[66] Very often this dynamic takes the form of public-private partnerships or other cross-sectoral arrangements.[67] As leading theorists of the nonprofit sector and civil society, Salamon and Anheier conceive of CSOs as the formal, nonprofit, and voluntary activity that is not part of the state, private sector, or households and is commonly used throughout the Global North.[68]

Some economists such as Robert Eastwood and Michael Lipton view the decentralization, devolution, and privatization of state programs and operations as an opportunity for community organizations to increase democratic participation.[69] However, for other more critical scholars such as social theorists Susan Parnell and Jennifer Robinson, these shifts reflect the state's move toward a more laissez-faire economy whereby local initiatives can operate without any real impact or directive.[70]

Neoliberal approaches to social service delivery are especially prevalent in urban governance in order to manage significant urban challenges with a smaller role for government.[71] More than half of the world's population currently lives in cities, and it is expected that 68 percent will live in cities by 2050.[72] As the number of residents in cities grows and the location of global poverty becomes increasingly urban, scholars and policy makers have become more concerned that the urban governance of food, water, housing, transportation, and other basic needs will become strained over the next century. The urbanization of poverty has been a key fixture of this seismic demographic shift transforming the planet.[73]

Urban researchers such as Edgar Pieterse, Susan Parnell, Mark Swilling, and Mirjam van Donk have analyzed shifts within urban governance that include partnerships with private and nongovernmental organizations to deliver social services and programs. These scholars have examined how these management strategies aim to shrink the scope of government service delivery and reduce costs. In this way, these policy shifts are driven by economic motivations of financial stewardship and political motivations to limit the size and influence of government.[74]

CSOs have come under intense scrutiny for their lack of accountability, unclear impacts, corporatization, and neoliberal structure.[75] To start, scholars of civil society from the Global South have critiqued basic assumptions about the structure and design of CSOs. Mandla Seleoane, an expert on charity in South Africa, notes that resources do not always flow from rich to poor communities. In addition, Seleoane states that the nuclear family may not always be the typical household in South African contexts, as extended family and neighbors interact and care for each other in ways that reflect local customs and traditions.[76] Also, John L. Comaroff and Jean Comaroff, leading theorists on civil society in Africa, suggest that civil society is culturally distinct and a reflection of the unique historical and cultural factors that shape each place. In this way, comparison between civil societies may be limited.[77]

In the context of North America, a number of scholars have examined how CSOs operate in urban food systems. Prominent food scholar Julie Guthman has written extensively about the ways in which state institutions use CSOs to depoliticize, devolve, decentralize, and privatize agrofood philanthropy.[78] In addition, academic Rachel Slocum has explored the ways in which alternative food movements have reinforced exclusionary practices based on race and gender in city spaces.[79] Also, geographer Jerry Shannon's work on food deserts and obesity has highlighted how CSOs can reinforce problematic framings of food inequality when they focus on individual health decisions at the expense of the structure of the broader food system.[80]

Food banks, a type of CSO, have expanded across many higher-income countries in North America and Europe.[81] In many cases, they have become a central component of neoliberal food system governance as they are promoted as a replacement for the social welfare state and key mechanisms to reduce food insecurity and food waste.[82] In some cases, as food banks have developed, state welfare food programs have grown smaller.[83]

In this way, the state co-opts the food bank's programs as its own or utilizes the food bank as a means to deflect pressure from its own institutional failures or policy gaps. This is unfortunate in that most people who work in the food charity sector aim to reduce food insecurity in a meaningful way. However, food bank staff are not naive, as they often recognize that food banks are not capable of replacing food and income support programs provided by the state. As noted by an administrator at the Ohio Association of Foodbanks, food banks are politically shielded from criticism in ways that the welfare state is not:

> The food bank system is a Band-Aid to fill what government will not fill in terms of basic needs. The defunding of [the] social safety net and shift in the structure of the economy has helped to facilitate the growth of food banks. There is a contradiction that [food stamps now known as] SNAP is unpopular politically, but food banks will never be slammed by any politician. There is a lack of political will to reduce food waste and food poverty. These issues are very solvable. We will not fix hunger with one more food donation or food drive.[84]

However, as noted by sociologist Janet Poppendieck in her influential 1999 book *Sweet Charity*, food banks developed as an emergency network to confront food insecurity, even as the state scaled back its support for food programs during U.S. welfare state retrenchment in the 1980s and 1990s. According to Poppendieck, food banks held this role even though they were not designed to be a replacement for state food programs.

Building on Poppendieck, Graham Riches, an academic writing on food banks in the Canadian context since the 1980s, has argued that the development of food banks in North America helped to diffuse debate about the causes of food insecurity and food waste. For Riches, discussion about the growth of food charity and record numbers of meals and pounds of food delivered helped distract the public's attention from the decline of support for state food and income programs and the state's failure to institutionalize the basic human right to food.[85] These concerns have been echoed by other food bank scholars such as Hannah Lambie-Mumford in Britain and Rachel Loopstra and Valerie Tarasuk in Canada, who have noted similar food bank–welfare state dynamics in those contexts.[86]

Although interrelated, food insecurity and food waste are the result of two separate sets of processes. Food insecurity is caused by poverty, low income, and economic and social inequality.[87] Declining rural economies, challenges to small-scale farming, lack of food availability, high food prices, expensive urban costs of living, and unhealthy food are all reasons why food insecurity persists in rural and urban areas.[88] Food loss and food waste are produced by inefficiencies and excesses in local, regional, and global food systems. Even though some of these factors are related to natural weather fluctuations or technical inefficiencies in the market, the structure of the global food system and its emphasis on corporate profitability and production contribute to the reproduction of waste across the food system.[89]

Food banks can work to reduce both food insecurity and food waste on a small scale; however, the redistribution of surplus food from corporations is not adequate to reduce global poverty or solve the global food waste crisis. Although food banks use an expansive and flexible definition of food waste in order to promote food rescue as a solution to the food insecurity crisis, food surplus is not interchangeable with food waste. Food surplus is any food that can be redistributed for human consumption. In this way, it is a small subcomponent of food loss and food waste.[90] Fundamentally, food banks operate by redistributing food surplus to food charities.[91]

Food banks are susceptible to challenges pertaining to limited institutional accountability, co-optation from the state, and mission drift.[92] Food charity expert Maggie Dickinson has critiqued food banks and their network of local food organizations for regulating and managing the poor or "secondary consumers" in what has become a "corporate food charity state." In this dynamic, people are divided between deserving and underserving poor and paid and volunteer or unpaid labor.[93] Volunteers and donors are often congratulated for their volunteer service, and society is persuaded to believe that charity effectively reduces food insecurity better than government food programs. Additionally, food charity expert Rebecca T. de Souza critiques food banks and food pantries for stigmatizing recipients and not integrating the knowledge, experiences, or perspectives of the food insecure seriously into the development of emergency food systems.[94]

Food banks have developed close relationships with the corporate food industry, to the point where they are dependent on them.[95] Corporations use food banks to promote corporate social investment, improve their brand, and deflect attention from poverty and income inequality. Also, food banks have become pass-through organizations for state policy to transfer resources and power to corporates through tax benefits, liability protection, federal food programs, and direct purchase of food from food corporations and farmers.[96] Food banks depend on corporations for food donations, financial support, and institutional legitimacy as well as support industries in transportation and logistics. In many contexts, corporations have successfully leveraged their board membership and significant financial and in-kind food donations to professionalize food banks and institutionalize corporate culture within food banks. Corporate influence has limited the advocacy and the type of work food banks pursue to safe nonpolitical arenas such as distributing corporate food waste and promoting food nutrition programs rather than engaging in highly political topics such as economic inequality or tax policies.[97]

As part of this reciprocal relationship with food companies, food banks have proactively reframed the economic, political, and social causes of global poverty and inequality in the global food system as technical problems to be fixed within the confines of the market.[98] Food banks promote themselves as the business solution to reduce food waste and insecurity.

Food bank umbrella organizations leverage global corporate expertise, and the FBLI is a place where food banks learn the value of corporate connections, and corporations learn the value of food banks.[99]

Other critical scholars have suggested that the institutional mission of food banks is easily compromised as food corporations successfully shape what food banks can and should be. Geographers George Henderson and John Lindenbaum have critiqued food banks as extensions of modern capitalism, and thus are more pessimistic about their role in society.[100] Andy Fisher, former executive director of the Community Food Security Coalition and a well-known writer on food charity, has argued that food banks need to incorporate more stakeholders and donors into their operations and governance structure. In this way, Fisher argues that food banks would then be in a better political and financial position to pursue living wage and antipoverty campaigns and advocate more directly for the food insecure.[101]

The mission of food banks has continued to evolve as they increasingly incorporate environmental or ecological impact metrics into their operations.[102] Where it was once viewed solely as a social institution that worked to fill gaps in the welfare state, the food bank has been increasingly tasked with fulfilling society's need to be environmental stewards to reduce food waste.[103] For food bank critics such as Graham Riches and Andy Fisher, these mission shifts are viewed as evidence that the food bank is prioritizing institutional self-perpetuation and relationships with the state and corporations more than the people they serve: the food insecure.[104]

Given that food banks typically work closely with large food corporations and often operate in cities where social welfare support is small or reduced, geographer Joshua Lohnes suggests that food banks may not have the capacity or incentive to overcome the structural causes of food insecurity, food waste, or social inequality.[105] For example, as noted by studies on food banks in Dayton, Ohio, and West Virginia, food banks in high-poverty, low-service areas are limited in their ability to navigate broader structural forces beyond their control. In these contexts, food banks play an outsized role in local food system governance.[106] For food scholars Julianne Busa and Rebekah Garder, these pressures reduce the potential for local food initiatives to reduce inequality or poverty.[107]

Although food banks play a small role in many contexts to reduce food insecurity and waste, some scholars have argued that companies and governments use food charity as a way to abdicate responsibility. As Andy Fisher notes, food companies have used charity to showcase the scale of their food donations rather than confront issues over high prices, financial speculation in food markets, low worker wages, and store closures in inner cities.[108] Additionally, Graham Riches notes that states have used food charity as a way to deflect attention from their own policy failures or gaps.[109]

In this book, I use multiple methods to examine the development of food banks across the world's regions.[110] I conducted hundreds of in-depth interviews with food banks, governments, food companies, informal vendors, households, and other key stakeholders in the food system.[111] In addition, I completed surveys to collect data on the mission, programs, and impacts of key food system players. When possible, I conducted ethnography with local food institutions to understand how people engage in food charity in communities. Last, I used basic descriptive statistical and spatial analysis to understand the structure of food systems. Importantly, this research is designed to provide new perspectives on the motivations behind food banks, food companies, governments, and other key food system stakeholders.[112]

The case studies illustrate how and why food banks have developed across the world. Through an analysis of different contexts, the chapters detail the process of food bank development in the world's regions and the roles that they play in each context. In addition, case studies provide data on the ways in which food companies and governments work with or against food banks to achieve their institutional goals. Given the limited impacts of food banks and potential pitfalls in many contexts, these case studies examine ways that food banks should be reformulated in food systems.

CHAPTER 2

FOOD BANKING IN THE UNITED STATES

In the United States, the emergency food system has transformed as the country's political, economic, and social structure has evolved. In line with these changes, conceptions of "deserving" and "undeserving" poor have shifted as well.[1] As noted by welfare historian Michael Katz, during the eighteenth and nineteenth centuries, only those deemed too old, disabled, or too sick were labeled as deserving food aid. Rugged individualism and the perspective that one's fate is the outcome of one's work ethic as well as racist attitudes toward non-White residents ensured that the deserving poor remained a small group. This began to change during the early to middle parts of the twentieth century, as widespread poverty in cities among working populations resulted in new, more inclusive definitions of "deserving poor." Since the middle of the twentieth century, this distinction has remained fluid, as race, class, and gender strongly influence how the deserving and undeserving poor are understood in U.S. society.

During the country's early history in the eighteenth and nineteenth centuries as a rural society, food relief was controlled by private philanthropy and charities. However, during the period of urbanization and industrialization in the late nineteenth and early twentieth centuries, poverty increased beyond the capacity of the voluntary sector. Additionally, as the country diversified with new immigrants from eastern and southern Europe and internal Black migrants from the U.S. South, the country's political climate changed. Increased support for an active central state resulted in the expansion of food relief through the growth of centralized food and income programs operated by the federal government during the early to mid-twentieth century.[2]

By the end of the twentieth century, political pressures shifted again as many key aspects of the welfare state were retrenched and devolved to private, nonprofit, and other local actors. Program changes included reductions in the size of benefits as well as new eligibility requirements.[3] Although key federal food and income programs remain a part of the U.S. welfare state in the early twenty-first century, private and nonprofit food assistance programs have also grown as well.[4]

The United States is the only Organisation for Economic Co-operation and Development (OECD) country and one of a few countries globally not to vote yes or ratify multiple UN resolutions on the access to food as a human right. U.S. president Jimmy Carter signed the International Covenant on Economic, Social and Cultural Rights in 1977.[5] However, the U.S. Congress did not ratify it because it was viewed as infringing on U.S. sovereignty. Although this covenant, along with many UN resolutions, is symbolic, the lack of U.S. support for it is important, in that it weakens the international movement to enshrine the basic human right to food in all countries on the planet.[6]

In addition, since the 1990s, food industry consolidation has resulted in fewer companies controlling the quantities, types, and prices of foods offered.[7] In addition, the locations of food retailers have become more unequal as well, as grocers close across many inner-city neighborhoods.[8] These trends have contributed to food insecurity in many places. Increasingly, food corporations have developed philanthropy programs in the area of food insecurity and waste; however, in what follows, these initiatives have been criticized by a range of scholars.

To start, as Andy Fisher notes, food companies have used food banks to distract from high prices, financial speculation in markets, low worker wages, and store closures in inner cities.[9] In this way, impressive food donation numbers help to recast food companies as part of the solution, not the problem.

Corporate sustainability scholars Güler Aras and David Crowther view this type of philanthropy as self-serving brand enhancement and distracting from the structural causes of food insecurity and waste.[10] Although food companies are designed to be profitable enterprises, business ethics scholars Peggy Simcic Brønn and Deborah Vidaver-Cohen suggest that food corporations have rebranded their social investment initiatives as sustainability programs in order to maximize short-term low-commitment projects with maximum visibility.[11]

Additionally, for Brønn and Vidaver-Cohen, these types of philanthropic initiatives tend to focus on narrow, company-specific technical fixes rather critically examining the company's broader role in the food system. Given their close relationships with food banks and their broader influence on their consumers, food corporations help to define when and where food insecurity and food waste initiatives are needed and how they are measured. In this way, food banks provide an important service for the food industry beyond repurposing food waste. Food companies use the positive reputation of food banks to reinforce their own legitimacy as ethical businesses, worthy of investment.[12]

The United States has never had a national approach to food waste reduction, as it has fundamentally devolved responsibility to local communities and households to process food waste as they see fit. Although the U.S. Environmental Protection Agency (EPA) has promoted its Food Recovery Hierarchy and other national best practices for more than twenty years, no federal-level policy exists that is legally binding. In some U.S. cities, food waste reduction efforts in the twenty-first century have been driven by the high cost of land or by local legal mandates; however, most places are governed in an ad hoc style where food waste is managed by an uncoordinated set of public, private, and nonprofit organizations.[13]

Very often, government and food companies point to the household as the main culprit of food waste, even though more than 60 percent of food waste comes from farmers, food manufacturers, restaurants, grocery stores, and other institutions across the food system.[14] Although households are clearly a part of the food waste problem, their behaviors are shaped by food retailers and are not the only cause of food waste. As noted by sociologist David Evans, the structural causes of food waste related to financial speculation in food markets, market pressures to produce excess food, and weak policies to govern food waste are as important as food waste decisions made by individuals.[15]

This chapter analyzes the development of three case study food banks in the United States, namely the Greater Chicago Food Depository, Freestore Foodbank in Cincinnati, and the Foodbank in Dayton. Each case study exemplifies the complex institutional roles that food banks play and the ways in which food banks benefit state and corporate players. Moreover, given the challenges associated with the COVID-19 pandemic, these case studies illustrate the limits of the charitable food sector to reduce food insecurity and waste.

THE GREATER CHICAGO FOOD DEPOSITORY

The Greater Chicago Food Depository, part of the Feeding America network, is one of the largest and most well-known U.S. food banks (see figures 6 and 7). Since its founding in 1979, it has grown rapidly and become one of Feeding America's most high-profile food banks, as evidenced by former president Obama's visit in 2018.[16]

During one's visit to the Depository, the sheer size of the facility is notable, as it takes up a full city block in the Archer Heights neighborhood in southwestern Chicago. The organization has a relatively high number of employees for this field, as it has more than a dozen highly paid professionals running its operations, with many more employees in the warehouse and in the field itself. Executive director and CEO Kate Maehr has managed the food bank since 2006.[17]

There are two main steps in the food redistribution process at the Depository. To start, food donations flow to the Depository's food bank warehouse. While most of the food is purchased (48 percent), government sources (28 percent) and donations (23 percent) are also important sources of food for the Depository. Then, at the Depository's food bank warehouse, 700 beneficiary organizations in the Greater Chicago region collect and redistribute 97.5 million pounds of food to give to their individual food recipients. Beneficiary organizations include pantries (79 percent), mobile programs (6 percent), group homes and shelters (3 percent), children's programs (2 percent), soup kitchens (2 percent), and other programs (8 percent).[18]

In many ways, the Depository has exemplified the broader shifts in food banking in the past twenty years. To start, the Depository's foods are

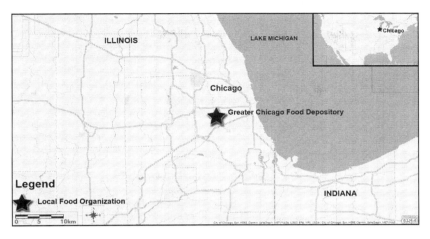

FIGURE 6. (*Above*) The location of the Greater Chicago Food Depository (courtesy of Warshawsky, 2020).

FIGURE 7. (*Left*) The Greater Chicago Food Depository (courtesy of Greater Chicago Food Depository, 2013).

increasingly healthy. As of 2022, while 45 percent of foods are shelf-stable core items, 36 percent are fresh produce and 19 percent proteins. As noted by an administrator with the Depository, this has been part of a deliberate effort by the Depository to provide healthy foods to its beneficiary organizations and the clients that they service, given the widespread obesity, hypertension, and diabetes that exist in the Depository's network.[19]

> The biggest shift in the food that we distribute is around the quality of the food that we distribute. . . . We have aggressive goals around distributing as much fresh fruits and vegetables as possible for us. The

next frontier for us is to diversify our supplier networks so that we can connect as much quality nutritious food [as possible] that is sourced locally to our partner organizations and the people that we serve.[20]

This dynamic was driven in part by the increased demand levels that the Depository experienced just before, during, and after the global recession of 2007–2009, as it was no longer sufficient to simply receive food. The Depository needed to purchase food to meet increased demand levels. As noted by a Depository administrator, it was during this process of purchasing food that the Depository started to take a more active role in the type of food delivered to its beneficiary organizations: "Increasingly, we are serving people who are employed. The new ugly truth is that the story of being hungry is America is also the story of working in America. . . . [During these years], it became more difficult for us to get food [to our beneficiary organizations because of the demand levels], so we began to purchase food."[21]

The Depository's shift to purchasing food is reflective of national trends where demand levels continue to increase unabated even though the economy has theoretically rebounded from the 2007–2009 global recession. However, it is also related to the Depository's financial position, as it is unusually large and robust for a nonprofit food bank. In 2022, its operating budget was $182.2 million per year, including $98.0 million from in-kind food donations.[22] The Depository received most of its resources from individual donors (58 percent), government grants and fees (25 percent), corporations and foundations (17 percent), special events (4 percent), and other (1 percent).

Importantly, the Depository has increasingly grown its private fundraising portfolio and reduced its dependence on government grants or any single financial source. This has allowed it to increase its purchasing of food and eliminate its shared maintenance or member fees where local food pantries and other local charities pay the food bank a small fee to receive food from it. Although they were approximately 20 cents per pound of food, these fees were a major source of concern for some beneficiary organizations before they were completely eliminated in 2020.[23] Also, this has provided the Depository with an opportunity to redirect beneficiary organizations toward a more collaborative and less punitive environment, which is realistically not an option for many other food banks that depend on member fees for a significant part of their income.

As noted by a Depository administrator, the Depository's elimination of member fees reflected a broader movement to develop deeper, less transactional relationships with local food pantries:

> [The elimination of member fees] is another strategic shift that we had made. And, what that has done is begin to shift from what has become a transactional relationship to a relationship that is a lot more about transformation. The policy and advocacy work is a big part of that. A whole set of strategies and community conversations about how we end hunger.[24]

The second shift regards advocacy. As noted by an administrator at the Depository, food policy advocacy has become a central part of its mission.[25]

> I would say that a significant shift is around our policy work and our advocacy work. It has become one of our most important strategies, and going forward it will be a bigger and bigger part of our work. It means we have a network that we collaborate with that focuses on federal conversations, state conversations, and local conversations on a range of issues.[26]

Even though this is a positive development in that its mission and strategic vision include advocacy as a key part of their future focus, CEO Kate Maehr still laments the many structural causes of poverty that remain outside of the Depository's mission or capacity to solve. This includes persistently low wages for the working poor, lack of support for a social safety net, and the demonization of the food insecure.[27]

Although influential in terms of food delivered and its network of stakeholders it can leverage to influence policy, the Depository's administrators are aware that its role as compared to federal programs is small.[28] They recognize that they are best positioned to fill a small niche. Yet, as noted by an administrator, people often falsely believe that food banks like the Depository can replace the programs that government operates:

> I think people want to think that food banks in this country can do it all, and we can't. SNAP provides significantly more support for men, women, and children. . . . I think we have to protect SNAP at all costs. The emergency food system would truly be an emergency

food system for people who do not qualify for nutritious programs or who have that one moment in their life when they are falling. Food banks would be smaller, and we would have a robust safety net that was meeting the needs of our neighbors.[29]

As expected, demand for food aid increased widely across the Chicago region as COVID devastated the local economy. In the first part of 2020, the number of people served through the Depository's network of local food agencies doubled at various points as compared to the previous year. To strengthen their network of food organizations, the Depository developed a coronavirus grant program to provide its member agencies small grants to help with operations. Sixty percent of funding was allocated for Black and Latino communities.

In addition, the Depository suspended fees for pantries to purchase food during the COVID crisis in 2020.[30] Even with these changes, almost 30 percent of food pantries were unable to remain open due to inventory, staffing, or health issues. The remaining 70 percent of network agencies remained open and managed to feed record numbers of people through the food bank system.[31] While many first-time food recipients utilized the Depository's food network in a variety of neighborhoods, the areas with the greatest increase in demand for food aid were in high-poverty food desert regions in south and west Chicago.[32]

As noted by CEO Kate Maehr, the COVID crisis created severe disruptions in the food system and subsequently limited donations of food exactly when they were needed most:

> We have had a real struggle accessing food here at our food bank. . . . What we see right now is that truckloads of food that we would have ordinarily ordered and then received in two weeks, we're now being told six weeks, ten weeks, twelve weeks to receive that food. . . . It is a reminder that we are all connected to this food system. And we need to understand the points of fragility within the system.[33]

Although the Depository actively worked to reduce food insecurity in the region, its smaller presence in the most vulnerable communities highlights the limitations of the charity-based food network.[34]

THE FREESTORE FOODBANK IN CINCINNATI

The Freestore Foodbank in Cincinnati is one of the most well-known food banks in Ohio and the United States more broadly.[35] As one of the founding members of Feeding America, the Freestore continues to be a both large and innovative operator. As of 2022, the Freestore served more than 37.7 million people per year across its twenty-county region through its network of more than 540 food pantries, shelters, and soup kitchens.[36]

Unlike the Depository, which is impressive in its size, the Freestore's accessibility is notable. Upon visiting the Freestore, it is clear that it is located strategically in a walkable part of Cincinnati near major bus lines and just a short distance from its service population. It is located just north of downtown Cincinnati in the densely populated Over-the-Rhine neighborhood.[37] The Freestore has a modest staff with a sizable volunteer contingent. CEO and president Kurt Reiber has managed the food bank since 2012.[38]

While it is not the largest food bank in Ohio, the Freestore is well known for its one-stop client center where people receive a range of wraparound services, including food, clothing, job training, health care enrollment, money management, transportation, and housing.[39] In addition to these services, the Freestore is unique in the number of partnerships it has with Kroger, one of the largest food retailers and food donors in the world, which is headquartered in Cincinnati. Given the Freestore's unique mission and programs and Kroger's innovative programs, Cincinnati is a good case study to examine further (see figures 8 and 9).

More than 90 percent of the Freestore's $65 million operating budget originates from individual donations, foundations, and corporations.[40] As stated by a Freestore administrator, Freestore staff attribute much of their success to their relationships with local leading corporations, such as Kroger. "We have a great community [with] many local corporations here that support our cause. But, without question, Kroger has been our number one partner. Kroger really understands the business of food and the business of hunger."[41]

To start, Kroger works with the Freestore to provide unsellable goods as part of the company's Zero Hunger/Zero Waste program.[42] In conjunction

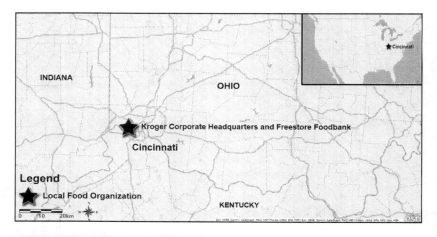

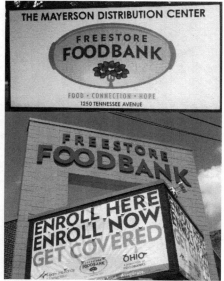

FIGURE 8. (*Above*) The location of the Kroger Company and the Freestore Foodbank (courtesy of Warshawsky, 2020).

FIGURE 9. (*Left*) The Freestore Foodbank (courtesy of Warshawsky, 2014).

with the Freestore, local food pantries, shelters, and soup kitchens pick up food that is near expiration, bruised, or damaged, but still edible. This program is operational at 99 percent of Kroger's stores in North America, collecting a total of 90 million pounds of perishable food donations in 2020.[43] In Cincinnati, the program donates 6.6 million pounds of food and has been operational since 2013. In addition, Kroger works with the Freestore to operate several in-store fundraisers throughout the year. These programs have been running for multiple decades and link the Freestore organization with Kroger more than any other company, since the Freestore is visible throughout Kroger storefronts, check-out aisles, and other displays for much of the year.

As only one of ten pilot food banks in the country, the Freestore is one of Kroger's reclamation hubs.[44] In the past, Kroger's Cincinnati regional warehouse sold many unsellable shelf-stable goods to a third-party vendor hundreds of miles away in northern Indiana to reclaim some profits in the secondhand market shops and dollar stores. As of 2013, all of these shelf-stable products were sent to the Freestore. This unique partnership not only increased donation volumes at the Freestore, as 500,000 pounds of food were delivered per year, but it has also set a new precedent for food donations nationally.

In 2018, as part of this push, Kroger announced it would establish a $10 million innovation fund through the Kroger Company Foundation, accelerate food donations to give 3 billion meals by 2025, donate more balanced and nutritious food, advocate for public policy solutions to address food insecurity and food waste reduction, achieve zero food waste status by 2025, and continue key partnerships with Feeding America, World Wildlife Fund, and ReFED to transform communities and improve health.[45]

While Kroger is aspiring to push forward to reduce food insecurity and food waste, many of the key specifics are not clear, as stated by Jessica Adelman, Kroger Group vice president of corporate affairs:

> We don't—and we won't—have all the answers. . . . While we are clear about our vision, we are flexible about how to get there. We are working closely with both Feeding America and World Wildlife Fund (WWF), our longstanding partners, to develop transparent metrics to track our progress. And we are inviting everyone who is passionate about feeding people and protecting the planet to join us in our mission to end hunger in our communities and eliminate waste across our company by 2025.[46]

As a founding member of Feeding America, the largest U.S. charitable food bank system, Kroger continues to be one of their largest donors. In

2020, Kroger donated 1.8 billion meals, with the expectation that this number would grow to 3 billion meals by 2025.[47] However, Kroger never defines how or why it counts the number of pounds donated or the number of meals distributed. It implicitly equates higher amounts of donated food with increased potential to reduce food insecurity, without evidence to make that connection. In addition, although Kroger points to a high diversion rate, that is, food not sent to a landfill, of over 81 percent, it is not clear how this is measured.[48] Through implementation of the EPA's Food Recovery Hierarchy, Kroger has developed a way to track its food waste, compare its waste to an industry standard, and promote its company brand and corporate stewardship.[49] According to Kroger, 51.7 percent of food waste ends up in a landfill or incinerator.[50]

When asked if the company's Innovation Fund would help contribute to solutions to reduce food deserts where Kroger has closed locations in many urban areas, the chief sustainability officer for Kroger said that the Innovation Fund is designed to create high-profile solutions to food waste, not to reduce food insecurity in high-need areas.[51] "The Innovation Fund is to fund new ideas about food waste reduction and to increase community involvement in Kroger and its food initiatives. The closure of grocery stores is always a tough decision, but this fund is not [designed] to fill the gap left by that process."[52]

This type of answer suggests that Kroger is, in part, using the sustainability initiative to draw positive attention to the company's philanthropy and away from store closures that have occurred across inner cities in the United States in recent years.[53] This has disproportionately impacted lower-income Black and Brown communities.[54] In this way, in line with business ethics scholars Güler Aras and David Crowther, the Zero Hunger/Zero Waste campaign could be viewed as a discursive tool to reproduce the company's legitimacy as an ethical and altruistic company.[55] Although food companies are designed to be profitable enterprises, Aras and Crowther suggest that green philanthropy can help deflect attention from places where companies make more significant impacts related to store location, food prices, and worker wages. Consumers expect companies to be socially, economically, and environmentally good actors, so brand enhancement is critical for long-term corporate profitability.[56]

Meanwhile, the Freestore's operations are quite reliant on the success of Kroger and other local corporations in Cincinnati. In line with food charity expert Poppendieck's critique of food banks, this creates dependencies where food corporations decide the type, amount, and timing of food donations that food banks like the Freestore must accept, even if they do not fit the needs of the beneficiary agencies or community members.[57] These tensions have been noted by some small food pantries in Cincinnati that have been forced to accept food donations and the Freestore's Feeding America bureaucratic structure.[58]

In part, these dynamics are shaped by the Freestore's laissez-faire management style, whereby the organization's operations have historically been decentralized and somewhat atomistic and based on unique unstructured social relationships. In some cases, this has resulted in increased food wastage, as noted by an administrator at a local food pantry in Cincinnati:

> The management of food rescue at the Freestore is laissez-faire. If there is extra food somewhere, the Freestore tells people [and organizations] they are welcome to take it. They don't care how they manage the relationships with the grocery stores. However, because of the Freestore's lack of proactive management, pantries would get massive quantities of (random) or half-rotten foods, and the pantries did not have the capacity to manage that [food waste].[59]

As noted by an administrator at a local food pantry in Cincinnati, the Freestore's moves to centralize decision making and partner with local power institutions, such as Kroger, have frustrated some smaller unaffiliated food pantries in the Cincinnati community, as a lack of management has turned to highly centralized management:

> There is tension between some local food nonprofits, in part because the Freestore is becoming more proactive about managing some of these relationships with Kroger, which is functionally trying to assert monopoly power. We as a food nonprofit sometimes feel like we are floating around the edges saying we have a good idea too. But we don't have resources to be impactful. There are a lot of relationships that happen at high levels between CEOs and boards such as Kroger and Freestore, and we are excluded.[60]

These frustrations are not just about money and resources. They are as much about power and the way emergency food services are delivered. There are many different ways to manage food aid. Some organizations prefer to have strong religious or political perspectives built into their organization, while for others, eligibility requirements, visit frequency, food types available, cost of services, and mode of delivery all vary. When large organizations such as Feeding America or the government become involved in food delivery, they introduce new modes of control. Also, large donors, such as Kroger, can then more strongly influence how food aid is managed. These are not necessarily negative, but they do have the potential to strongly influence how emergency food services are delivered.

In addition, given that many of Kroger's initiatives have succeeded at the Freestore exactly because of their location in Cincinnati, it is unclear how well some of their programs could be scaled out to other cities. This is clearly a goal for Kroger, as they would like to expand these philanthropic operations across the country.[61]

Like other food banks, the Freestore was overwhelmed with rapid increases in demand in 2020 due to COVID.[62] In March 2020, the food bank gave out six months' worth of food in one month. By April 2020, the food bank had only a three-week supply left.[63] As noted by CEO and president Kurt Reiber, higher demand was coupled with increased costs, decreased food donations, reduced numbers of volunteers, inadequate food storage facilities, and other pressures on the food system and the food insecure.[64] According to the Freestore, 75 percent of food recipients were first-time clients at the Freestore or its network of food charities.[65] As noted by a Freestore administrator, the COVID pandemic produced a serious of challenges for the food bank:

> The coronavirus pandemic has created a perfect storm for charitable hunger-relief networks. We rely heavily on large fundraising events, but those are at risk of being canceled. Donations from our grocery partners who typically provide excess food have now dwindled due to their empty shelves. Our food pantries are normally operated by elderly volunteers who are now sheltering at home. Children may not have access to replacement school meals; seniors, people living with disabilities, and other vulnerable populations cannot access

congregate feeding sites.... The foodbank is seeing a 35 to 40 percent increase in the demand for food.... We have spent over $1.5 million on food for a period that we would have spent $300,000.... The need just continues to escalate.[66]

To meet this higher demand and offset the lack of food and personnel at the food bank, the Freestore leveraged its increased visibility to fundraise record amounts of money. This was achieved quickly through generous donations from many of Cincinnati's largest corporations and foundations, as well as smaller individual donors in the community.[67] These fundraising efforts were put toward the purchase of large volumes of food to counterbalance fluctuations in the food supply chain. Whereas food supplies in prepandemic years were 50 percent from corporate and individual donations, 35 percent from government programs, and 15 percent from purchased food, food supplies during 2020 shifted dramatically, as purchased food increased to 40 percent and donations declined to 15 percent of overall food supplies.[68] In addition, to mitigate the 10 percent closure rate of food charities, reductions in volunteers, and steep increases in need for food relief, the Freestore increased its delivery of food and emergency food boxes, and the Ohio National Guard assisted in food delivery on multiple occasions.[69]

Although Cincinnati has long had a relatively high poverty rate, especially among children, COVID pushed the city into the top ten of poorest large U.S. cities.[70] Thus, the economic fallout from the pandemic increased pressure on the charitable food relief network. As noted by an administrator at the Freestore, the COVID crisis pushed the Freestore to reevaluate what it had been doing and what it should be doing following the pandemic:

> Right now, we spend 60 to 65 percent on food resources and 30 to 35 percent on wraparound supportive services and workforce development programs. I could see us getting to a 50/50 percent split, or at some point it could be a 60/40 split the other way in order to treat the causes, not the symptoms. I think that is something that a lot of food banks across the country are saying: "What are we going to own and lead?" I would say that the pandemic has accelerated this internal reflection at the Freestore.[71]

Thus, the impact of the COVID pandemic on the Freestore has been significant in that it stretched the capacity of the network to feed people, and it forced the food bank to change its operations and reflect on the value of its programs, given that the demand for food aid continued to increase. However, although the Freestore managed to increase its institutional foothold within Cincinnati during 2020–2021, it is unclear whether it has the capacity or long-term support to broaden its mission or impact in the community.

Meanwhile, panic buying, disruptions in food supply, and reduced numbers of volunteers to transport food decreased Kroger's capacity for donations. To mitigate the impacts of the pandemic on its food bank partners, Kroger developed the COVID-19 Response Fund to provide approximately $10 million for food relief efforts across the country.[72] The Freestore has been the fortunate recipient of many of Kroger's in-kind donations and innovative programs. As with previous investments, Kroger's COVID-19 Response Fund provided the Freestore with financial support in partnership with the Greater Cincinnati Foundation.[73]

Although COVID increased costs for Kroger, it also produced record sales, as household demand for food increased dramatically during 2020.[74] These record profits are worth noting as they theoretically place Kroger in a better position to grow its philanthropic enterprise. The Freestore, in some ways, is simply a pass-through organization for Kroger to meet its broader company goals. In addition, like food bank networks in other cities such as Chicago, the Freestore Foodbank network has faced criticism from some of its network agencies and other nonaffiliated food organizations in the city. While this is not unique to Cincinnati, it does highlight the challenges of working with so many different stakeholders.

THE FOODBANK IN DAYTON, OHIO

The third food bank examined in this chapter is the Foodbank, located in Dayton, Ohio (see figure 10). By many measures, the Foodbank, founded in 1976, has been ranked as one of the leading food bank institutions, especially given its relatively small size, as the smallest of twelve food banks in Ohio.[75] In 2018, the Foodbank was ranked as the second-best food bank in the country, according to Charity Navigator, due to the quality of the

Food Banking in the United States 47

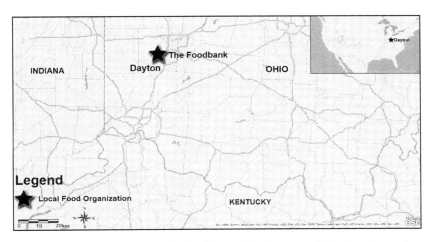

FIGURE 10. The location of the Foodbank in Dayton, Ohio (courtesy of Warshawsky, 2020).

organization's operational and financial efficiency and management.[76] It has also received positive press for its dynamic leadership and its capacity to redistribute large volumes of food given its small size.[77]

The Foodbank compares well with other food banks in Ohio. It is the fourth largest food bank in the state in terms of pounds delivered, yet it is the seventh largest in terms of households served and ninth largest in terms of member agencies served.[78] Thus, the Foodbank provides more food to a somewhat smaller region of only 740,000 people. The Foodbank distributed over 15 million pounds of food through its network of more than ninety-two member agencies across the three-county region of Montgomery, Greene, and Preble counties. Approximately 196,000 households are served through this distribution network.[79]

The Foodbank warehouse sits on an old industrial site in the near west side of Dayton, just outside downtown. Although it is imposing in its size, it is both centrally located for food pickup and delivery and home to spaces for food composting, urban gardening, and public art.[80] The organization employs forty-five people, and its leadership is well recognized.[81] Chief executive officer Michelle Riley has managed the food bank since 2011.[82] Riley is a bold leader and not afraid to speak hard truths to her employees, food recipients, or the public. Given her connections to Feeding America, she is knowledgeable of the Foodbank's role from a broader regional, state, and national perspective.[83]

To fulfill its mission to relieve hunger through the acquisition and distribution of food to hungry people in the Dayton region, the Foodbank distributes food through its network of member agencies.[84] Forty percent of this food is fresh fruits and vegetables, in part because it is free for member agencies to pick up at their location.[85] The evidence of this significant fresh food push is seen literally in front of the food bank, as the public art sculpture created by local artist Chad Johnson and the local Garden on Hope highlight the food bank's fresh food initiative (see figures 11 and 12).

The Foodbank's member agencies operate a range of programs through food pantries, mobile farmers markets, meal sites, shelters, mass food distributions, congregational feeding programs, food relief through area hospitals, SNAP outreach, Kids Cafe, Drive-Thru food redistribution, and Good-to-Go Backpack programs. These programs collectively result in donations for more than 650,000 meals served across the region.[86] Food originates from five main food streams, including the Ohio Association of Foodbanks Agricultural Program and Ohio Food Program, more than sixty local food retailers such as Meijer and Kroger, U.S. Department of Agriculture Emergency Food Assistance Program, food drives and donations, and wholesale product distributions.[87]

In fiscal year 2022, the Foodbank's operating budget was $25.8 million per year, with 72.1 percent from in-kind donations, 19.1 percent from financial contributions, 8.2 percent from governmental grants, and less than 1 percent from other sources.[88]

Although significantly smaller than food banks in larger cities such as Chicago or Cincinnati, the Foodbank has a major presence in the Miami Valley region, which has some of the higher levels of food insecurity in the state.[89] The Dayton region has had a higher than average rate of poverty and food insecurity for decades, since deindustrialization started to decimate the region beginning in the 1970s and continuing today.[90] Dayton's ranking as the ninth most food-insecure metropolitan area in 2014 shocked many policy makers, social service deliverers, and activists and was a wake-up call to the level of need in the region.[91] According to this report, 22.6 percent of residents in the three-county region were food insecure.[92]

FIGURE 11. (*Left*) Chad Johnson, *The Apple*; nutrition as public art at the Foodbank (courtesy of Warshawsky, 2016).

FIGURE 12. (*Below*) The Garden of Hope, an urban garden at the Foodbank (courtesy of Warshawsky, 2016).

Since 2014, Dayton–Montgomery County Public Health, local food advocacy organization Hall Hunger Initiative, and other community stakeholders in the Dayton region have taken on food insecurity as a central political, public health, and service delivery issue.[93] Although the impact of these initiatives has been mixed, the role of the food bank is as critical as it has ever been in the region, especially as many other food initiatives are not viewed as realistic or profitable.[94] While Foodbank staff are aware of the limited role that they can play in reducing food insecurity, they also recognize the challenge of overcoming more structural challenges associated with food access. This perspective is articulated by an administrator at the Foodbank:

> We are distributing 10 million pounds of food. How many pounds of food do you think we should distribute in addition to food stamps before people start saying you are either not doing it right or you really don't care if you shorten the line? And I do care, but the problem here locally is that they want a grocery store and they need three actually. . . . Why haven't we done it? Because you can't make money at it.[95]

Yet, there are some staff at Dayton area food advocacy organizations who are concerned that the Foodbank's ties to Feeding America have the potential to micromanage food aid eligibility and delivery processes, as stated by an administrator at a local nonprofit food advocacy organization: "I am a big supporter of the [Dayton] foodbank and its programs and its advocacy, but many beneficiary agencies in the community are limited by their relationship with the Foodbank and Feeding America's rules. This is especially a problem for those recipients who do not have identification, undocumented immigrants, or refugees."[96]

As in Chicago and Cincinnati, these concerns revolve around the independence of food charities to determine how they implement food aid when Feeding America controls the rules and regulations in food rescue and recovery. While the Foodbank is an example of a local food bank working beyond the scope of its mission, local and state food bank leaders in Ohio have pointed out that government food assistance through SNAP and the minimum wage are the two most important ways that food insecurity can be reduced in the state and the nation.[97]

In short, the Foodbank has arguably maxed out its potential in terms of reducing food insecurity in the Dayton region. As a highly efficient organization, the Foodbank works as one of the leading food advocacy organizations in the region. Most local nonprofits in the Dayton region are supportive of the Foodbank and realize that its role in the region is invaluable beyond its food rescue mission. Its successes highlight the limited potential of food banks to be the solution to food insecurity. It can and should be a key part of food insecurity reduction in the Dayton region, but clearly part of Dayton's challenges have to do with much broader issues, including declining wages and employment opportunities related to deindustrialization, inadequate government support for food assistance programs and the minimum wage, and lack of private sector investment in food retail grocery and fresh food options in a region with food deserts in urban and rural communities. In this way, the experiences of the Foodbank in Dayton are reflective of many other U.S. contexts where the food bank system works to deliver food aid in the context of deeply entrenched structural challenges related to poverty, structural unemployment, and food insecurity.

In 2020, the COVID pandemic decimated the local economy and contributed to increased unemployment and lost wages for many households.[98] Food insecurity rates rose dramatically from March to May 2020, with some estimates pointing to a doubling of hunger in the state of Ohio due to the pandemic.[99] This produced dramatic increases in food bank usage across Ohio and extremely long car lines in the Dayton area, with hundreds of cars lined up for the Foodbank's Drive-Thru food services.[100]

The Foodbank played a key role in addressing dramatic increases in food insecurity in 2020, as it was one of the first institutions that people went to during the economic collapse that followed the health crisis.[101] Yet, although the charity-based patchwork of food relief helped many during the pandemic, the crisis also revealed the structural weaknesses of a network that is based on in-kind and financial donations and volunteers.[102] These were the exact resources that dwindled in 2020, as noted by Foodbank development manager Caitlyn McIntosh and grant and advocacy manager Emily Gallion:

> We could never have prepared for the extent to which it would impact our own operations. . . . Traffic at our on-site drive-thru has reached

an all-time high [triple what it was before COVID]. . . . At that time, we were seeing demand steadily increasing at the same time as many of our main sources of food procurement, such as food drives and grocery store donations, dwindled or were stopped completely.[103]

In addition to the food bank central warehouse near downtown Dayton, operations at the one hundred member agency food pantries, soup kitchens, and shelters struggled as well, with many agencies closing altogether due to lack of staff and volunteers and an inability to operate with recommended social distancing and public health guidelines. The agency closure rate reached 70 percent in March and April 2020, although many have since reopened with new models of delivery such as drive-through and scheduled appointments.[104] As stated by McIntosh and Gallion, these dynamics forced the Foodbank and its member agencies into a very challenging position:

Only 75 of our 110 partner agencies are still open [in May 2020]. The others have been forced to close due to a variety of reasons, such as the closure of their parent organization or concerns for their own volunteers. . . . With agency closures taken into consideration, our agencies that are open are serving over twice as many individuals as this time last year.[105]

The food bank network was not only strained but also smaller due to agency closures while the food bank fed record numbers of people. The Foodbank estimated that food relief increased across its network because of higher food demand from low-wage workers, service workers, and those who stopped working to take care of those at home.[106] Also, as with other food banks, the Foodbank was confronted with severe disruptions in the food supply chain. Although it was able to purchase food through an increase in fundraising, the charitable food network showed its vulnerability at the exact moment it was needed the most by the food insecure.[107] On top of COVID, inflation has contributed to increased costs for food recipients and the Foodbank since 2021.[108] For these reasons, the Foodbank has been working with partners to fundraise for a new, larger facility to cope with increased food demand.[109]

CHAPTER 3

FOOD BANKING IN ISRAEL AND SOUTHWESTERN ASIA

This chapter analyzes two food bank networks, the first of which is located in Israel. It is called Leket Israel (LI) and is part of the Global FoodBanking Network (GFN). In contrast to most food banks across the world, its focus is on fresh food redistribution.[1] Since 2003, it has gained notoriety around the world for this unique mission.[2] Yet its impact has been small given increasing poverty in the country and the amount of food waste in Israel.[3] Moreover, the Israeli government and corporations have been lukewarm about supporting food initiatives, thus further limiting more meaningful change in the food system.[4]

The second network is called the Food Banking Regional Network (FBRN). It is headquartered in Dubai, and has a network of thirty-nine food banks located in thirty-seven countries across southwestern Asia, South Asia, and Africa, although FBRN staff define its primary service area as the Arab region.[5] While the FBRN has a wide geographical distribution of operations, many of its food banks are smaller, unstable, and not well supported or monitored by the FBRN network.[6] Additionally, given the lack of state support and political instability in many autocratic regions where it operates, it must develop strong ties with corporations and individual donors. This is an uphill battle, given the scale of food insecurity in the Arab region and the small size of the social welfare state there.[7]

Given the social and economic fallout from the COVID-19 pandemic, this chapter underscores the institutional challenges philanthropic initiatives such as food banks must face in order to operate well or at all.

LEKET ISRAEL

Leket Israel, formerly known as Table to Table, emerged in 2003 when a New York immigrant named Joseph Gitler settled in Israel and was shocked by the level of food waste in a country where food insecurity remained a problem.[8] Approximately 35 percent of food is wasted in Israel, which ranks as one of the highest food waste rates in the world given its level of development.[9] Gitler started to save food that he found at corporate cafeterias and catering halls. He then stored the food in refrigerators in the parking lot at his home and distributed it to charities himself. Within one year, Gitler expanded the operations as LI bought a warehouse and trucks.[10] For his leadership at LI, Gitler has been recognized with numerous awards within Israel.[11]

The LI employees are well-versed in the nonprofit fundraising landscape, not only in Israel but internationally in the United States, Canada, and parts of Europe as well. This skill set has given LI an advantage in that it can effectively communicate its mission in English, discuss operational challenges and opportunities, and advocate for financial support in a wide-ranging number of contexts beyond Israel.[12]

LI is currently one of the most well-established food banks in the world and has been on the radar of the GFN since the GFN was founded in 2006.[13] In addition, given LI's unique focus on the redistribution of fresh fruits and vegetables through gleaning and hot meals, LI has garnered international attention from GFN and its other member food banks as a model to replicate.[14] LI's administrators are well aware of their uniqueness as a food bank:

> I think people in the [GFN and the global food banking community] are astounded that we can move as much of the food as we do for the number of meals and produce that we redistribute. That is why we have a lot of people inquiring [from around the world].... The GFN is often sending us people who physically come and visit us or share information such as best practices.[15]

Food Banking in Israel and Southwestern Asia 55

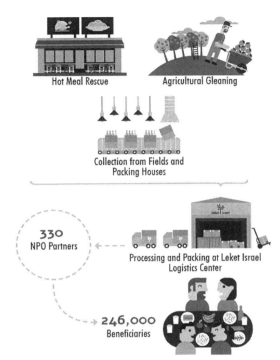

FIGURE 13. Leket Israel organizational structure (courtesy of Leket Israel, 2021).

The mission of LI is "to lead the safe, effective and efficient collection and distribution of surplus nutritious food in Israel, to those who need it."[16] This is accomplished through the harvesting of surplus agricultural produce and the collection of cooked meals for people in need. The former is funneled through one of LI's warehouses, whereas the latter are given directly to people in the 263 charities spread across the country (see figure 13). In all of its operations, the focus is on nutrition, an aspect that separates LI from other food bank operations around the world.[17] This distinctive mission has been recognized by the GFN's CEO Lisa Moon:

> Leket's approach is really unique, because they focus on fresh fruits and vegetables and working with local producers and focusing on nutrition with the people they are serving. . . . That's why GFN is so passionate about promoting this model to communities around the world. [Leket has a] unique method of collecting fresh, rescued food from the top of the food chain at the level of agricultural production.[18]

According to statistics from 2022, LI has rescued 26,064 tons of fruits and vegetables and delivered 1,710,000 hot meals to more than 223,000 food recipients.[19]

LI's operating budget in 2020 was 49,924,000 shekels or U.S.$15,532,270 per year.[20] Importantly, only 41 percent of funding for LI comes from within Israel, as the United States accounts for more than 45 percent of funding, with Canada, the United Kingdom, and other countries accounting for the rest. Moreover, 50 percent of financial support originates from individual or private donors, 33 percent from foundations, 8 percent from corporations, 5 percent from federations, and 4 percent from churches and synagogues.[21]

Although LI has grown significantly in recent years, it has faced substantial challenges. To start, in the years before COVID-19, demand levels increased dramatically due to the emergence of the working poor population within the country.[22] While poverty in the country is moderate as compared to its peer countries, economic growth in Israel has not benefited everyone, as the cost of living has hit the working poor especially hard. According to the Organisation for Economic Cooperation and Development (OECD), Israel had a relative poverty rate of 16.9 percent in 2019, which ranked it in line with countries such as Turkey and Mexico. Additionally, the OECD noted that Israel had one of the highest costs of living, as the country had food prices 19 percent higher than other OECD countries.[23]

In 2020, the COVID pandemic created extreme pressure on LI and its network of food agencies to collect and distribute food.[24] Although LI redistributed record amounts of food, multiple challenges limited its operations. Demand for food relief increased more than 50 percent as compared to the previous year due to sharp increases in unemployment and food insecurity. In 2020, 510,000 Israelis left the labor market, and approximately 2 million people reported a loss of income in a country of only 9 million people.[25] At the same time, donations of unused prepared foods from hotels, companies, and army bases decreased by more than 50 percent.[26] With limited food supplies and staff and volunteers, more than 50 percent of food charities within the LI network closed at some point.[27]

To offset these limitations, LI was forced to raise money to purchase food, something that was not part of their typical operations. Although fundraising doubled to approximately $2.5 million in 2020, it was not clear if this would result in sustained support, even as the levels of food insecurity and unemployment were likely to persist after COVID's impact decreased.[28] As noted by an LI administrator, this uncertainty placed LI in a precarious situation moving forward:

> Right now [in 2021], we're the flavor of the month. I've never seen food banks get as much attention as they've received over the last year. The question will be, when people's lives go back to some sort of normality, where does that leave us? Our fear is that our donors might not be able to extend themselves like they did in 2020. We feel like the need is going to be very high in Israel, and we really have no clue what the fundraising is going to look like.[29]

The charity-based food bank system in Israel has been forced to cope with a food insecurity crisis well beyond its capacity. This has been compounded by the Israeli government's inadequate response to the crisis.[30] Although the Israeli social welfare state is moderately sized, with a range of income support programs for those eligible, no direct food aid is provided by the state. In addition, the Israeli government has not adequately funded the welfare state to sustain these programs, especially in light of increases in poverty across the country.[31] As the Israeli state has pushed a "social investment" approach to reduce welfare loads and increase participation in the labor market, the social welfare state is being systematically transformed into a workfare state.[32] These collective decisions have undercut support for the vulnerable in Israeli society when support is most needed to confront the high cost of living, relatively low wages, and social inequality that many Israelis confront on a daily basis across the country.[33]

Even with increasing demand levels both before and during the COVID pandemic, LI struggled to gain financial support among food corporations. This has persisted, in part, because LI deliberately created a model where food companies and their surplus food are excluded from the LI redistribution system. Food companies are not integrated into LI's mission as they are in other food banks, since LI does not redistribute dry goods or foods from the food supply chain. Although food corporations contribute a significant amount of food waste in Israel, LI made the decision to focus on fresh food only.[34] As explained by an LI administrator, the lack of corporate support makes LI unique in its structure and operations:

> We really don't [have corporate food or funding support] yet, in part because we are not a traditional food bank. Our emphasis is all fresh food [and hot food]. [We don't do dry goods.] That is where we put our resources. Ninety-five percent of our food is nutritious food. There are other organizations that do the dry foods. We are unique because we focus on the fresh and healthy foods.[35]

While the government passed the Food Donation Act in 2018, which made Israel one of only five countries in the world to have food donation liability protection for corporations, LI CEO Gidi Kroch has been frustrated with the Israeli government for multiple reasons.[36]

To start, Kroch would like the Israeli government to be more proactive about developing a food policy that aims to reduce food poverty and waste while also promoting healthy eating.[37] As Kroch notes, the right to food is not mentioned explicitly, nor is it a key part of the country's budget priorities through the National Insurance Institute or the Ministry of Welfare and Social Affairs.[38] Although Israel signed and ratified the International Covenant on Economic, Social and Cultural Rights in 1991, Israel does not have any language recognizing the right to food as a human right in any of the country's welfare policies.[39]

In addition, while LI aims to work with government officials across a range of political perspectives, frequent turnover in the Israeli government has the potential to reduce the effectiveness of lobbying and advocacy. As noted by an LI administrator, this dynamic has stymied potential opportunities for LI to collaborate with government:

> We would like stronger ties with different governmental officials. There's probably going to be elections here in Israel again. A lot of people that we have already been working with the last number of months or years have already resigned. I'm afraid that will probably have some negative impact on some of the progress and commitments that we have received. I hope we don't have to start again from tabula rasa.[40]

Although Israel's governmental structure ensures that change is often slow or nonexistent, the COVID crisis created an opportunity for LI to increase the visibility of its programs and impacts. As noted by an LI administrator, the staff at LI were hopeful this increased attention would increase LI's access to government funding and amplify its voice in the social welfare discussions taking place in government: "The silver lining was whereas before COVID-19 we didn't have direct communication or any active partnership with municipalities, now this crisis has given us a foray into that world. Now we're not just recognized by a few local charities we are working with, as the whole municipality knows who we are and what we're doing and our impact."[41]

In addition to these tensions with the Israeli government, LI has also faced challenges with the diversity of organizations that it serves. As LI has worked to expand its reach across the country, some charities have been unable to redistribute perishable or hot foods in line with basic food safety and storage requirements, as staff training or warehouse storage is inadequate.[42] Even with these limitations, it is likely that LI will remain a leader in the food banking world given its significant financial support from funders in Israel, North America, and Europe. Joseph Gitler has shown resilience in working through different institutional challenges, as resource limitations, tense government relations, and unstable beneficiary organizations are somewhat typical for many food banks across the world. Its challenges, especially during the COVID crisis, have shown that even seemingly robust food bank systems like the LI may be unable to significantly reduce food insecurity or food waste levels, which both remain very high.

THE FOOD BANKING REGIONAL NETWORK

While the GFN is arguably the largest and most influential food banking network in the world, it is not the only multicontinent food bank alliance in the Global South. The FBRN has food banks across southwestern Asia, South Asia, and Africa.[43] Although it is an independent network of food banks, the FBRN is a partner with the GFN in its global hunger reduction mission. The origins of FBRN started in Egypt in 2006, where a group of successful businesspeople launched the first food bank in Egypt to address the significant food insecurity crisis there.[44] As the Egyptian Food Bank expanded in size and notoriety, the FBRN was founded in 2013 to further expand the mission to the broader region of South Asia, the Middle East, and much of Africa.[45] The key proponents of the FBRN had extensive experience in the hotel and tourism industries and therefore could convince them to reduce food waste in their industries in Egypt and additional countries.[46]

Moez El Shohdi, founder and CEO of the FBRN, has managed its network of food banks since it was founded in 2013. With a staff of only a few people, El Shohdi manages the daily operations of the organization, including media appearances and visits to member food banks around the world, at the same time he also continues his daily job as president of the Middle East and Africa division of Style Hotels International, which he has held since 1993.[47] With his PhD in hotel management and over thirty years' experience in the hotel and tourism industry, El Shohdi speaks from a position of knowledge about how, where, and when food is wasted. He has used this knowledge to foster a passion for reducing food waste in the business and tourism sectors.[48]

Across the FBRN network, 5.5 million families are fed monthly through the work of 17,400 volunteers.[49] The network's mission is to "eliminate regional hunger through the founding, development and support of food banks in the region in cooperation with a broad spectrum of partners, sponsors and members."[50] As part of this broader vision "to create a region free from hunger," FBRN promotes a number of pillars or types of programs to fight hunger.[51] Although these pillars continue to evolve in form and number, they currently include feeding, food waste reduction, development and capacity building, humanitarian relief, community engagement, and sustainable philanthropy and investment.[52] These pillars are associated with FBRN's key performance indicators associated with more coverage of their key regional coverage areas in southwestern Asia, South Asia, and Africa.[53]

Food banks have developed within each country in the FBRN network as a result of outreach from wealthy businesspeople, government embassies, or nonprofits already existing in the country.[54] Given the range of these different institutional players, the structure and orientation of regional food banks varies across each country. As part of their development with new food banks, the FBRN identifies and trains new staff on the mission and management of food bank operations, maintains a central database to measure programs in each country, and takes the lead to manage collaborations and fundraising initiatives with corporations.[55]

The FBRN's yearly operating expenses were approximately $1.46 million according to figures available in 2015, with approximately 50 percent from wealthy individuals, 30 percent from corporations, companies, and hotels, and the remaining 20 percent from investments.[56] As noted by an FBRN administrator, the FBRN positions itself as a business-minded nonprofit organization that leverages corporate and individual wealth to feed and empower people: "We were businessmen of different backgrounds and successful in our businesses. So, we decided to take the responsibility to take the model to solve the problem [of food insecurity]. We came up with this model [with pillars] to solve the problem [of food insecurity and food waste]."[57]

As stated by El Shohdi, the FBRN focuses on what he describes as the Arab region. In his view, the Arab region is in great need of a charitable food network that can address widespread food insecurity there:

> We don't find one Arab organization competent in fighting hunger and providing food security for indigenous peoples and underprivileged groups; FBRN takes the lead to present an Arab model for organizing charity work randomness, unifying efforts and encouraging cooperation between different sectors for protecting the right of people to feed themselves in dignity. From this point, food banks operating under the FBRN umbrella are [aiming to] achieve food sufficiency, secure the environment, and [help] needy people.[58]

As of 2019, the Arab region had a poverty rate over 20 percent. Although many regional economies in southwestern Asia and North Africa have expanded, the depth of poverty is vast, as many economies have high levels of inequality and struggle to absorb their relatively young populations, migrant workers, lower-income residents, elderly, and high numbers of refugees.[59] While parts of the region produce enough food for their residents, food availability is a serious problem there. Political instability has limited consistent food production in countries such as Syria, Yemen, and Lebanon.[60]

In addition, an extreme desert climate has forced Gulf countries, such as Saudi Arabia, Oman, the United Arab Emirates, and Qatar, to import significant volumes of food from Europe, including wheat from Russia and Ukraine, given the lack of land suitable for agriculture.[61] This trade relationship has opened up the region to increased price volatility as the Russia-Ukraine war has destabilized food markets.[62] It should be noted that food prices were a key reason why political unrest swept across the region during the Arab Spring of 2010 to 2012.[63] Most countries in the region have technically ratified the International Covenant on Economic, Social and Cultural Rights, including countries as varied as Algeria, Bahrain, Egypt, Iraq, Jordan, Kuwait, Oman, and Qatar. However, Egypt is the only country that has an explicit recognition of the right to food as a human right in its constitution.[64]

Rather than forcing local food banks to fit the traditional North American model of food banking, where food corporations drive food charity, FBRN works within each country's political, economic, and social context to figure out how and where it can be useful. Because the FBRN spans multiple countries in the region, its structure is more ad hoc and less centralized. FBRN's food banks have significant autonomy to implement food redistribution in ways that meet their mission. Depending on the context and needs of local partners, different FBRN pillars are prioritized. However, development of individuals is a key part of the FBRN's mission regardless of context.[65]

In Egypt and wealthier Gulf states such as Bahrain, Saudi Arabia, and the United Arab Emirates, food banks prioritize the waste reduction and sustainable philanthropy and investment pillars. In these contexts, the catering and tourism industries provide significant volumes of food for redistribution to charities. These food waste reduction efforts have received recognition from the FAO.[66]

In conflict regions, such as Lebanon, Syria, and Yemen, the feeding and humanitarian pillars are pursued, as emergency food assistance provides food to people where war or political instability have produced famine or extreme food insecurity. Throughout these war-torn regions, FBRN's food banks play a supportive role to assist other international relief efforts.

In southern Asia, in countries such as Bangladesh and Pakistan, food banks promote the feeding and development and capacity-building pillars. Given that people access food daily in sprawling informal food economies, food banks work with local communities to feed the poor and provide opportunities for the unemployed.

While the GFN covers much of the world, the FBRN leadership makes it clear that it will manage food bank development in its defined region of South Asia, the Middle East, and much of Africa. As noted by an FBRN administrator, the FBRN has a sense of territoriality when it compares to the GFN:

> We are entitled to cover the region of Middle East, Asia and South Asia. We transfer [our food bank] model to the GFN and they share their information with us so that we can cover the whole world with our activity. They are entitled [to their regions and we are entitled to ours]. That's why we make sure that we are transferring the model everywhere.[67]

Although FBRN technically has a presence across much of Sub-Saharan Africa, FBRN is more focused on the Arab region and less focused on ongoing development or support of its other member food banks in newer parts of its network. In this way, FBRN's food banks in Sub-Saharan Africa are likely not as developed as they are in the Arab region. As noted by an administrator at a global food advocacy organization, FBRN's governance style is relatively laissez-faire once the food bank starts its operations in the local context: "FBRN is more about initial development, not about ongoing support. I'm not saying that FBRN wouldn't support ongoing technical assistance and guidance, but they are not going to drive resources, funding, and food to their countries. They're more about introducing concepts and helping to get food banks launched."[68]

In addition, the FBRN network's food banks face significant resource and operational challenges when working in violent conflict zones, such as Syria and Yemen, and areas where large numbers of refugees have arrived, such as Iraq, Jordan, and Lebanon.[69] Also, in countries such Algeria, Egypt, Libya, and Tunisia, periodic political instability has created significant barriers to the operation of food banks.[70] As noted by an FBRN administrator, these external political factors influenced the FBRN to scale back its goals of food insecurity reduction: "The vision [to reduce hunger] by 2020 is [not realistic]. We are currently revisiting the vision and will extend it to later dates."[71]

The existing vulnerabilities within the FBRN meant that it significantly struggled in the initial months of the COVID pandemic. The rapid decline in oil prices before COVID and the economic fallout combined to severely disrupt food systems in the Arab region.[72] As a result of the pandemic, it is estimated that an additional 14.3 million people in the Arab region became food insecure. This increased the region's total number of food-insecure residents to 115 million people or 32 percent of the region's overall population, a number that is expected to remain high for years.[73] COVID's impact on food access for the young, women, migrants, and refugees has been especially severe.[74]

Although a 2020 United Nations report stated that the Arab region's high levels of poverty and inequality called for increased state support of social welfare programs, governmental investment in income and food relief has been limited.[75] Social welfare spending has averaged below 5 percent of GDP among countries in the Arab region, which is similar to other regions in the Global South but significantly lower than other OECD countries.[76] Moreover, given that every country in the Arab region except Lebanon, Morocco, and Tunisia is classified as either partially or fully authoritarian in the Economist Intelligence Unit's *Democracy Index*, the motivations of states such as Algeria, Iran, Libya, Qatar, Saudi Arabia, and the United Arab Emirates are not always transparent or reflective of popular opinion.[77]

To meet the increased need and operational constraints during the COVID pandemic, the FBRN increased its fundraising with corporations and private companies. In addition, FBRN developed the Daily Labor Support program to assist those who lost their jobs due to the pandemic.[78] Food banks within the FBRN network have continued to operate; however, it is unclear how well they have been able to meet the increase in need, given the scale of the health and economic crisis.

CHAPTER 4

FOOD BANKING IN GERMANY AND DENMARK

In contrast to countries such as the United States, which has a relatively smaller welfare state and different approach toward public assistance, central and northern European nations tend to have some of the largest social safety nets in the world. In countries like Germany and Denmark—the two case studies in this chapter—the idea that the government should take care of its most vulnerable residents is fairly commonplace. Because Germany spends 29.6 percent and Denmark spends 31.4 percent of GDP expenditures on social protection benefits respectively, the strength of these countries' social safety nets might suggest that they do not need food banking systems.[1] However, as explained in the case studies, both countries have experienced a series of political, economic, and social issues that have challenged the welfare state.

The welfare states in Germany and Denmark are not just very large; they are also quite comprehensive in terms of the scope of their coverage. Both operate government initiatives pertaining to maternity, families, health, disability, work injuries, old age, social assistance, and unemployment.[2] However, the welfare state in each country has been challenged by political parties on the political center-right as being too large or covering too many people. Since the 1990s, ideological pressures from the United States and United Kingdom have influenced German and Danish governments to consider reducing the size of government programs.[3] The arrival of new residents from other countries in central and northern Europe due to increased immigration and refugee resettlement have combined to increase the racial and ethnic diversity of Germany and Denmark. As a result, political parties in each country have disagreed over social welfare program eligibility, as different perceptions on race, identity, and nationality influence support for central and northern Europe's newest residents.[4] More recently, the COVID crisis has increased the social pressure on these large welfare states, as significant stimulus measures were taken to strengthen the social safety net.[5] This chapter examines how German and Danish food banks have navigated these dynamics in order to remain relevant and push toward a path of institutionalization in each country.

THE FEDERAL ASSOCIATION OF GERMAN FOOD BANKS

The Federal Association of German Food Banks, or Tafel Deutschland, is one of the largest food bank systems in Europe. It was founded in 1993 after a member of a Berlin charity called the Berlin Women's Initiative Group returned from the United States and became inspired to replicate the model of the New York City–based City Harvest food redistribution system. Following a lecture by German politician Ingrid Stahmer about homelessness in Berlin, Sabine Werth and other members of the charity decided that a more formalized structure could be developed in Germany to repurpose surplus food. This led to the development of the Berliner Tafel in 1993, with three more food banks developed in 1994. By 1995, thirty-five food banks existed, and the national German Round Table Association was founded to facilitate food bank information and resource sharing.[6]

The Tafel organization is highly professionalized and very adept at media and public relations. Although the Tafel has not been led by one person throughout its history as has been the case in other countries, it is managed by a team of well-educated staff who are keenly aware of the ways that food bank supporters and its critics view their work. The Tafel leadership are politically savvy in their efforts to position the organization in a society where many ask whether the food bank is good for society.[7]

According to 2013 statistics, Germany's Tafel has grown to become one of the four largest food bank systems in Europe, along with those of France, Spain, and Italy.[8] Tafel's 2020 statistics suggest that it remains one of the largest food bank systems in Europe.[9] While the Tafel had been independent for many years, it decided to join the European Food Banks Association (FEBA) network in 2018.[10]

The Tafel provides over 265,000 tons of food to more than 1.65 million people through its 960 beneficiary organizations. This is accomplished with more than 60,000 volunteers across the country.[11] In 2020, the budget was €16.42 million or U.S.$18.2 million, with 84 percent donations, 10 percent grants, 1 percent membership fees, and 5 percent other income. Most of the resources for the Tafel come from private or individual financial or in-kind donations.[12]

The Tafel's stated mission is to reduce food poverty and food waste. It promotes four values as part of its mission: sustainability, humanity, justice and participation, and social responsibility.[13] Although the national Tafel umbrella organization facilitates donor relationships and advocates for food banks at the national level in Germany, the Tafel's network of over 900 member charities or individual Tafel food banks do the on-the-ground work to redistribute food to households (see figure 14).[14]

There are two pathways for food to reach households through the Tafel food bank system. First, in some cases, large German food manufacturers contact the national Tafel office to alert them of surplus food. From there, the twelve regional Tafel distribution centers work with the 900 local Tafel food banks to collect, store, and then distribute the surplus food items to households. Second, in other situations, the local Tafel food banks collect food directly from neighborhood supermarkets and grocery stores and then redistribute this food to households.[15] In either case, the eligibility requirements, structure of operations, and pickup or delivery options are determined by individual Tafel food banks at the local level.[16]

Tafel management say it is not designed to work in place of government services, but this highlights the inherent contradiction of food banks—that they would not be necessary if the government adequately provided for people. As noted by a Tafel administrator, food charity is designed to complement the social welfare state in Germany:

> I think the role of charity is different, because there is a big social safety net in place, and the people who come to the Tafel will generally

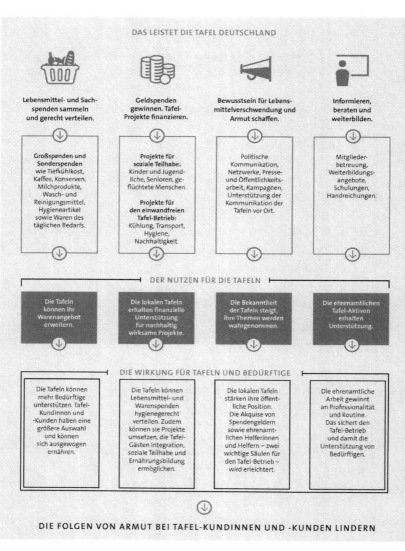

FIGURE 14. The Tafel's food bank structure (courtesy of Federal Association of German Food Banks, 2021).

have to prove that they are on some sort of public assistance. It's widely accepted in Germany that it is primarily the government's job and responsibility to provide for people who cannot provide for themselves. The role of the Tafel is to help people who fall through the social safety net but have not found a place in the private economy.[17]

Although Germany signed and ratified the International Covenant on Economic, Social and Cultural Rights in 1973 as well as many other UN resolutions since that date, Germany does not have any constitutional language recognizing the right to food as a human right in its country's constitution.[18]

Statistically, the severe deprivation rate in Germany has remained below 6 percent since 2009.[19] However, this masks the rapid increases in demand for food aid from vulnerable populations, as 20.7 percent of the population were at risk of poverty as measured in 2021.[20] Though the Tafel states that its mission is to fit within the existing German welfare state and focus on reducing and redistributing food waste from the corporate sector, it has struggled to keep up with the demand for food. In addition to increases in single-parent households and the working poor, the percentage of pensioners receiving aid at Tafels increased from 12 percent to 23 percent between 2007 and 2015, as the population grew older and retirement benefits were lowered by the German government.[21]

In addition, between 2015 and 2018, Tafels served between 220,000 and 280,000 new refugee clients each year. This represents approximately 19 percent of the total population served by Tafels in a given year. Although most refugees were from Syria, other people fled Afghanistan, Iran, the western Balkans, Somalia, Eritrea, and the Ivory Coast. The growth of food-insecure populations in Germany and their impacts on the nonprofit network of charities have been noted by many academic and news outlets.[22]

These tensions exploded in 2018, when one food bank in the Tafel network decided not to serve non-German citizens.[23] The backlash was swift and deep and even forced Chancellor Angela Merkel to note that while food banks should not restrict access, increased food demand was a reality for the country's charities.[24] Although the food bank somewhat quickly changed course to open again to all Germans regardless of country of origin, the crisis placed the food bank squarely in the middle of the political debate over who deserves to be served at the Tafel's network of food banks and within Germany more broadly.[25]

In the face of these extreme political, economic, and social pressures on the Tafel's operations, they are actively lobbying and, when necessary, working with government to promote various food-related issues.[26] In the case of food waste, the Tafel has actively worked with the German government to develop the National Strategy for Food Waste Reduction.[27] Although the initiative is continuing to evolve, the Tafel aims to make the policy legally binding in order to reduce food waste and ensure a stronger flow of surplus food to the food bank system.[28]

However, some scholars studying the development of food banks in Germany have argued that the Tafel has become too large and institutionalized. In particular, German social scientists Fabian Kessl, Stephan Lorenz, and Holger Schoneville contend that the growth of the charitable food sector in Germany contributes to welfare state retrenchment and legitimizes reductions in food and income support programs.[29] Although German Chancellor Gerhard Schröder and his coalition government promoted U.K.- and U.S.-style "third-way" approaches toward poverty management in the 1990s and early 2000s, and the state continues to reduce support for pensioners and other vulnerable populations, social welfare remains a priority in Germany.[30]

While Tafel staff are supportive of the welfare state and its role in German society, the Tafel notes that the food bank system is a necessary part of society moving forward. As noted by a Tafel administrator, the food bank system has become a permanent institution in Germany:

> Even in a country [like Germany] where there's a lot of social welfare and a lot of safety net support, there's going to be people who fall through the cracks and there's going to be food wasted for a long time. So, as long as we can continue to keep pairing those two, I think that the Tafel will still be here, unfortunately.[31]

The COVID pandemic severely impacted the operations of the Tafel food banking system.[32] As noted in one of their COVID bulletins on the Tafel's webpage, the speed and depth of the pandemic caught the Tafel off guard and became the greatest institutional crisis in the history of the organization:

People are asking for support from the food banks who were not previously dependent on external help.... At the same time, it shows that people who came to the food banks before the Corona pandemic are currently not being reached.... Many food banks lack helpers, as more than two thirds of the 60,000 active volunteers are elderly and thus belong to the group worth protecting.... Normal operations that reach the same number of Tafel customers as before the pandemic are currently not possible.[33]

The German government passed one of the world's largest stimulus packages in 2020 to support lower-income residents. Valued at approximately 60 percent of its GDP, Germany spent €236 billion in direct fiscal measures, €500 billion in tax deferrals, and €1.32 trillion in other liquidity and guarantee measures.[34] These measures helped furloughed workers and struggling businesses, as demand for food relief increased dramatically in the first months of the COVID pandemic.[35] Some vulnerable groups, such as the elderly, had difficulty accessing food in person at the local food bank location, known as a panel, for fear of contracting the virus. Thus, logistical challenges of distributing food aid emerged as a significant hurdle, as food banks were compelled to quickly establish food delivery, food distribution outside, and prepackaged food packs.[36] As a result of increased visibility due to the COVID crisis, fundraising at the Tafel increased by 59 percent in 2020, with 400 companies and 9,300 private individual donors contributing to the food bank network.[37]

In March and April 2020, almost half of the 948 food banks in Germany closed due to staffing and other logistical issues, as most volunteers at the Tafel are senior citizens. These challenges were compounded by declines in food donations and increased costs in many contexts. For these reasons, the Tafel was not able to serve as many people as beforehand even though the need was higher than ever.[38] As noted in the Tafel's 2020 report "Overcoming the Crisis Together," the closure of food banks had negative impacts on food insecurity, mental health, and community connectedness:

Over 400 of the 948 local Tafel food banks and pantries in Germany were forced to temporarily close their doors. It has been the greatest challenge the Tafel organization had faced since it was founded twenty-seven years ago. Having to abandon people in need was especially painful for our volunteers.... It's far more than just a food pantry. It is a place to meet and socialize, a community space central to the lives of many of our beneficiaries.

Even with these challenges, the Tafel remains one of the largest and most well-developed food bank systems in the world. Yet, as evidenced in during the COVID pandemic, the structural vulnerabilities of the food bank system are significant and suggest that the Tafel is not a sufficient solution for addressing food insecurity in Germany.

THE DANISH FOOD BANK

The Danish Food Bank (DFB), or the FødevareBanken in Danish, is one of three major food bank systems in the Nordic region.[39] It is an important case study given that it is in one of the most food-secure regions on the planet. According to statistics from 2020, Denmark had a severe material deprivation rate of 2.4 percent, which was one of the lowest rates in the European Union.[40] As of 2022, only Denmark and Norway had registered food banks with FEBA.[41] Although Denmark signed and ratified the International Covenant on Economic, Social and Cultural Rights in 1972 as well as many other UN resolutions since, Denmark does not have any constitutional language recognizing the right to food as a human right in its country's constitution.[42]

In the case of Denmark, food bank development is a relatively recent phenomenon. The DFB was founded in 2008 by Danish resident Thomas Fremming. During a visit with family in Canada, he volunteered at a local Canadian food bank. Upon his arrival back in Copenhagen, he hoped to work in a food bank, but soon realized that no food bank system existed in Denmark. To fill this gap, Fremming developed partnerships with food corporations and local charities for most of 2008 and 2009 in order to raise the funds necessary to build out the food bank model.[43] Within just a few years, the DFB became the largest food bank system in the Nordic region.[44]

Upon visiting the DFB, it was notable that the food bank was located in a residential neighborhood of northwestern Copenhagen called Bispebjerg, rather than an industrial or central location like many food banks in other countries. Its Copenhagen offices housed both the professional staff and the food bank's main warehouse. In addition, as compared to the large food bank warehouses in North America and many parts of Europe, the Copenhagen warehouse was quite small. Yet, the DFB staff were highly professional, well educated, and very attuned to the landscape where food banks operate in Scandinavia. This has given them a strong position to fundraise and develop partnerships across the country.[45]

As of 2020, DFB had approximately 311 member organizations that receive food directly from the food bank and then give food to their clients.[46] These organizations focus on groups such as the homeless, children, the aged, refugees, orphans, and other socially vulnerable populations. The DFB does not mandate any rules for its beneficiary organizations in terms of eligibility; however, each charity is required to follow strict food safety standards. The DFB promotes food traceability via electronic goods registration, refrigeration chain management, and mandatory hygiene courses for member organizations.[47] Importantly, the DFB does charge member fees of DKK10,000 per year, or approximately U.S.$1,500 per year as of 2020.[48] This is not insignificant and has caused some organizations to stop working with the food bank.[49]

According to the 2020 annual report, the DFB's annual operating budget totaled DKK15,314,690 or approximately U.S.$2,294,000 per year in 2020. This included 33 percent from private foundations, 29 percent from corporate subsidies, 18 percent from public pools and funds, 18 percent from logistics or member fees, and 2 percent from donations, member support, and income supports.[50] The DFB has approximately twelve paid employees and 272 volunteers.[51]

The mission of the DFB is to reduce food waste and food poverty. In their redistribution system, the DFB receives most of its food from producers, farmers, and wholesalers. In comparison to food bank systems across Europe, the DFB receives only a small amount of food from retail sources.[52] Although the reduction in food insecurity inspired much of its work as an organization, the DFB shifted tactics in order to remain viable. During DFB's early years, it strategically emphasized food waste reduction as a way to sidestep criticism that it was duplicating government programs provided by the Danish social welfare state.[53] As noted by a DFB administrator, the food bank recognizes that it needs to position itself as complementary to the welfare state:

The government [would not] buy food with public dollars in Denmark, because people would say we have a very expensive welfare system. This is an old argument from the 1980s that we don't need the food bank because people are well taken care of here. So, the government would not support buying food, given the size of the social welfare safety net, but food that would otherwise be thrown out [is easier to support politically].[54]

However, more recently, the DFB was buoyed by two broader trends in Danish society. First, the Danish government, in line with many other countries across Europe, was keen to find ways to reduce the size of the welfare state.[55] Although the DFB was relatively small, it was courted by the Ministry of Social Affairs in the Danish government in part because it could help to facilitate the neoliberal changes to the welfare state. Importantly, the DFB provided political cover for the government to reduce the size and eligibility of some social welfare state programs.[56] In addition to cutting spending, the Danish state has moved toward workfare-style programs espoused by the United States and the United Kingdom.[57] As noted by a DFB administrator, the backlash against the cost and size of government programs provided an opening for food charity to grow in the Danish context:

When the [food bank did develop in Denmark], it happened in part because we were in the process of scaling back the welfare state. There have been some social welfare reforms in Denmark. Part of it is the increase in costs from refugees, but it has been moving this way anyways, and some view the state as too expensive. The antiwelfare movement has been growing in the last few years.[58]

Second, food waste started to became an issue of broad public concern across Europe, especially in Denmark. This food waste movement has been led by Stop Wasting Food, the key food waste advocacy organization in Denmark. Reports on the amount of food waste in Denmark showed a significant decline of almost 25 percent at the household level between 2012 and 2018.[59] Thus, food waste reduction is an issue with significant support among the public in Denmark.

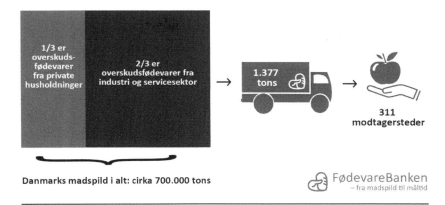

FIGURE 15. The Danish Food Bank model and its impacts on food waste reduction (courtesy of Danish Food Bank, 2021).

According to 2020 statistics, approximately 700,000 tons of food are wasted each year in Denmark, one-third of it from private households and two-thirds from the food industry and service sector. Yet given the enormity of the food waste issue and the relatively small size of the DFB, the Danish food bank system was only able to save 1,377 tons, less than 1 percent of the approximate 470,000 tons of food that went to waste (see figure 15).[60] In this way, although the DFB is the largest food bank system in the Nordic region, its impact is quite small in comparison to the scale of food wastage in the country. As noted by DFB administrators, the Danish food bank's facilities and staff are relatively small, and without more financial and human resources to grow, the logistical capacity of the food bank will remain limited.[61]

Unlike other food banks in the United States and Europe, it has taken time for the DFB to convince food corporations that the work of the food bank is supplemental and advantageous to the brand and overall efficiency of the corporate food system.[62] As noted by a DFB administrator, this complicated food bank–food corporation relationship has evolved over time.

> Early on, many corporates did not want [to partner with the food bank]. It was originally seen as admitting that you were not doing

your job as you should be. For corporations, it is about [brand enhancement]. Corporations have to use more manpower to donate food. So, it has to be motivated by PR. Many of the food corporations that support us have the business sensibility and they know there is a value in supporting us.[63]

The food bank's dependence on government and corporate support places pressure on the DFB to be relatively apolitical or nonparticipatory in advocacy or lobbying. Geographer George Henderson argues that food banks, like other charities such as Habitat for Humanity, the Salvation Army, and the United Way, are institutionally limited by their own partnerships that fund and support them.[64] Even if lobbying or advocacy is technically legal, food charity experts Joshua Lohnes and Andy Fisher claim that the fear of retribution from government and corporate partners reduces the incentive for food banks to engage in politically charged issues such as living wage campaigns, tax increases, or social or economic justice movements.[65] In line with these concerns, they focus on their food redistribution efforts exclusively and are careful not to advocate for any causes that might offend their partners, as noted by a DFB administrator:

We do some advocacy, but we are mainly a logistics organization. We are fairly moderate in our advocacy because we are placed at a point where we don't want to offend anyone. If we wanted to be more outspoken and be more aggressive in terms of blaming, we might have a problem in terms of getting [corporate food or government support].[66]

As stated in their 2022 report, the DFB has spent the last ten years working to achieve its primary goals to increase funding and scaling out its operations.[67] As noted by a DFB administrator as early as 2016, the Danish food bank has been actively pursuing new entrepreneurial opportunities as a way to increase its impact and improve its financial position:

We have explored other options that would reduce food waste and reduce poverty in some degree, but also make money. We have toyed with the idea of a social supermarket like in Stockholm where they sell the food for profit that goes into the organization. The client would pay for it. The idea is that we would get the food for free and we would sell it at 30 percent [of its typical consumer] cost. Socially vulnerable people could buy it at that price, so it would benefit them. And we could also make some money.[68]

Key studies produced by the Nordic Council of Ministers have reaffirmed these concerns about increasing the food bank's capacity while also expressing hope that the untapped potential of food bank systems can grow in the Scandinavian region.[69] The Nordic Council of Ministers, an international regional network of leaders in Scandinavia, have been studying this issue in order to streamline food safety protocols, develop regulations that facilitate food bank development, and promote best-practice models based on FEBA, GFN, and other international leading food bank initiatives. These food waste reduction programs are part of the Nordic prime ministers' Green Growth initiative to promote sustainable development and the green economy.

While these initiatives are clearly embraced by many Scandinavian governments, it is unlikely that food banks could be as large as they are in the United States, United Kingdom, or other countries with a less developed social safety net. Instead, food banks in the Nordic region have developed a targeted mission to reduce food waste in the corporate sector. As of 2022, most of these Scandinavian food banks are small in size and impact; however, increased resources could provide them with an opportunity to broaden their operations.[70]

The COVID pandemic increased food insecurity dramatically in the country. Estimates in 2021 suggested that as much as 10 percent of Denmark's residents experienced food insecurity because of increased unemployment and lost income due to the economic and social fallout from the pandemic.[71] In addition, COVID also produced increased costs for the DFB network. Even with these challenges, the DFB increased its capacity to meet the rapid increases in demand for food aid.[72] As noted by DFB director Karen-Inger Thorsen and Church Crusaders head Helle Christiansen, food charity leaders in Denmark wanted the government to confront food insecurity, not the nonprofit sector.

> [Due to COVID], the FødevareBanken had to [increase] its activities tenfold. But we actually do not want that. Our mission is to turn food waste into meals for the most vulnerable in our society for the people who fall through the safety net of welfare. . . . In a welfare society like

the Danish one, it is unheard of for 100,000 households to be so vulnerable that they are regularly challenged to get food on the table. . . . It is simply too many to leave to charity in one of the world's richest and best welfare systems.[73]

Although the DFB increased its scale of operations, it was unable to meet the higher demand levels. Ultimately, the COVID crisis reinforced that the Danish welfare state is the only institution capable of or politically responsible for income and food support in Denmark.

CHAPTER 5

FOOD BANKING IN ITALY AND HUNGARY

This chapter examines two additional European countries: Italy, which has a large social safety net but persistent poverty, and Hungary, which has both a limited safety net and higher poverty. Food banking networks in both countries are part of the European Food Banks Federation (FEBA).

As compared to its northern neighbors, Italy, along with Spain and Portugal, has higher unemployment, persistent poverty, and a well-developed social safety net by European standards, as 28.8 percent of GDP spending goes to social protection benefits in Italy.[1] However, the EU has pressured Italy to impose austerity measures to rein in costs and remain financially stable. This has resulted in some reforms to the welfare state to reduce the eligibility, type, or size of income benefit programs; yet the social safety net in Italy remains relatively strong.[2] According to statistics from 2021, Italy had an unemployment rate of 9.5 percent, which, along those of with Spain and Greece, is one of the highest rates in Europe.[3]

As part of Viktor Orbán's leadership, the Hungarian government has promoted a socially conservative, anti-immigrant, anti-NGO, and antipoor agenda.[4] This occurred as the country confronted a severe material deprivation rate of 8.0 percent, one of the highest in the European Union, and a relatively low 17.4 percent percentage of GDP spending on public assistance programs.[5]

Although Italy and Hungary have always had higher poverty and unemployment rates compared to northern and central European countries, both were especially hard hit during the 2007–2009 global economic recession and were slow to recover.[6]

THE ITALIAN FOOD BANK NETWORK

The Italian Food Bank Network (IFBN), or the Banco Alimentare, is one of the most well-established and largest food bank networks in Europe.[7] The IFBN was founded in 1989 by leading Italian philanthropists in Milan. After learning about food banking in Barcelona, Cavalier Danilo Fossati, the president of the Star food corporation, and Monsignor Luigi Giussani, founder of the Communion and Liberation international Catholic movement, decided to open up a similar food redistribution system in Italy.[8] Food banks expanded rapidly in Italy, and became one of the four largest systems in Europe, along with those in France, Germany, and Spain.[9]

The IFBN staff is highly educated and knowledgeable about the problems facing the food bank system. They are not only aware of the roles that food insecurity and food waste play in Italy, but they also recognize the institutional challenges that food banks confront politically in Europe and the role that the IFBN plays as one of the largest food bank systems on the continent.[10] The 2023 secretary general of FEBA previously worked in a leadership role at IFBN before she left for her current FEBA post in 2018.[11]

Given its size and relative age compared to other European systems, the IFBN has been of great interest to scholars who have examined its development, mission, and structure.[12] For this reason, the IFBN is detailed as a case study to explore the development and challenges associated with food bank development in southern Europe.

Importantly, Italy has signed and ratified the International Covenant on Economic, Social and Cultural Rights in 1978 as well as many other UN resolutions since that date. Although it does not specifically recognize the right to food as a basic human right within the country's constitution, there is language that indicates that Italian citizens deserve basic social assistance.[13]

The mission of the IFBN is to recover surplus food from the agriculture, production, distribution, and catering sectors of the food supply chain and redistribute this unused food to charitable organizations in need across the country. The IFBN's mission is designed to provide four types of benefits to its stakeholders. First, the IFBN provides social benefits to people in need through the delivery of healthy food to charitable organizations. Second, the IFBN provides economic benefits to the food supply chain stakeholders as storage and disposal fees are reduced and food is used rather than wasted. Third, the IFBN provides environmental benefits to reduce negative externalities associated with landfill waste, carbon emissions, and wasted energy. Last, the IFBN provides educational benefits to facilitate charity and social inclusion.[14]

To pursue this mission and set of goals, the IFBN operates three types of programs.[15] First is the redistribution of excess food through its partner food businesses from the agriculture, production, distribution, and catering sectors of the food supply chain. Second, the IFBN manages food drives such as the National Food Collection Day, known as the Giornata Nazionale della Colletta Alimentare.[16] Third, the EU's Fund for European Aid to the Most Deprived (FEAD) provided €3.8 billion or U.S.$4.3 million in funding for EU member states to supplement their emergency food programs between 2014 and 2020. It was then renewed until 2022, at which point its future remained uncertain.[17] In Italy, the FEAD program provided 85 percent of the funding, €670.6 million or U.S.$758.3 million, to complement the Italian government's 15 percent funding, €118.3 million or U.S.$133.8 million.[18] This amounted to significant funding support for IFBN and other key Italian poverty relief organizations. Italy, in fact, had the highest FEAD allocation of any EU country, given its disproportionate number of people in extreme poverty.[19]

Each of these three programs collectively contributes significant amounts of food resources to the food insecure in Italy. According to statistics from 2021, the IFBN collected and redistributed approximately 126,000 tons of food per year to its twenty-one food banks across the country. These food banks gave food to about 7,600 local charities that provided food to approximately 1.7 million people.[20] The staff included about 1,800 daily volunteers. In 2021, the operating budget was €9.1 million or U.S.$10.8 million.

This includes 49 percent from fundraisers, 46 percent from private sources, 2 percent from public entities, and 3 percent from other sources.[21]

Over the past couple of decades, the Italian welfare state has been reformed to reduce the size and scope of income support programs. As part of this process, the EU has pressured Italy to impose austerity measures in order to ensure its expenditures remain sustainable.[22] Even with these changes, the Italian welfare state remains relatively large by European standards.[23] However, as noted by an IFBN administrator, the IFBN view their food bank system as a necessary complement to fill gaps in the welfare state: "In Italy, we need civil society organizations [like our food bank system]. Our welfare system is not perfect. It is not as good as many other states in Europe that are [more] perfect. I think there will always be a role for nonprofit organizations to play [even if their role] changes over time."[24]

Also, while a significant amount of funding and resources originate within Italy, the EU FEAD has been an important source of funding for the Italian food bank system and many other food banks across the continent.[25] However, it has been rife with significant political tension, as many governments across northern Europe are not supportive of what is sometimes viewed as a handout for its poorer southern neighbor countries.[26] While it has been reconstituted as a social policy to reduce poverty rather than an agricultural support policy based on surplus food, it remains highly politicized and unevenly implemented.[27] In these ways, the growth of the IFBN is connected to the politics and broader political economy of Europe as a whole. Staff at the IFBN recognize the importance of advocacy and lobbying at the national and continental scales.[28]

While the IFBN is working through its significant institutional limitations associated with increased demand levels and the politics of food aid in Europe, it has been very successful at lobbying against food waste. One of its greatest successes has been the passage of Law Number 166 in 2016, also known as the Gadda Food Law.[29] In contrast to the French law on food waste that punishes food vendors who do not donate food, the Italian law on food waste uses incentives to facilitate increased food donations. Specifically, this law creates a regulatory framework to regulate fiscal incentives associated with food waste, civil liability, and hygiene and food safety procedures. It also creates a clearer set of definitions and guidelines on donation and dating food as "best before" and "use by."[30]

Beyond the typical challenges that all food banks face in their operations related to resources and staffing, there are some key issues that are specific to Italy and southern Europe.[31] To start, the poverty rate in Italy remains very high. According to statistics from 2021, 25.2 percent of Italians were at risk of poverty.[32] This ranks Italy among the worst in Europe. Although the economies in southern Europe have always had higher levels of poverty compared to northern Europe, the 2007–2009 global recession produced significant increases in the levels of unemployed, underemployed, and working poor individuals and families, with the southern European unemployment rate peaking at 17.6 percent in 2013.[33]

However, the geographical contrasts between north and south are significant. In southern Europe, the severe deprivation rate increased to a high of 12.7 percent in 2014, while it only increased to 3.7 percent in northern Europe during that same period. Although the severe deprivation rate slowly decreased to 7.6 percent in southern Europe and 2.6 percent in northern Europe by 2020, just before the COVID-19 pandemic started, poverty remained elevated for years in southern Europe.[34] Unlike in Germany, increasing demand levels in Italy were not due to a rise in migration or refugee populations, as many of those groups traveled farther north to wealthier European countries.[35]

These dynamics were only further reinforced with the uneven impacts of COVID on the European continent.[36] Given Italy's relatively high poverty and unemployment rate, the impact of the COVID pandemic in 2020 and 2021 was especially severe. It was one of the earliest countries to experience high infection and death rates in March 2020. The subsequent economic and social fallout of the public health crisis produced significant challenges for food insecurity. Figures from August 2020 suggest that poverty may have doubled to almost 10 million people.[37] This included vulnerable populations such as the homeless, elderly, working poor, and a large growth in furloughed or recently unemployed people.[38]

To confront these crises, the Italian government passed multiple stimulus aid packages targeted to help the businesses and people impacted by the economic shutdown.[39] This included money to help struggling businesses and furloughed workers as well as some specific food aid programs with help from the EU's FEAD.[40] In comparison to other European countries, the Italian stimulus was medium sized.[41] While many Italians changed their eating habits to reduce food waste through innovative cooking techniques or more efficient food purchasing, government support programs and consumer-based practices had their limits as a food waste and hunger reduction mechanism given the spread of poverty across the country.[42]

Between March and June 2020, IFBN fed more than 2.1 million people, which is 600,000 more than before the crisis. Network food banks noted increases in demand for food aid of more than 50 percent, and 70 percent in some southern parts of Italy.[43] As noted by IFBN president Giovanni Bruno, increased costs, reduced resources, and other logistical pressures reduced the IFBN's capacity to meet the need for food aid:

> We have to cope with pressing demands for food, but we don't have infinite resources. There has been a great response from companies and also from individuals . . . but we are worried. . . . [We have shortages in donated food.] The problem of respecting distances and safety measures makes everything more difficult. . . . All this has costs.[44]

Although IFBN fed more food-insecure people in 2020, the limits of the food banking network were stretched as increased demand, uneven food donations, lack of protective gear, inadequate numbers of volunteers, and increased costs stressed the emergency food system operations of IFBN.[45] In addition, many food banks within the IFBN network closed for a few weeks or months, although there was significant variation across the country in terms of the number and duration of closures.[46]

In the face of these challenges, the IFBN was forced to increase human and financial resources for its struggling food banks. This included the incorporation of more young volunteers into its network, implementation of a record-breaking fundraising campaign leading to a 213 percent increase in income, to €12.7 million or U.S.$14.5 million in 2020, and collaboration with the Italian government to form the Municipal Operations Centers (COC) to centralize food aid and volunteers (see figure 16).[47] As noted by an IFBN administrator, the IFBN leveraged the COVID pandemic to expand its relationships with a range of new corporate and nonprofit partners: "The IFBN has shown itself to be a partner capable of dialoguing and interacting with . . . both corporate and third sector entities. . . . This path of awareness was accelerated by the pandemic. [The pandemic] was an

FIGURE 16. The Italian Food Bank Network (courtesy of Italian Food Bank Network, 2021).

opportunity that highlighted various needs and urged companies to take responsibility."[48]

The IFBN has managed to increase the amount of food redistributed and number of partnerships with different institutions across society in the face of high poverty and unemployment, increased demand due to COVID, and diverging perspectives on the role of the welfare state in Italy. However, although the IFBN has grown significantly over the past few decades, it remains unclear whether more meals served can be equated with lower food insecurity and food waste levels in Italy.

THE HUNGARIAN FOOD BANK ASSOCIATION

The Hungarian Food Bank Association (HFBA), or the Magyar Élelmiszerbank Egyesület in Hungarian, operates a food redistribution network with local charities across the country. HFBA started in 2005 and became a member of FEBA in 2006. HFBA started in Budapest after a prominent local resident named Balázs Cseh founded the organization in response to the high levels of poverty he saw in Hungary and the presence of food banks in other countries across Europe.[49] While the food bank initially started in Budapest, it quickly spread across the country, as other charities learned of the food redistribution work at the food bank in the capital city. Since its founding in 2005, Balázs Cseh has remained the president of the HFBA.[50] In addition to his leadership on food banking within Hungary, he has also served on the board of FEBA since 2009.[51]

Upon visiting the HFBA in Budapest, the building appeared noticeably small and nondescript. It was located on the outside of Budapest in a low-density, somewhat rustic neighborhood called Rákosliget. The staff there was relatively small, and they spoke very carefully about their work as they did not want to overtly politicize the HFBA's role in what is generally considered a country hostile to nongovernmental organizations, especially those that work in the area of poverty or social welfare.[52] The HFBA has continued to downplay its social welfare role within the highly reactionary political climate in the country. Importantly, although Hungary signed and ratified the International Covenant on Economic, Social and Cultural Rights in 1974, Hungary does not have any constitutional language recognizing the right to food as a human right in its constitution.[53]

Since its founding, HFBA has continued to focus on implementing its mission to feed the hungry and reduce food waste.[54] In this way, HFBA focuses on both the social and environmental impacts of food waste. However, as noted by an HFBA administrator, their message is communicated differently depending on the audience, often trying to depoliticize or broaden the number and range of stakeholders who would see value in the HFBA:

> We [prioritize] both [the social and environmental aspects of food waste]. Our mission is to reduce surplus food by not overproducing and not throwing out food. But it actually depends who we speak with. If we speak with food producing or distributing companies, we always try to make them understand that it's not a shame that you have a food surplus or food waste because that's what happens, but it's a shame if you waste that food.[55]

As of 2021, HFBA had distributed 89,400 tons of food worth over $168.7 million to over 300,000 people in need.[56] The process of food redistribution starts at the country's main large supermarkets, known as hypermarkets, factories, and processing plants where excess food is transported to the main food bank warehouse in Budapest. Although most food is stored in the main warehouse in Budapest, some foods are supplied directly to charities, given the size of the country and the potential for certain foods to spoil in transport over long distances. As part of these processes, HFBA operates food waste redistribution, nonprofit wholesale, and express distribution of surplus food from supermarkets when necessary.[57] In all cases, food redistribution works through charities, not individuals. HFBA's vast network of 550 charities span the country. The HFBA works with charities to provide free food, as there are no member fees for its beneficiary organizations.[58]

Importantly, the HFBA gives its local charities the independence to determine how they distribute food and to whom they will give food. In this way, there are no universal eligibility requirements for food aid within the HFBA network. Although the Hungarian state has increasingly promoted rhetoric that is hostile to immigrants and the poor, the HFBA has remained steadfast in its support of its charities and their decision to redistribute food to a wide range of people with different races, ethnicities, religions, and places of origin.[59] During both the 2015–2018 Syrian migrant crisis and the Ukraine-Russia war as of 2023, charities associated with the HFBA have redistributed large amounts of food to refugees and asylum seekers.[60]

Two waves of uncertainty made the years from 2007 to 2022 turbulent for HFBA. To start, the 2007–2009 global economic recession undoubtedly increased demand; however, the actual economic status of the country remained not only uncertain but, at times, deliberately mischaracterized for political purposes. As noted by an HFBA administrator, this created a dynamic where nonprofits like HFBA could not publicly discuss rising food insecurity, as it might be viewed as antigovernment sentiment: "It's quite hard to get reliable information on this, because the propaganda thing is working quite strong here. It's not easy to get proper information. But what we saw after 2008 was struggle. Now, things seem to be a bit better than it was in 2008, but I guess it's no better than it was before 2008."[61]

Undoubtedly, the 2007–2009 global economic recession and the subsequent influx of refugees from Syria placed a significant strain on the organization, as it not only had to find the resources to feed more people, but it also had to figure out a way to navigate what had become a highly politically charged arena of social support for refugees. As noted by an HFBA administrator, this placed the HFBA in a difficult political position:

> [The government] made a political thing out of [refugees], but [our organization is] not political. It was quite hard for us to have a statement on this. We supported certain initiatives that started to help the refugees. But we don't publicize this, because we don't want to be attacked from the [government] or from the general public. In Hungary, the whole refugee thing is dividing the whole society as one part [of society] think refugees should go, and they should never enter [the country again].[62]

As noted by social welfare historian Michael Katz and food scholar Rebecca de Souza in the U.S. context, food banks and their network of food charities have to navigate highly charged political environments in many contexts where food recipients are often unfairly classified as undeserving poor if their race, ethnicity, language, religion, or place of origin is different from those in power.[63]

In addition to these challenging political and social dynamics, the HFBA has historically struggled to persuade corporations to partner with the food bank network. Although HFBA is designed to repurpose waste from the food industry, Hungarian food companies have been traditionally unaware of the work that food banks do and therefore resistant to collaboration with the HFBA. As noted by HFBA administrators, some food corporations have viewed HFBA as just another charity asking for food or resources.[64] Nevertheless, after years of lobbying from HFBA, food companies have finally started to partner with the HFBA. However, without full partnership with the food industry, HFBA cannot expand significantly, as it needs financial and food donations to grow in size.

While food corporations are slowly coming to work with HFBA, the Hungarian government is a different story, as HFBA operates in an environment where the state is relatively hostile to NGOs focused on welfare or food relief.[65] As mentioned by the director of FEBA, this has been a common problem among many former communist countries in eastern Europe, where there is significant distrust of NGOs, especially those with ties to western Europe or the United States, such as Estonia and Slovenia.[66] Even though HFBA is a locally founded organization, its administrators believe the Hungarian government is hostile to HFBA because it is viewed as an extension of the West, especially given that FEBA, its main international partner, is based in western Europe.[67] Moreover, given its role as a food relief organization, the HFBA is directly in the crosshairs of the state as its presence highlights the failure of government to feed its own people, and it works with vulnerable populations that the state does not want to serve, such as refugees or homeless persons.[68]

The HFBA has experienced organizational challenges associated with limited human resources, including retaining paid staff and recruiting volunteers, as well as fundraising hardships. Although many food charities across the world struggle with resource limitations, the political climate in Hungary creates additional fundraising challenges for HFBA. Given that the state is suspicious of funding flows from non-Hungarian sources and there are different perspectives on who should receive food aid in the country, HFBA has to constantly convince its donors of its value in the most nonpolitical way possible.[69] In this way, the Hungarian state creates a culture of fear among donors and the HFBA more generally, which combine to narrow the scope of HFBA's operations and limit the range of institutions that will support the food bank network.

In sum, food banks in Hungary are a particularly illuminating case, because they underscore the point that food banks so often rely on corporations and the state in order to carry out their goals. When state or corporate entities do not see the value of food banks for society or themselves, food banks often struggle to operate.

The COVID pandemic created additional challenges to food banking in Hungary as the economic and social fallout initially increased food insecurity and unemployment across the country. To reduce the burden on struggling businesses and the unemployed, the Hungarian government passed a stimulus bill in 2020.[70] However, the bill was somewhat modest in its direct assistance to the food insecure, and Hungary also actively blocked EU COVID relief packages for political purposes.[71] Within this context, the HFBA worked to acquire food donations where possible and limit network closures, although human resources declined precipitously as volunteers were unable to assist in the distribution of food.[72]

Building on these challenges, Hungary has seen record levels of inflation due to the Russian war in Ukraine and COVID supply chain issues. As of December 2022, inflation was 24.5 percent, the highest rate in Europe.[73] This placed increased pressure on HFBA as food banks and other emergency safety net providers struggled to meet increased demand for food aid and other basic social services.[74] Moreover, the future of HFBA remains uncertain given the lack of government support.

CHAPTER 6

FOOD BANKS IN INDIA AND SOUTH AFRICA

The final case studies analyze food banking in India and South Africa. Both countries are part of the Global FoodBanking Network (GFN) and have robust informal economies where people are employed in jobs unregulated or protected by the state.[1] Although India is often lauded for its economic growth and its emergence as a global economic powerhouse, it continues to have one of the highest rates of food insecurity in the world. The Food and Agriculture Organization of the United Nations stated that 209 million people or 15.3 percent of the Indian population was undernourished as of 2021. In addition, 31 percent of children under age five had stunted growth.[2] Meanwhile, India's spending on social welfare was less than 3 percent. Although average as compared to other countries in the Global South, it is far less than what OECD countries or other emerging upper middle-income countries such as China, South Africa, or Brazil spend on social protection.[3]

Studies have revealed that food insecurity rates in South Africa are approximately 26 percent overall, with another 28 percent at risk of hunger in the country.[4] These numbers are slightly higher in rural areas, although the percentage of people vulnerable to food insecurity in cities remains over 25 percent in many contexts.[5] To confront these significant food insecurity challenges, the South African state has developed one of the largest social grant systems in the Global South, as more than 18 million South Africans receive some type of social grant.[6] In addition, it has developed a series of other urban agriculture, school feeding, health support, and food parcel programs. While the state has spent significant resources to support these programs, it has been criticized for its corrupt misuse of social support programs for political gain and failure to meaningfully reduce food insecurity in society.[7]

THE INDIA FOOD BANKING NETWORK

Although the International Covenant on Economic, Social and Cultural Rights was signed and passed through accession in 1975 and the right to food is mentioned in the Indian Constitution, food insecurity has been a persistent and unrelenting challenge for both rural and urban areas in India.[8] These issues associated with persistent food insecurity and economic inequality have been well documented by researchers.[9] The Global Hunger Index ranks India 107 out of 136 countries, a composite score based on malnourishment, child wasting, child stunting, and child mortality.[10]

It is within this broader context of extreme food insecurity that the India FoodBanking Network (IFBN) officially formed in 2011, after three years of development.[11] Sam Pitroda, a wealthy Indian telecommunications engineer and entrepreneur, led the process of developing the food banking system in India. Through his extensive corporate connections and his position as special advisor to the former Indian prime minister for infrastructure, technology, and innovation, Pitroda chaired the IFBN Planning Forum in New Delhi in 2009. This meeting brought together key corporate, government, and nonprofit players, including representatives from the GFN, to discuss the potential for a national food bank network in India.[12]

As a philanthropist with many nonprofits in India, Pitroda viewed the IFBN as an innovative market initiative to reduce food waste in a highly food-insecure environment. However, the IFBN took significant time to develop due to significant resource and logistical issues noted later in this section.[13] IFBN, along with Feeding India by Zomato and No Food Waste, is one of three GFN-certified food bank systems in India.[14] Vandana

Singh, a highly educated leader with a range of corporate, government, and nonprofit experiences, has been the CEO of the IFBN since 2012.[15]

As of 2022, the IFBN had opened food banks in forty-four cities across India.[16] This includes food banks in the largest urban areas of the country. While food insecurity is clearly a significant problem in rural areas, the IFBN started in cities since the network of food redistribution is easier and already built in some form.[17] The aim of the IFBN system is to "eliminate hunger in India by 2030."[18] The network attempts this primarily by redistributing unused food products to individual beneficiary organizations located across each metropolitan region. This collection of more than 150 beneficiary organizations includes feeding programs at homeless shelters, old age homes, schools, orphanages, hospitals, and other charities.[19] In addition, the IFBN facilitates school feeding programs, most often to fulfill corporate social investment objectives for companies.[20]

Although IFBN staff have been interested in the development of food banking for more than ten years, food bank development is not a given in India. To start, the food system is structured differently in India than in North America and Europe. In India, people access fresh food in local markets on a daily basis rather than buying food from large grocers once or twice a week. While the IFBN has developed partnerships with the GFN and other Indian companies and government departments, the IFBN's development has been slower in part because the GFN needed time to understand how food banks could operate in a context so different from those of North America or Europe.[21]

There are a few key reasons for this dynamic. To start, the structure of India's food system is fundamentally different from those of countries such as the United States, Canada, and Australia, and other countries where the GFN operates. This was an initial concern among Indian food bankers, as there seemed to be a significant disconnect between the GFN's model and what would work in India.[22] Over time, the GFN and its staff realized that a new model or set of models would be needed in India. As noted by a GFN administrator, food banks can only work if they are adapted to fit the local Indian context:

> The traditional model of food banking doesn't work in India, because food banks are dependent on packaged food, not prepared food. The

typical Indian goes to shop every day and buys what they need that day, and virtually everything that they buy is fresh. Food banks are going to be smaller operations even though this is the country with the highest number of hungry people. The whole concept of food banking has to get scaled down to a more localized environment. Logistics and food handling procedures need to be adapted to be more focused on fresh products rather than packaged products.[23]

GFN staff noted that the country is decentralized politically and culturally, so any change to the food system needs to emerge from local communities.[24]

There have been problems distinct to the corporate food sector in India as well. It is relatively small in size given the population, but even in cases where it is developed, food corporations are not necessarily keen to donate food for fear that it will hurt their brand if people get sick.[25] As compared to the United States or Europe, Indian food corporations are not as experienced with the process of surplus food redistribution, given that the country's food system is based on daily fresh food consumption.

In addition, food redistribution can be politically charged, as the legacy of the caste system in India can create perceptions that the food insecure are receiving inedible food waste, rather than food that is for human consumption. As noted by anthropologist Dolly Kikon, the origin, smell, taste, size, and feel of food is strongly tied to social hierarchies in India. According to Kikon, dietary culture is more than just food consumption but rather a reflection of how people see themselves and others.[26] Academic Christina Sathyamala highlights how some people are identified as less valuable when they eat certain types of meat such as beef or foods such as amphibians, rodents, or insects that are labeled traditional or unmodern.[27]

For this reason, food banks have worked to explain the value of high-quality surplus food redistribution. Companies have many charities to donate to, which are equally pressing, but when they donate, they often want to support visible projects, not day-to-day operations or staff.[28] As noted by an IFBN administrator, donors' restrictions on how and when funding is spent limits the growth of food banks:

> We are in the cities where land costs are extremely high [to build warehouses]. What food comes in, goes out immediately [because we

don't have the space to store it]. We say we need funding to have two people to manage the food bank or do fundraising to speak to the food companies, but that is something that is not visible to [corporate sponsors], so they don't support it.[29]

In addition to the aforementioned challenges associated with food corporations, the government of India has been slow to support the IFBN, in part because there are many other existing charities in the country and the IFBN needs to prove its worth. As stated by an IFBN administrator, food banking in India is small relative to the size of government food programs:

> The government said [what we were doing] was a great idea, but you are just starting out. So everybody wants a proof of the concept. [Our impact] will always be very little as compared to what the government is already doing, and therefore the government views us as a minor partner. It can never really emerge into a big partnership. When I tell the government that I am reaching out to 200,000 children, it is like nothing for them.[30]

The Indian social welfare state has grown notably since 2000, with most increased spending for product-based subsidies for food, fuel, and fertilizer rather than people-based subsidies such as cash transfers. As noted by academics Ashima Majumdar and Saundarjya Borbora, this approach has been criticized for its fragmented design and poor implementation, as limited spending has been invested in health, education, and sanitation. Importantly, social assistance programs have struggled to reach people who work in the informal economy, the largest and most financially unstable workforce in the country.[31] In addition, although there has been discussion about both increasing support for cash transfers and developing a more systems-based approach that would be more in line with other peer middle-income countries, the Indian welfare state remains small by global standards.[32]

Though far from adequate, the Indian national government has taken steps in recent decades to address food insecurity. Most notably, this included the National Food Security Act (NFSA) of 2013.[33] Central to the NFSA bill has been the redistribution of food parcels to both rural and urban food-insecure people through the subsidy of foodstuffs produced by the Indian agricultural sector as well as large school feeding schemes.[34] Although these food initiatives are clearly a significant step in the direction of the government's acknowledgment of the persistence of food insecurity and the need to address it in some form, these programs have been criticized as politically motivated, prone to corruption, favoring corporate agribusinesses over small farmers, and inadequate to meet the causes of food insecurity.[35]

It should be noted that the Food Safety and Authority of India, which regulates the food industry in the country, is supportive of the IFBN and the general issue of food waste reduction. Although there is no Good Samaritan Law in India, which limits food donation liability, the Food Safety and Authority of India promotes food donations to its food businesses.[36]

While the IFBN's impacts are small in comparison to the scale of hunger and food insecurity in India, IFBN can play a niche role to reduce food insecurity and food waste. This point has been articulated by an IFBN administrator:

> There are two gaps that food banks can fill. One is the food that goes to waste in the food businesses. That is something that the government is not looking [at] at all: food corporations and food businesses. So, that is an area where we can make a difference, as we are the only organized charity in the country doing that work. A second issue is that within the government programs a lot of people get left out, because of their different vulnerabilities, such as homeless or orphans. So it is there that food banks and other charities can play a very important role in reaching out to the hungriest and the most vulnerable.[37]

The IFBN developed in one of the most food-insecure regions of the world, yet it was slow to develop due to lagging support from the corporate and government sectors. While the economic growth over the last two decades has provided increased economic opportunity for many people in the middle and upper classes in India, food banks have developed programs to complement feeding schemes run by the government and network of charities across the country.

Food bank growth has been stalled in part because the Indian government has not developed legislation to facilitate corporate food donations or integrate food banking into the large food programs it already operates. India's Ministry of Food Processing Industries 2016 study on food waste estimated that approximately 927 billion rupees or U.S.$13.8 billion worth of food was lost annually. Although many types of food were wasted, fruits and vegetables, beans, peas, cereals, and poultry meat had the highest levels of food loss, ranging from 4.6 percent to 15.8 percent.[38] According to IFBN staff, a significant amount of this food waste could be salvaged if the Indian government utilized the food bank or other charities to redistribute some of these foodstuffs.[39]

In addition to lack of support from government, food corporations have not yet provided food banks with meaningful amounts of food or money. Given that the scale of food insecurity is so significant in India, there is only so much impact the IFBN can have given the limited support it receives from the government and the food industry. In this way, the Indian case study is another illustration of how food banks are dependent on state and corporate interests.

The impact of COVID-19 on food insecurity in India has been severe for several reasons.[40] As the lockdown started in March 2020, reductions in the physical availability of food increased as farmers confronted labor shortages, reduced demand from restaurants and local food vendors, and left unused food to rot in the fields.[41] Most problematically, the lockdown disrupted many people's informal livelihoods and opportunities to earn money. For many informal street vendors who sell food, rickshaw drivers who transport people, cleaners who sweep streets, day laborers who build structures, and domestic workers, employment stopped without any notice.[42]

This produced rapid increases in food insecurity practically overnight as many households did not have the discretionary income to purchase food in the market. Given that 380 million people or 80 percent of India's workforce is employed in the informal sector without any formal contract or income security, the scale of this crisis was extreme.[43] In addition, governmental reforms to liberalize the farming sector produced large-scale protests in 2021 among the country's numerous small-scale farmers.[44] Although the government eventually backed down, small-scale farmers were brought to the brink as their livelihood was challenged.

In all, these dynamics have created an environment where malnutrition, hunger, and extreme poverty persist.[45] As of 2023, reports suggest that hunger rates remain high in India, as people eat less high-quality food, as high costs, inadequate availability of food, persistent unemployment, and lack of income contribute to high food insecurity levels for many households.[46]

To confront economic, social, and health crises associated with food insecurity, the Indian government passed new legislation in 2020 to provide both direct food relief of rice, wheat, and dry beans and peas as well as small cash transfers for those who were eligible.[47] Although significant, the government intervention has been criticized for its relatively small size, given that it equates to approximately 1 percent of the country's GDP, well below the 10 to 15 percent of other European and Asian countries. In addition, in a country where 58 percent of people have inactive or no bank accounts at all, cash transfers are likely to be unavailable for those that need them most. Also, this plan did not provide unemployment insurance for those in the informal sector, even though 80 percent of the country works in the informal sector.[48] Moreover, existing government food programs, such as the school feeding program, have been hampered by long delays and an inability to reach families while children are out of school. In line with these issues, the International Commission on Jurists, an international human rights NGO based in Geneva, has argued that the Indian government did not meet its legal or ethical obligations to adequately provide food for its residents during the COVID crisis.[49]

As expected, IFBN's operations were significantly impacted by COVID. In addition to increased demand, IFBN was faced with reductions in food supplies and logistical challenges. To meet these needs, the IFBN expanded from fourteen to forty-four cities and distributed ration kits of nonperishable foods. Between April and August 2020, IFBN provided 3.7 million units of food in ration kits to more than 1 million people, totaling 300 metric tons of food.[50] In addition, when schools were closed due to COVID and children were learning remotely, IFBN provided Nutri Kits to children and their families as part of a revamped school feeding program.[51]

Although the IFBN worked to move toward more perishable foods, it simply did not meet the increased demand levels during the COVID crisis. As stated by the director of a member food bank in the IFBN, the increase in demand for food aid in 2020 due to COVID was more than the food bank system could handle: "With our existing resources and the increased demand for support from community, we are not able to meet the [food] requirements. We are trying to bring in more resources. We have initiated a fundraising campaign exclusively for emergency food relief."[52]

On top of all of these preexisting conditions, the COVID crisis and its impact on food system output, informal livelihoods, and food insecurity highlighted the structural limitations of a charity-based food relief system in India. In a country with such extreme food insecurity challenges, it is not clear whether food banks can or should be more than a small niche component of the food relief system in the future.

FOODFORWARD SOUTH AFRICA

Food banks exist in South Africa's largest cities and some small rural areas as well. The Gauteng food bank was founded in the industrial suburb of City Deep just south of Johannesburg's downtown in a 700,000-square-foot public market called the Joburg Market, the largest in Africa.[53] The staff at Johannesburg's food bank included well-educated nonprofit professionals as well as a range of fieldworkers and physical laborers.[54] However, rural food banks such as the Agri-FoodBank developed in remote KwaZulu-Natal on unpaved roads hours from any city, in contrast to the gritty, sprawling streets of Johannesburg. Staff at these food banks were disconnected from formal training or the national food bank headquarters in Cape Town, where most of the globally connected nonprofit professionals work.[55]

Although the food banks in Gauteng and KwaZulu-Natal have since moved or closed, the dynamics at play in South African food banks reflect the extreme inequality that persists across the country's urban and rural areas.[56] While some food bank partners promote FoodForward South Africa (FFSA), other stakeholders in the community express frustrations that the food bank is too bureaucratic, is disconnected from communities, or excludes the knowledge or experiences of Black residents.[57]

Following the fall of apartheid in the 1990s, food insecurity in South Africa's cities has remained high as food access has been limited by the rising cost and reduced availability of nutritious foods in formal and informal markets.[58] Recent studies have confirmed the persistence of food insecurity, with studies in 2019 and 2023 suggesting the risk of hunger in

South Africa is between 20 and 30 percent, with some metrics suggesting that half of the country is at risk of food insecurity.[59] Importantly, these studies suggest that food insecurity predated the COVID crisis and remains elevated.

These inequities are most notable in the townships and informal settlement regions, which are growing the fastest and have the weakest infrastructure to provide stable high-quality foods.[60] While many wealthy suburban enclaves have a range of retail and fresh food options that are similar to those in cities in North America or Europe, food access is starkly divided by race and class in South Africa's cities. The markets in townships and informal settlements are often unstable, sprawling, and limited in terms of food availability.[61]

The drivers of food insecurity in South Africa's rural areas originate from the colonial and apartheid systems of development, which resulted in the uneven development of agricultural systems and land distribution, underdevelopment of Black homelands, and marginalization of traditional farming.[62] Today, South Africa's farming sector is primarily divided between White-controlled fertile farms that produce food commodities for internal consumption and export, and the remaining rural lands that are primarily farmed by small-scale Black residents who often do not have the capital, technology, or markets to farm as efficiently or effectively as those on large corporate-controlled farms.[63] Although people living in rural areas engage in a range of livelihood strategies to secure incomes, these farming inequities reproduce the underdevelopment of the landscape and contribute to stagnant poverty rates in rural areas.[64]

Even though geographers Patrick Bond and Richard Peet have suggested that the South African state has engaged in a process of neoliberalism, the size of social spending has been significant and is more likely to be characterized as an ineffective system or a corrupt or crony system given the political use of food programs to reinforce the power base of the African National Congress (ANC).[65] In many respects, South Africa's constitution is recognized as one of the most progressive in the world when it comes to food and other basic needs, as the right to food is written into it. In addition, South Africa signed and ratified the International Covenant on Economic, Social and Cultural Rights in 2015. However, it is not clear whether these developments have resulted in anything tangible, beyond their symbolism indicating the importance of food as a basic human right.[66]

Food waste is also quite high in South Africa.[67] According to studies, South Africa's food waste totals approximately 9 million tons per year.[68] As noted by urban planner Faranak Miraftab, South Africa has institutionalized a neoliberal approach to manage social service delivery, including food waste mitigation. For Miraftab and development expert Thomas Mogale, this means that the South African state has privatized, devolved, and decentralized responsibility for basic services, such as sanitation, power, and refuse collection, to local government and nongovernmental institutions as a way to reduce the size and scope of government.[69]

In line with the Waste Act of 1998 and the National Waste Management Strategy of 2011, municipalities have been mandated with the primary responsibility of reducing organic waste (including food waste) in landfills.[70] To achieve these waste reduction goals, local municipalities must organize waste policy in line with international standards, which includes waste prevention, minimization, reuse, recycling, and treatment, with disposal only as a last resort. In Johannesburg, this has resulted in the passage of the City of Johannesburg Integrated Management Policy.[71] Fundamentally, this policy aims to streamline and increase waste removal processes. Waste services include collection of household waste and recycling, building rubble, garden waste, illegal and toxic waste, street cleaning, and animal carcass collection. Thus, food waste is only a small part of this waste strategy.

Once the GFN was founded in 2006, its leaders focused on identifying countries that fit the criteria for the successful development of a food bank. This included the presence of a well-developed corporate food sector, strong set of civil society organizations, stable political environment, and high food insecurity and food waste levels. In 2006 and 2007, South Africa had seemingly met these criteria, and some South African NGOs were actively looking to build a food bank system in the country.[72]

By 2007, FFSA (initially called FoodBank South Africa) was formed. Between 2007 and 2011, food bank locations were opened in the country's major cities, including Cape Town (the headquarters of FFSA), Johannesburg, Durban, Pietermaritzburg, Port Elizabeth, Rustenburg, and Polokwane, although the Pietermaritzburg has been folded into the

102   CHAPTER 6

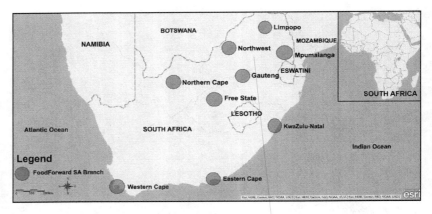

FIGURE 17. The locations of FoodForward South Africa food banks (courtesy of Warshawsky, 2020).

Durban branch. As of 2022, FFSA operated food banks in all nine provinces (see figure 17). Currently, each food bank collects and redistributes food to FFSA's network of 2,750 beneficiary organizations (see figure 18).[73]

Since its development more than a decade ago, FFSA has always played an important role within the GFN. As noted in the 2016 GFN report called "Two Projects That Transformed Food Banking Globally," the GFN describes FFSA as one of its first successful international test cases: "The South Africa project eventually became the model for future projects to establish new food banks. GFN's Feasibility Analysis Toolkit, a guide for assessing the feasibility of food banking in a community/country and an outline for developing a business plan, was designed around the South Africa experience."[74]

In addition to the core food bank mission to warehouse and redistribute food and the secondary program to manage school breakfast programs for 75,200 students daily, FFSA operates three programs in South Africa.[75] This includes the FoodShare program, which reduces food waste by connecting beneficiary organizations to retail stores using virtual technology; the Second Harvest program, which addresses food waste in rural areas; and the Mobile Rural Depots program, which makes food more accessible in rural areas.[76]

Food Banks in India and South Africa 103

FIGURE 18. The FoodForward South Africa network of food banks (courtesy of Food-Forward South Africa, 2021).

Importantly, the FFSA positions itself as the foil to the government. Whereas the FFSA critiques the South African state for its underdeveloped or ineffective programs and strategies, the food bank emphasizes that the FFSA can be efficient, flexible, ethically managed, and in line with the needs of communities.[77] Although FFSA is professionally managed, academics Sheryl Hendriks and Angela McIntyre suggest that the impact of FFSA is small when compared to the size of South African government programs.[78]

In this way, as noted by food charity experts Graham Riches and Tiina Silvasti, food philanthropy cannot provide food or income support at the scale of government because it does not have the institutional capacity or resources that governments have across the world.[79] As noted in FFSA's 2020 publication called "Major Shifts in Poverty Highlighted by COVID-19 Necessitate the Need for New Social Paradigms," South African food banks depend on the South African government in order to implement meaningful reductions in food insecurity at a larger scale:

> With the help and support of well-organized civil society organizations and social enterprises, these organizations can act as an extension of government at [the] community level, providing much needed social services. . . . There is an opportunity here for government . . . to explore social paradigms with social partners that will bring about the needed change in under-served communities.[80]

FFSA's operating budget was 23.9 million rand in 2021. This included 70 percent from donations, 26 percent from grants, 2 percent from membership fees, and 1 percent from service agreement revenue.[81] FFSA received 0 percent from government grants. This was a significant shift from its early years, when the government was a financial and political supporter. FFSA actively avoids partnerships with government, as it views the state as corrupt, inefficient, and not accountable.[82] Although governmental programs have been limited by these aforementioned issues, South Africa has implemented one of the largest income support systems in the Global South through its social grant programs. In this way, although FFSA has been critical of the South African state's lack of political commitment toward food insecurity programs, the impact of governmental income support programs is significant even when it is flawed.

FFSA has actively grown its private and individual donations to bolster its operating reserves and independence from government. As noted by an FFSA administrator, FFSA has used a range of different income-generating strategies to diversify its sources of funding:

> We have scrubbed every single government contract because of corruption, because of bad administration, and we just could not work with them. This forced us to diversify our incomes to include recurring funding from individuals and corporates, service delivery fees, monthly membership fees, and major yearly fundraising events. So we spread our risk quite broadly to make sure we are not beholden to anyone.[83]

Between 2009 and 2013, FFSA's operating budget fluctuated between $1,000,000 and $3,500,000 as funded support was uneven and operational expenses were high. This led to erratic and uneven service delivery, turnover in management, reduction in staff and food bank locations, and a dire financial position for the organization. As of 2023, FFSA is in a better financial position given that it has successfully tightened its operating budget through consolidation and streamlining of its services and grown its funding sources through a diversification strategy following the 2009–2013 institutional budget crisis. Its somewhat precarious financial position was disclosed in its own audited yearly financial statements.[84]

FFSA continues to push an ambitious program for expansion.[85] This includes an expansion of its existing food redistribution programs through more corporate food partnerships and development of more food warehouses in more cities. As part of their most recent five-year plan, FFSA aims to reach 1 million people through a network of 2,000 beneficiaries by 2025.[86] Compared to its pre-COVID size in 2019, this represents a four- to fivefold increase in size. Although FFSA initially overextended itself and was arguably overambitious in terms of its desire to expand to twenty cities in its original plans, the management at FFSA believe they are now in a better strategic position to expand its operations and programs.[87]

Moving forward, FFSA's challenges regarding expansion are somewhat typical of food banks in North America and Europe, as it is difficult to expand at a pace that is manageable and can be supported by donors. Most corporate donors do not want to support operational expenses or staff support even though these are critical to growth and sustained success of local food organizations (LFOs).[88]

Given FFSA's location as the most institutionalized food bank in Sub-Saharan Africa and its historically important role as one of GFN's first successful test cases globally, FFSA has recently emerged as a regional leader along with GFN in Africa for food banks. As noted by an FFSA administrator, FFSA is helping to develop food banks in Botswana, Kenya, and across Sub-Saharan Africa. "We are also now in talks with GFN to set up a regional cooperation of food banks in Botswana, Kenya, and other countries to set up food banks. We are trying to play a pivotal role in the region to strengthen food banks."[89]

As in other countries across the world, the COVID pandemic has produced significant economic and social fallout across South Africa. The country's economy shrank 17.6 percent in the second quarter of 2020, and 47 percent of households did not have enough money to buy food in April.[90] Lines of food recipients stretched miles across various places in South Africa as many people's livelihoods, especially those in the informal sector, disappeared with no warning.[91] These metrics suggest that South Africa struggled more than other comparable middle-income countries such as Brazil or Turkey.

In 2020 and 2021, FFSA ramped up the number of people it serves, significantly increasing its food redistribution.[92] According to its statistics, FFSA fed 950,000 people through 48 million meals and 12,015 tons of food distributed in 2022. This was completed with FFSA's network of approximately 2,750 beneficiary organizations focusing on aged care, disability care, early childhood care, institutional support, home-based care, after-school care, shelters, skills development, and youth development.[93]

To offset the impact of COVID on businesses and low-income residents, the South African government passed large stimulus measures to provide increased unemployment insurance, health support programs, small business support, and income and food assistance. In comparison, this package was 10 percent of South Africa's GDP, significantly larger than that of any other peer middle-income nations such as Brazil, Indonesia, Argentina, Turkey, Mexico, or India.[94] However, these efforts were in part negatively impacted by corruption.[95] As noted by researcher Channing Arndt and the team of researchers studying the impact of COVID in South Africa, government programs for the poor can have a significant impact on people's lives if they are extended permanently.[96]

In 2020, FFSA positioned itself as an adept, localized, and efficient institution to increase its visibility during the COVID crisis and to fundraise to expand its impact.[97] As noted by FFSA in their 2020 report "Food Poverty Is Emerging as a Significant Threat alongside the COVID-19 Pandemic," FFSA raised more than 50 million rand in order to expand its programming:

> A total of R53 million was raised in response to our Special COVID-19 Appeal. These funds will put FoodForward SA in a much stronger position to respond rapidly to meet the growing demand for food across South Africa. Taking an eighteen to twenty-four month view, we still need to raise an additional R43mn to be in a position to scale

up further. We rely on your continued support to help us repair the social fabric in under-served communities.[98]

FFSA has since increased its ambitions to scale up its operations to reach more people and create more efficient applications and monitoring procedures of its food banking network.[99] It is unclear, however, whether FFSA will acquire the funding or develop the capacity to scale up its operations.

By its own measures, FFSA has met its goals in terms of food delivered.[100] However, it experienced significant problems in its first ten years pertaining to financial support, government political interference, tension with community-based organizations (CBOs), and an inability to reach beyond urban centers. These dynamics are explored through the two subsequent examples of the food bank in Johannesburg and the Agri-FoodBank in KwaZulu-Natal.

The Gauteng Branch in Johannesburg

Along with food banks in Cape Town and Durban, Johannesburg's food bank is both one of the oldest and largest in South Africa (see figures 19 and 20). However, although it opened in 2009 to much fanfare and positive publicity, it initially struggled to develop consistent funding and efficient food donation processes. In part, this was due to struggles with the quality of management at the Johannesburg branch.[101]

While some of these issues were overcome with FFSA's consolidation into a centralized national management structure, the Gauteng branch in Johannesburg (formerly known as FoodBank Johannesburg) continues to face key challenges as it develops its donations and fundraising and its legitimacy within the region.[102]

In addition to issues pertaining to stable resource allocation and financing, the food bank in Johannesburg has had to manage the positive and negative impacts of the South African state's political influence. In the early years of the food bank, the state was a clear supporter of the food bank as it provided both political and financial support for development.[103]

However, support from the state has come with conditions, as the state has utilized the food bank to achieve its broader political agenda to reconsolidate its power as a legitimate institution in the battle against poverty and food insecurity. While the government's initial support of the food

FIGURE 19. Original location and name of FoodForward in Johannesburg, South Africa (courtesy of Warshawsky, 2009).

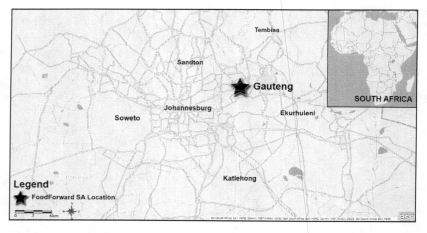

FIGURE 20. FoodForward South Africa in Johannesburg, South Africa (courtesy of Warshawsky, 2021).

bank could be viewed as genuine, as the state viewed FFSA as a viable solution to reduce food insecurity and food waste, the food bank also conveniently fits into the state's broader agenda to achieve two goals.[104]

First, the state has used food programs as political tools to reinvigorate its ANC base through food parcel delivery. Second, food banks facilitate

FIGURE 21. Community-based beneficiary organization in Johannesburg, South Africa (courtesy of Warshawsky, 2009).

the state's broader political agenda to depoliticize and offload food insecurity programs to LFOs and other local actors. As noted by an FFSA administrator, FFSA chose to break its ties with the South African government in order to maintain its political and institutional independence:

> We are not going to partner with government, because the programs are not focused on food security. It is for political ends. For example, the Department of Social Development [has used] its huge budget on food security... to buy food in ANC strongholds to win elections, to buy local elections to give people food parcels. We cannot be part of that dynamic. We do not see government as a real partner. They are more of a liability.[105]

Also, the experiences of many CBOs within FFSA's network in Johannesburg suggest that the food banking network may be vulnerable to key problems (see figure 21). Importantly, most of the CBOs within the FFSA network operate a range of services such as care for children, elderly, disabled, sick, unemployed, or youth in conjunction with their food programs. While FFSA typically operates at a high bureaucratic level with food corporations and government, CBOs are on the ground with people who are food insecure.

For this reason, CBOs can be viewed as the front lines of food insecurity and hunger in South Africa. They are typically funded by one or just a few people within the community. Although it is possible for money or in-kind donations to originate from the community at large, such as church funds, CBOs do not have fundraising structures or the capacity or time to apply for large amounts of money. As noted by an administrator at a CBO based in Johannesburg, CBOs are often highly unstable and susceptible to turnover.

> Turnover is high. Many CBOs receive food or money once every month or two. That means they operate on their own without any assistance. They buy food from surrounding spaza shops, which is expensive for the organization's manager. Most funding comes from the community, especially churches or the manager, so resources are thin and often nonexistent. For this reason, the organizations often do not last long.[106]

In addition to funding and operational instability, some CBOs within the beneficiary network have struggled to meet new bureaucratic rules promoted by the FFSA itself. This includes new required membership fees for beneficiary organizations and increased oversight and compliance measures implemented as part of FFSA's changed management structure. In addition, CBOs have to pledge to promote the self-reliance of food recipients and improve the employability of those that receive food.[107]

While some of these measures are part of FFSA's more efficient systems, they have the capacity to be quite burdensome for CBOs given their already limited capacity. Although there are broader expectations among many donors that LFOs push to professionalize their operations, it is unclear whether this is realistic or appropriate for CBOs that operate in extreme uncertainty in a range of cultural and social contexts. As documented elsewhere, it is not always evident that staff at the FFSA have visited or are knowledgeable about the type of work that food beneficiaries operate in their communities.[108] As noted by a stakeholder at a Johannesburg-based

CBO, this creates friction between FFSA and the food charities that already exist in the community:

> Some organizations will hate the food bank, as soon as you create a bureaucracy that will discourage some people from belonging. Many of the community-based organizations are not represented with the food bank structure.... If they [operate in a space where others already work, the community will not be pleased].... They [should have spoken to people and organizations] who deal with food every day.[109]

Part of this challenge is that CBOs often exist in informal settlements or townships far from the food bank warehouse or administrative offices. Also, sometimes, racial and ethnic divisions reinforce the disconnect between communities. In South Africa, many food bank professionals are White or Coloured, whereas most of the recipients are Black. These racial and ethnic categories are distinct to South Africa and continue to be used in the country's census statistics.[110] As noted by a stakeholder at a Johannesburg-based CBO, it is critical for food charities to recognize racial and ethnic differences between different communities if they are to be trusted:

> You send white people to farmers, because they know how to speak their language, and you send Black people to Black-owned businesses and CBOs. If you cannot mention the name of a Black township, then you will have [no standing] with the donors or the people you serve. If they ask you where in Soweto you serve and you do not know ... you must know the beneficiaries to prove to donors and stakeholders that you understand hunger. If you fail to answer, you will not get nothing.[111]

Although these tensions are not necessarily unique to Johannesburg, the cultural and sociodemographic differences between neighborhoods in the city are quite extreme and more reflective of cities in the Global South, especially those with colonial histories. Both the managers and the clients of the CBOs live in communities with food insecurity and interact with people who experience food insecurity. Also, CBOs are more in touch with people's cultural taste preferences for the types of foods that people want to eat and various types of food interventions that would work or are needed in communities. Given that food banks such as FFSA are often given whatever food manufacturers and retailers cannot sell, FFSA is more likely to adhere to the food preferences of its donors given that they keep the organization afloat.

The Agri-FoodBank in KwaZulu-Natal

Between 2007 and 2012, the combined forces of reduced private corporate donations due to the 2007–2009 global economic recession and an overextended programming infrastructure collectively precipitated an institutional crisis for FFSA as it was simply unable to meet its financial obligations in 2012. This was compounded by the fact that the South African state decided to stop funding FFSA given its overly urban focus at the same time. While both rural and urban food insecurity have remained critical problems in South Africa, the central state has continued to reinforce the idea that food insecurity is primarily a rural problem. Given that the state provided more than 70 percent of FFSA funds in 2012, FFSA simply ran out of money.[112] As noted by an FFSA administrator, FFSA mismanaged its operations and almost stopped functioning:

> Between 2009 and 2013, we were running quite an elaborate model that was quite an expensive model. It was not sustainable. By 2013, the organization was technically insolvent. There was not enough money to run the organization except for two weeks. New leadership was brought in to look at the model and to make it more efficient and more cost effective.[113]

In the years that followed this crisis, FFSA reduced its operations and staff as well as diversified its financial portfolio to include more private and individual fundraising, membership fees, and service fees. In addition, FFSA consolidated its existing warehouses into one centralized warehouse to streamline and cut costs.[114] As stated by an FFSA administrator, FFSA's reorganization was necessary and ultimately improved the stability of the institution:

> The model just wasn't working. Everyone was doing their own thing. There was no unity around standard operating procedures, around engagement with food donors and actual donors. Now, we manage

everything from a central office. At the national office, we have five departments that we did not have before, including IT, fund development, marketing, finance, beneficiary development, and an operations department.[115]

However, although these changes made a significant impact on FFSA's overall financial viability, staff and board members within FFSA grew concerned that its mission needed to expand to meet the expectations of funders. The Agri-FoodBank concept was developed to incorporate small-scale rural farmers in lower-income regions to bring their products to FFSA's markets, which would then feed the poor. FFSA administrators hoped that this could position the organization as a more development-oriented LFO, which helped both rural and urban areas.[116]

Given FFSA's limited expertise and capacity, FFSA collaborated with TechnoServe, an international nonprofit that works on poverty reduction through private sector partnerships, and the South African Department of Agriculture, Forestry and Fisheries.[117] The Makhathini Flats in Jozini and Vulamehlo in Ugu in rural KwaZulu-Natal were chosen as they would be paid for by the provincial government and were deemed high-poverty areas (see figure 22).[118]

The structure of the Agri-FoodBank is relatively straightforward in that food produced by small-scale farmers flows through the Value-Added Center warehouse to the FFSA's network of beneficiary organizations; government health, education, and social development program recipients; and formal and informal vendors in markets (see figure 23).

It was the South African state that had the potential to scale out the program to make it feasible. For this reason, FFSA and TechnoServe were content for the Department of Agriculture, Forestry and Fisheries and the Department of Social Development to promote and take credit for the Agri-FoodBank program. According to FFSA and TechnoServe, government buy-in was critical in order to see the project through to its completion, given that the state had the resources and capacity to make the project succeed.[119]

Although the Agri-FoodBank was designed to be completed in 2014 after three years of development, it never came to fruition. While it is true that cooperative farmers in Jozini planted a range of fruits and vegetables,

114 CHAPTER 6

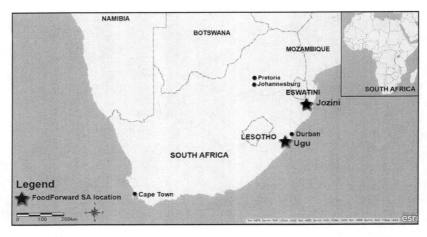

FIGURE 22. Location of the Jozini and Ugu Agri-FoodBanks (courtesy of Warshawsky, 2020).

FIGURE 23. Small-scale farmers in Jozini, South Africa (courtesy of Warshawsky, 2012).

the Agri-FoodBank in Ugu was never built. The problems that developed were multiple. To start, the farmers were never connected adequately to the various markets, and many of the farmers did not have the skill set or expertise to produce the expected results.[120] Also, the role of government never materialized, as it both was unable to fulfill its commitments and had suspicious motivations.[121] According to various stakeholders, the location of the project was chosen in part because it was in a region where the ANC was trying to assert its political influence. KwaZulu-Natal not only was President Zuma's home province, but it was an area where the ANC always felt that it needed to build a stronger political presence. The Agri-FoodBank gave the state a project that could fill that role while also appearing to be committed to poverty reduction.[122]

With the lack of project realization and frustration by its partner organization, the Agri-FoodBank project collapsed. FFSA walked away from the project and later moved on to other rural projects, such as the Second Harvest project mentioned earlier.[123]

This can be seen through South Africa's food policy initiatives that developed with great fanfare without ever being realized. As noted by an FFSA administrator, the government engaged in a process to create food policies without any real consultation with people or organizations that were knowledgeable about food insecurity:

> The government set up a food security committee ... [with] ministers who knew nothing about food security.... Then, they came up with a plan to address food insecurity. The plan went nowhere. Government really needs to be an enabler of what civil society is already doing. Government needs to see that when they address food insecurity, they need to see food banking as a viable model.... We can be a tool in their arsenal if they use it properly.[124]

Both the FFSA Gauteng branch in Johannesburg and the Agri-FoodBank in KwaZulu-Natal are examples of food banks that did not become institutionalized because their missions clashed with that of the state, underscoring the symbiotic relationship that needs to exist for food banks to take hold.

Moreover, with all of these growing pains and new innovative programming such as FoodShare, Second Harvest, and Mobile Rural Depots, FFSA remained financially viable for no more than a few months at a time. Additionally, there was no guarantee that their newer programs would operate successfully, especially in rural areas as the infrastructure was significantly underdeveloped given the widespread poverty and other logistical and social challenges in those contexts. Moreover, in a country that has the right to food enshrined in its constitution, it is not clear whether food charity represents a step toward this goal.[125]

Importantly, even with these challenges, FFSA remains one of the most important case study food banks, as noted by GFN administrators.[126] It is often used as the prototype for food bank development in other parts of the world, especially the Global South. If FFSA represents the model food bank in the Global South, that is concerning given that it has all of the aspects of a seemingly successful food bank system, such as a strong corporate food sector, active civil society, stable government, and high need, yet it has struggled to meet its own expectations. In comparison to South Africa, most countries in the Global South have a less developed corporate food sector and experience continuing political, economic, and social crises related to extreme health and poverty concerns, ineffective or corrupt governance mechanisms, and lack of social service delivery.[127] Given that many contexts in the Global South often have the weakest infrastructure and highest need, it is exactly in these locations that food banks are likely to fail operationally.

CONCLUSION

PUTTING FOOD BANKS IN THEIR PLACE

This book has examined the historical development, mission, structure, and outcomes of several global food banking systems—the core food banking regions of North America and Europe and emerging food bank regions in Asia and Africa—to understand how and why they have expanded rapidly across the globe. The analysis investigated who benefits the most from food bank development and how.

Importantly, as mentioned throughout this book, food banks play a niche role in many contexts to reduce food insecurity and food waste. Although many food banks point to record amounts of food delivered or persons served as evidence of their impact in communities, these metrics reflect the growth and institutionalization of food banks more than their capacity to reduce food insecurity or food waste. In most contexts, the impact of food banks is small, especially when compared to the size of government food and income support programs.

The COVID-19 pandemic has further highlighted the structural weaknesses of food banks.[1] Food banks struggled to cope with rapid increases in demand, inadequate food supplies, lack of financial and human resources, higher costs, and the closure of some local charities.[2] These dynamics have underscored that charity-based food bank systems are more of a patchwork than a systematic network that can effectively reduce food insecurity and food waste on a large scale.

Given the challenges and limited effectiveness of food banks, this book sought to shed light on the dynamics that contribute to their continued promotion as a panacea for addressing food insecurity and waste across the globe. I have shown that food banks are often promoted as replacements for social welfare programs.[3] Food banks contribute to the depoliticization of food insecurity when governments use them as a way to deflect from accepting responsibility for their own policy failures. Also, although food banks participate in some advocacy, it is not clear whether food banks can expand the scope of their advocacy beyond safe nonpolitical issues, as their ties to corporations, governments, and other powerful entities determine their existence.

In the United States, food banks emerged in large part because of the devolution, decentralization, and privatization of the social welfare state. Their early development coincided with economic recessions in the 1970s and 1980s and neoliberal welfare retrenchment policies in the 1980s and 1990s. In the twenty-first century, U.S. food banks represent one of the largest charities in the country and are supported in part through government in-kind donations through farm commodity programs and other tax incentives.[4]

In Israel and the Arab states in southwestern Asia, food banks have developed systems with limited support from government. Although the Israeli welfare state is moderately sized, the government has not adequately funded food support programs as it pursues a more workfare-oriented welfare state.[5] Given that Israel has high costs of living, Israeli food banks play a small role when compared to the levels of poverty in the country.[6] In the Arab states, food banks have developed without support from government. Social welfare states are underdeveloped as compared to other peer countries in the world with similar economies. This has been exacerbated by pressures to keep expenditures lower to maintain high financial standing.[7]

In Germany and Denmark, food banks have developed alongside well-developed welfare states. Although Germany has faced political pressures to reduce and reshape welfare state programs and limit eligibility, it remains one of the largest welfare states in Europe. However, German food banks have become politically charged as they try to navigate different perspectives on the role of government assistance, food charities, and who is eligible for food aid.[8] Similarly, in Denmark, food banks have emerged in the context of one of the most well-developed social welfare states in the world. As the social safety net has faced increased pressures to reduce spending and eligibility, the Danish government has promoted food banks as a means to reduce food insecurity and waste in the country.[9]

In contrast to those of northern and central Europe, food banks in southern and eastern Europe have faced a range of political, economic, and social challenges. In Italy, high unemployment and pressures to reduce the size and scope of the social safety net have created instability for food banks.[10] Yet food banks have become one of the most well-developed systems in Europe. In Hungary, persistent poverty, relatively small social welfare state spending, and antipoor sentiments have combined to marginalize food banks.[11] This has limited food bank development in Hungary and much of eastern Europe.

In India and South Africa, food banks have faced a range of challenges in their development. In India, although the government has increasingly developed school feeding and other direct food aid programs with potential to feed hundreds of millions of people, the social welfare state is small when compared to other middle-income countries.[12] In addition, the government has viewed food banks as small operations with little impact, given the scale of food insecurity in the country. In South Africa, the social welfare state is one of the largest in the world as compared to other middle-income countries.[13] Although the state initially promoted the food bank system for political purposes, food banks have parted ways with the government due to its lack of commitment to food security, its corruption, and its inefficiencies.

Moreover, food banks often elide the difficult questions surrounding the root cause of food inequality in cities and the role that their closest partners, namely food corporations and private industry, play in perpetuating high food prices and uneven food access in some contexts.[14] Food banks are in large part an outgrowth of the corporate charitable sector and are subject to its idiosyncrasies and contradictions, as corporate wealth and excess are a key part of the food bank's financial and in-kind resources flows. Food banks are therefore dependent on food corporations to operate.[15] In many cases, corporations have utilized their board memberships and financial influence to change how food banks operate, as the scope of activities remains limited to safe zones such as nutrition and food donations rather than politically laden issues such as economic inequality or tax policy.[16]

Meanwhile, corporations use food banks to improve their own market value, brand, and sustainability initiatives and to capture tax benefits, liability protection, and other food resources available to them through food banks.[17] Food corporations promote the idea that food insecurity and waste issues can be solved via the market with technical business solutions.[18] Although it may beyond the capacity of food companies to overcome, the political, economic, and social causes of food insecurity and waste are not sufficiently addressed by the food industry. Instead, food banks focus on building larger organizations with an emphasis on institutional growth, corporate partnerships, and the priorities of donors.[19] Importantly, since food banks operate within the existing corporate food system structure, it is doubtful that food banks have the ability or incentive to overcome the structural causes of food insecurity, food waste, or social inequality in many locales.

In the United States, food banks have developed close partnerships with food corporations, as the latter provide funding and surplus food. This has empowered the food industry to use food banks as marketing tools within their broader sustainability initiatives and increasingly penetrate the daily operations of food banks through board control and lobbying limits.[20]

In Israel and the Arab states in southwestern Asia, the relationships between food corporations and food banks have varied. In Israel, food banks have developed without significant corporate support, given that their mission is to save fresh food rather than surplus food from industry. In the Arab states, food banks have developed close partnerships with food corporations in order to provide money and in-kind donations. Given that food banks work without government support, food corporations are essential to the operations of food banks in this region of the world.

In Europe, food corporations have increasingly supported food banks as a way to reduce food waste in line with their sustainability initiatives. This has empowered food banks in Germany and Italy to grow significantly. Although there was some initial hesitation among Danish and Hungarian food corporations to support food banks, they have increasingly supported their mission as well once they became familiar with their operations and realized the services food banks provide to the food industry. In the European context, even though food banks have been used to legitimize welfare state retrenchment, food banks play a key role in reducing food waste in the corporate sector, which would probably have been ignored by the state and corporate sectors. For this reason, it is likely that food banks will continue to grow in Europe, even as they face pushback from a range of political movements from both sides of the ideological spectrum.

In India and South Africa, food corporations have developed different relationships with food banks. In India, food corporations have not partnered with food banks given concerns over liability. In addition, the Indian food system's fresh food and lack of prepackaged foods have combined to limit the potential for food bank development. In South Africa, food corporations have developed a strong connection to food banks. The formal food sector is well developed in South Africa and well aware of the value that food banks bring them in terms of brand enhancement and food waste reduction. However, as in India, food banks have struggled in informal economies and rural areas in the country where food insecurity is the highest.

Data from this book suggest that whether food banks are institutionalized and seen as legitimate is dependent on the size and wealth of the corporate food sector and financial and political support in a particular context. Ironically, food banks have become most institutionalized in North America and Europe, where the government already provides a strong social safety net and where the economy is generally more robust.

Over the past few decades, food banks have become increasingly institutionalized in North America and Europe, as Feeding America and the European Food Banks Federation (FEBA) have developed strong connections with the corporate sector and some support from state governments. The developments in Israel, southwestern Asia, India, and South Africa suggest that the experiences of food bank development are more varied in the rest of the world.

Although the Global FoodBanking Network (GFN) and Food Banking Regional Network (FBRN) have actively worked to develop food banks around the world, some food bank networks have struggled to find financial and human resources to remain financially viable due, in part, to uneven support from food corporations, central states, and challenges associated with working with both corporate donors and local beneficiary community-based organizations (CBOs). Even in South Africa, one of GFN's earliest test cases and one that is often touted for its development by GFN for its successes and program rollouts through FoodShare and Second Harvest, the food bank system is only financially viable for short periods of time.

This evidence points to a central contradiction: the places with the greatest excess of food and money are the places where food banks are most likely to be embraced. I have argued this is because the state uses food banks to distract from their own policy failures and the root causes of food insecurity or food waste.

REFORMULATING THE ROLE OF THE FOOD BANK

As food banks continue to expand in size and scale across the globe, policy makers and researchers need to critically assess the limits of food banks as institutions and identify what roles they may be able to play in food systems and food policy formation, especially in the Global South, where informal food pathways are so critical to food security.

The uneven development and institutionalization of food banks thus far has aligned with each food bank's placement in the global economy and geopolitics of the region. Generally, the development of the food corporate sector or support from government has played a significant enabling or disabling role. Also, demand levels are extremely varied in terms of the number and type of food-insecure people that each country faces. While it seems possible that there may be a role for food banks in limited or niche roles, the scale and structure of development will likely not be uniform across the world. In addition, food banks may or may not resemble the large food bank systems in North America. Food banks should be understood and conceptualized as civil society institutions in local contexts, influenced by unique historical, political, economic, social, and cultural factors.

Although it is true that food banks have been used as a rationale for welfare state retrenchment in some contexts, they have also developed a small role in food waste reduction in the corporate sector. In addition, even though food waste is generated across the industrialized food system and the scale of corporate food waste is significantly larger than food banks can manage, food banks can contribute to some food waste mitigation at one very specific point at the end of the food system in some places. In this way, food banks can play an extremely specialized role in some local contexts, given that corporate food waste will likely never disappear completely. Since food corporations have the most well-developed infrastructure in metropolitan regions, food banks will likely continue to be located in cities as wasted food is collected faster and at greater volumes within urban areas.

Given the limited impacts of food banks and potential pitfalls in many contexts, I suggest that we need to reformulate the role of food banks. Although some scholars suggest that food banks should be eliminated, I argue that food banks should not be completely removed from the global food system.[21] Instead, I suggest that food banks can play a very small role in some parts of the world if they are reconceptualized. There are a few important reasons why food banks should be reimagined.

To start, the mission of food banks needs to be both clearer and more realistic, as food surpluses can never realistically reduce food insecurity in a meaningful way. Rather, food redistribution can be understood as a complementary small-scale function provided by food banks. While they can help fill small gaps in food aid, they will never come close to replacing the size, scope, or capacity of government food programs.[22] To this point, the COVID pandemic has reinforced the significant impact of government food and income support programs and secondary roles that food charity responses play in emergency food relief.

In addition, food banks need to regain their institutional independence from food corporations. Although the food industry has provided food banks with significant financial and in-kind resources, they are becoming too involved in the daily operations of food banks.[23] This has changed the mission of food banks and limited their advocacy for important food justice issues. Food banks should not continue to be an extension of food corporations or reinforce state welfare retrenchment. For this to happen, food banks will have to make difficult decisions about their mission, size, and impacts. They should not grow just for the sake of growing, but rather become more focused on food redistribution in contexts where food surplus is discarded. If food banks develop a stronger mission that is more independent from the state and food corporations, they can more actively promote the right to food, conduct living wage campaigns, and critique government and corporations when necessary.

Also, food banks need to more adequately incorporate the knowledge and experiences of the food insecure in the daily operations of the food system. In some contexts, food banks are reproducing new bureaucracies, stigmatizing food recipients, sidelining existing food charities, or excluding the hungry from their network.[24] As charities, food banks should be empowering the poor and food insecure, not demeaning them. Given that many people who work at food banks and food beneficiary organizations are both knowledgeable about the critiques of food banks and passionate about helping the food insecure, a revamped and refocused food bank system would enable food bank staff and volunteers to contribute to a better emergency food system in many contexts.

Although these dynamics are present in various contexts around the globe, food bank development in the Global South is the most concerning. Unlike North America and Europe, it is unclear that food banks can work or should exist in parts of Asia and Africa, as food systems are designed differently in these regions.[25] Given that food banks need surplus food to operate, the lack of a well-developed food industry in many countries in the Global South suggest that food banks may not function well there. Additionally, as evident in places such as India, where the informal food sector is strong, food banks may not fit the existing food system. Although more research is needed in countries with strong informal economies, underdeveloped formal food economies, and high poverty rates, evidence in this book suggests that food banks may not be appropriate for many contexts in the Global South. This is critical, as food banks are not a magic bullet to reduce food insecurity and food waste. Rather, their successes are on a small scale and limited to some regions of the world.

In North American and European contexts such as the United States, Denmark, and Italy, food banks have increased the efficiency of food donation systems in many cities and repurposed corporate food waste that would otherwise be landfilled. In Asia, Israeli food banks have salvaged food from the agricultural sector, while food banks in other parts of southwestern Asia and Sub-Saharan Africa have increased the number of institutional stakeholders involved in food waste mitigation efforts. Thus, even though food charity has clear limits, food banks have contributed in meaningful ways in some contexts.

REFORMULATING THE ROLE OF THE STATE

Evidence in this book suggests that new approaches need to be developed to increase accountability of all food system institutions. Critical collective solidarity can focus the discussion on who benefits from food bank development and why, as it is an integrated approach across institutions and all people rather than an uncritical solidarity that supports corporate philanthropy.[26]

Specifically, more responsibility and accountability need to be placed on the state. Government food and income support programs must be supported adequately and right-to-food guidelines should be backed through global agreements, national constitutions, and tangible food policies.[27] As the representative of the people, governments need to be ethically, legally, and politically accountable for the well-being of their residents. This includes access to food and other basic human rights such as water, health care, sanitation, and housing.

Though far from adequate, countries around the world have developed programs to promote food security. In the United States, this has included the Supplemental Nutrition Assistance Program (SNAP) as well as other farm commodity and direct feeding programs for children.[28] Although many of these programs are directly tied to the U.S. Farm Bill and the interests of the food industry, they do provide important food aid in the country.[29] Like food banks, these programs also need to be reformulated and politically supported as part of a broader reconceptualization of the U.S. social safety net. Given that the United States is one of a few countries globally not to vote yes or ratify multiple UN resolutions on the right to food as a human right, more work is needed by the United States to commit to food security.[30]

In contrast to the United States, most European states have developed a more comprehensive social safety net, including a wide range of social assistance programs for the poor or other vulnerable populations.[31] Although many European states have committed to UN right-to-food resolutions, this has not always resulted in stronger food policies in practice.[32]

In Israel, the state has shown uneven support for the poor, while the state has largely been absent in many other regions of southwestern Asia.[33]

In India and South Africa, two countries with large food-insecure populations, each respective government has increased its role in social protection. In India, this has included national policies to increase food redistribution and school feeding.[34] Although it is a large operation, the program's impact remains small given the high levels of food insecurity in the country's cities and rural areas. In South Africa, social grants have contributed to one of the largest social support systems in the Global South. However, corruption, extreme poverty, and inefficiencies have limited their impact.[35] This suggests that a strong governmental role in food protection and social assistance is necessary but not sufficient to reduce food insecurity on a large scale, especially in the high-poverty regions of the world.

While the COVID pandemic has highlighted the structural weaknesses of food banking as a solution to hunger, it has also presented an unusual opportunity for states to take a stronger role in providing for their residents. I have noted throughout this book that food insecurity increased at the start of the pandemic, but a September 2021 report about household food security in the United States found that food insecurity across the entire population for the entire year of 2020 was not higher than prepandemic levels.[36] This is in contrast to what has happened following past recessions, when food insecurity increased. Poverty researchers Patrick Cooney and Luke Shaefer have suggested that the expanded safety net that the U.S. government provided during 2020—which included direct payments to families and individuals—are the reason for the surprising stability in food insecurity that year.[37] This supports the argument that, in order to address food insecurity, the state needs to take the lead in alleviating economic insecurity and poverty.

Similarly, severe material deprivation rates were relatively stable in most of Europe, although there was some variation by country. In places where large amounts of stimulus were given to protect unemployed, food-insecure, and other vulnerable populations, poverty rates remained relatively similar to prepandemic metrics.[38] Although Israel's stimulus measures were more modest, poverty rates also remained flat there.[39]

In contrast to the United States, Europe, and Israel, food insecurity has remained elevated in many portions of the Global South, including southwestern Asia, India, and South Africa.[40] Government interventions were significantly smaller in these places, and the scale of poverty is much greater.[41] In addition, these regions have larger informal economies. These factors make it more difficult to meaningfully reduce food insecurity. According to data, poverty was projected to rise in most of southwestern Asia due to COVID as the stimulus measures were insufficient or nonexistent to help those already food insecure.[42] Additionally, in India, food insecurity remained elevated, given the insufficient size of the government's stimulus measures.[43] Although South Africa passed a relatively large stimulus measure to mitigate COVID's negative impacts on unemployment and food insecurity, lack of preparedness, inefficiencies, corruption, and the scale of poverty across the country has limited the impact of these measures.[44] Even though poverty would surely be worse in places like India and South Africa without government intervention, state programs are important yet not sufficient to significantly reduce food insecurity as underdeveloped economies and high levels of poverty blunt their potential impacts.

A number of food-related social movements—such as the food sovereignty movement and the right to food movement—have drawn a clearer connection between poverty and food insecurity as they push governments to provide more meaningful food and income support programs and operationalize more effective food policies.

Since the 1990s, the food sovereignty movement has formulated a political vision that highlights the right of local households to be in control of the nature of production, distribution, and consumption, all of which influence how and what people can eat in various contexts.[45] The political movement has its origins in rural peasant communities in Latin America and across the Global South as a resistance to global neoliberal influences.

Over the past three decades, the food sovereignty movement's counterhegemonic messages have spread globally as rural and urban residents contest how food systems are organized and controlled.[46] Even though many of its tenets focus on local control of food production, food sovereignty has become institutionalized in some countries in government constitutions.[47] Although not specifically about food banks, the food sovereignty lens provides a critical perspective to examine what types of institutions should participate in food systems. Given that food bank systems are connected to global corporate food flows, food banks could be critiqued as oppositional to food sovereignty.

In addition, for more than seventy years, scholars and activists have promoted right-to-food social movements that highlight food as a basic right that all humans have.[48] Within three years of the development of the United Nations, Article 25 of the Universal Declaration of Human Rights in 1948 clearly stated the right to food as a basic human right.[49] Since then, numerous legally binding global agreements have been reached among the UN's member countries to promote and protect the right to food. This has included Article 11 in the International Covenant on Economic, Social and Cultural Rights.[50] The covenant has been ratified by 171 states, although the United States is the only OECD country and one of a few countries globally not to vote yes or ratify multiple UN resolutions on the right to food as a human right.[51] Thirty countries explicitly recognize the right to food in their state constitutions.[52]

As codified in international law, the right to food movement demands that all institutions, especially governments, accept their political, social, and moral responsibility to ensure all residents are food secure. Although food scholar Graham Riches has pointed to the right to food movement as a legally binding vision with significant potential to transform societies, other scholars such as Katharine S. E. Cresswell Riol argue that its support has been more symbolic than concrete.[53] Unlike the food sovereignty movement, right to food advocates have overtly criticized food banks as institutions that depoliticize hunger and deflect attention from the state's responsibility toward food security and the right to food. While some food bank administrators advocate for the right to food abstractly, food researcher Karlos Pérez de Armiño and other right-to-food movement advocates see this as uncritical solidarity, as food banking is strongly associated with corporate philanthropy, not social justice.[54]

Although from different perspectives, both food sovereignty and right to food movements express concern that the food insecure are not fully integrated into food relief systems.[55] From this point of view, food recipients need to be understood as active participants in the food system—without secondary status or gendered, racialized, or classed stigma—and be a key part of food system development, identification of challenges, and possible solutions to issues of food waste, food insecurity, and social inequality.[56] This is especially critical as food banks operate in local contexts in the Global South, far from the North American or European cities where food banks first developed decades ago. Food recipients in informal settlements or small rural areas in the Global South interact with food differently, and food relief organizations need to understand these different cultural and social foodways.[57]

Most importantly, it is imperative that government food and income support programs are supported sufficiently and enshrine the international right to food in state constitutions. Although the structure of economies significantly impacts the opportunities, livelihoods, and income of people living in various cities, towns, and rural areas across the world, governments can make a significant impact with targeted income and food interventions. While it is important to expand job opportunities given that food security is strongly tied to income, social safety nets make a significant difference in poverty levels, as seen during the COVID pandemic.[58] Importantly, it is the state that is ultimately responsible for the well-being of its residents, as it has a moral, legal, and political responsibility to ensure that people are food secure.[59]

NOTES

INTRODUCTION

1. Food and Agriculture Organization, "The State of Food Security and Nutrition in the World."
2. Riches and Silvasti, "Hunger in the Rich World"; Riches, *Food Bank Nations*.
3. Hebinck and Shackleton, "Livelihoods, Resources, and Land Reform."
4. Crush, Frayne, and Haysom, "Introduction to Urban Food Security in the Global South"; Frayne, "Pathways of Food."
5. Moragues-Faus and Battersby, "Urban Food Policies for a Sustainable and Just Future"; Crush and Frayne, "Urban Food Insecurity and the New International Food Security Agenda."
6. Gustavsson et al., "Global Food Losses and Food Waste"; Lipinski et al., *Reducing Food Loss and Waste*.
7. United Nations Environment Programme, *UNEP Food Waste Index Report*.
8. European Commission, *Recommendations for Action in Food Waste Prevention*; Gunders, *Wasted*.
9. Evans, "Blaming the Consumer—Once Again; O'Brien, *A Crisis of Waste?*; Spring et al., "Food Waste"; Stuart, *Waste*.
10. United Nations, *Sustainable Development Goal 2*.
11. United Nations, *Sustainable Development Goal 12*.
12. Flanagan, Lipinski, and Goodwin, "SDG Target 12.3 on Food Loss and Waste"; Flanagan, Robertson, and Hanson, *Reducing Food Loss and Waste*; Food and Agriculture Organization, "Food Security and Nutrition"; ReFED, *A Roadmap to Reduce U.S. Food Waste by 20 Percent*.

13. EPA, "Putting Surplus Food to Good Use"; European Union, "Directive 2008/1/EC of the European Parliament."
14. Food Waste Reduction Alliance, "Messy but Worth It!"
15. Crush and Frayne, "Urban Food Insecurity and the New International Food Security Agenda"; Wiskerke, "Urban Food Systems."
16. Tefft et al., *Urban Food Systems Governance*; Moragues-Faus and Morgan, "Reframing the Foodscape."
17. Beall, Crankshaw, and Parnell, *Uniting a Divided City*; Parnell and Robinson, "(Re)Theorizing Cities from the Global South."
18. Food and Agriculture Organization, "Food Security and Nutrition."
19. United Nations, "68% of the World Population Projected to Live in Urban Areas by 2050, Says UN."
20. Atkinson, "Approaches and Actors in Urban Food Security in Developing Countries"; Drakakis-Smith, "Urban Food Distribution in Asia and Africa"; Frayne, "Pathways of Food"; Sonnino, "The New Geography of Food Security."
21. Hoover, *Estimating Quantities and Types of Food Waste at the City Level*; Warshawsky, "The Devolution of Urban Food Waste Governance."
22. Global FoodBanking Network, "The State of Global Food Banking."
23. Global Food Banking Network, *Waste Not, Want Not*; Global FoodBanking Network, "About GFN."
24. European Food Banks Federation, "Members"; Food Banking Regional Network, "Current Food Banks"; Global FoodBanking Network, "Our Global Reach."
25. Lohnes and Wilson, "Bailing Out the Food Banks?"
26. Loopstra and Tarasuk, "Food Bank Usage Is a Poor Indicator of Food Insecurity."
27. Riches, *Food Bank Nations*.
28. Huang, Liu, and Hsu, "Understanding Global Food Surplus and Food Waste"; Teigiserova, Hamelin, and Thomsen, "Towards Transparent Valorization of Food Surplus, Waste and Loss."
29. Lohnes, "Regulating Surplus"; Tarasuk and Eakin, "Charitable Food Assistance as Symbolic Gesture."
30. Warshawsky, "Food Waste and the Growth of Food Banks."
31. Caraher and Cavicchi, "Old Crises on New Plates"; Tarasuk and Eakin, "Charitable Food Assistance as Symbolic Gesture."
32. Beasley, "WFP Chief Warns of Hunger Pandemic as COVID-19 Spreads"; Forero, "In Developing World, Coronavirus Slams Workers"; United Nations, "Policy Brief."

Notes to Pages 5–10   133

33. De Sousa, "World Hunger Could Double"; Food and Agriculture Organization, "Impacts of COVID-19 on Food Security and Nutrition."
34. Abi-Habib, "Millions Had Risen Out of Poverty"; Dahir, "'Instead of Coronavirus, the Hunger Will Kill Us'"; Worley, "COVID-19 Threatens Decades of Progress."
35. European Food Banks Federation. "Present Challenges and Urgent Needs"; Feeding America, "Feeding America Network Faces Soaring Demand"; Global FoodBanking Network, "The COVID-19 Pandemic Is Deepening the Hunger Crisis."
36. Reiley, "Full Fields, Empty Fridges"; Yaffe-Bellany and Corkery, "Dumped Milk, Smashed Eggs, Plowed Vegetables."
37. Clapp, "Spoiled Milk, Rotten Vegetables and a Very Broken Food System."
38. Anderson, "To Fight Waste and Hunger, Food Banks Start Cooking"; Corkery and Yaffe-Bellany, "'We Had to Do Something'"; Wharton, "Meet the Gleaners, Combing Farm Fields."
39. Administrator, Global FoodBanking Network, interview with Daniel Warshawsky, January 19, 2021. As in this interview, most interviewees preferred to remain anonymous and be identified by their institutional role only. See chapter 1, notes 110 and 111 for more detail.
40. Global FoodBanking Network, "The COVID-19 Pandemic Is Deepening the Hunger Crisis," 1.
41. Global FoodBanking Network, "Strengthening Food Donation Operations during COVID-19."

CHAPTER ONE

1. Global Food Banking Network, *Waste Not, Want Not*; Global FoodBanking Network, "About GFN."
2. Lougheed and Spring, "Conduits That Bite Back."
3. Feeding America, "Our History"; Wan, "America's Top 100 Charities."
4. Feeding America, "Our History."
5. Feeding America, "Our History."
6. Katz, *In the Shadow of the Poorhouse*.
7. Poppendieck, *Sweet Charity*.
8. Poppendieck, "Food Assistance, Hunger, and the End of Welfare."
9. Wolch, *The Shadow State*.
10. Kodras, "Restructuring the State."
11. Lindenbaum, "Countermovement, Neoliberal Platoon, or Re-gifting Depot?"

12. Feeding America, "Our Work"; Wan, "America's Top 100 Charities."
13. Feeding America, "About Feeding America," 1.
14. Feeding America, "2022 Annual Report"; Feeding America, "Our Work."
15. Administrator at Feeding America, interview with Daniel Warshawsky, August 1, 2019.
16. Feeding America, "Appropriations, Budget, and Taxes"; Feeding America, "Advocating for a Hunger-Free America"; Feeding America, "Leading the Movement to End Hunger."
17. National Council member at Feeding America, interview with Daniel Warshawsky, May 20, 2019.
18. Feeding America, "Federal Food Assistance Programs"; U.S. Department of Agriculture, "FNS Nutrition Programs."
19. Leone, "Feeding America Statement on Congress' Passage of CARES Act"; Leone, "Feeding America Statement on Able-Bodied Adults without Dependents Proposed Rule."
20. National Council on Nonprofits, "Federal Law Protects Nonprofit Advocacy and Lobbying."
21. Lohnes, "Regulating Surplus."
22. Global FoodBanking Network, "GFN Marks a Decade of Global Food Banking"; Global FoodBanking Network, "The Making of The Global FoodBanking Network."
23. Global FoodBanking Network, "FY2022 Annual Report."
24. The following countries are part of GFN: Argentina, Australia, Bolivia, Botswana, Brazil, Bulgaria, Canada, Chile, China, Colombia, Costa Rica, Dominican Republic, Ecuador, El Salvador, Ethiopia, Guatemala, Ghana, Guinea-Bissau, Honduras, Hong Kong, India, Indonesia, Israel, Jordan, Kenya, Madagascar, Malaysia, Mexico, Mozambique, New Zealand, Nicaragua, Nigeria, Panama, Paraguay, Peru, Philippines, Russia, Singapore, South Africa, South Korea, Sri Lanka, Taiwan, Thailand, Turkey, United Kingdom, Uruguay, and Vietnam (Global FoodBanking Network, "Our Global Reach").
25. Global FoodBanking Network, "FY2022 Annual Report."
26. Global FoodBanking Network, "The State of Global Food Banking"; Global FoodBanking Network, "Our Global Reach."
27. Global FoodBanking Network, "Training and Knowledge Sharing."
28. Global FoodBanking Network, "Training and Knowledge Sharing."
29. Global FoodBanking Network, "Financial Statements."
30. Global FoodBanking Network, "IRS Form 990"; Global FoodBanking Network, "Reflections"; Administrator at Global FoodBanking Network,

interview with Daniel Warshawsky, June 27, 2019; Global FoodBanking Network, "Financial Statements."
31. Global FoodBanking Network, "Food Banks Strive for the Gold Standard of Food Safety."
32. Global FoodBanking Network, "Our Global Reach."
33. Global FoodBanking Network, "The Food Bank Leadership Institute."
34. Global FoodBanking Network, "FY2022 Annual Report"; Global FoodBanking Network, "The Food Bank Leadership Institute."
35. Riches, *Food Bank Nations*.
36. Administrator at Global FoodBanking Network, interview with Daniel Warshawsky, June 27, 2019.
37. Global FoodBanking Network, "About GFN."
38. Global Food Banking Network, *Waste Not, Want Not*, 3.
39. Jeff Klein, as quoted in Global FoodBanking Network, "Reflections," 1.
40. CEO at Global FoodBanking Network, interview with Daniel Warshawsky, August 8, 2012.
41. Administrator at Global FoodBanking Network, interview with Daniel Warshawsky, June 27, 2019; administrator at Global FoodBanking Network, interview with Daniel Warshawsky, August, 8, 2012.
42. Global FoodBanking Network, "FY2022 Annual Report"; Global FoodBanking Network, "The State of Global Food Banking."
43. Global FoodBanking Network, *Advancing the Sustainable Development Goals*; Global Food Banking Network, *Waste Not, Want Not*.
44. United Nations, *Sustainable Development Goal 2*.
45. United Nations, *Sustainable Development Goal 12*.
46. Global FoodBanking Network, "FY2022 Annual Report."
47. Administrator at Global FoodBanking Network, interview with Daniel Warshawsky, June 27, 2019.
48. Food and Agriculture Organization, "COVID-19 Series/Identifying and Addressing the Threats."
49. The following countries are members of FEBA: Austria, Belgium, Bulgaria, Czech Republic, Denmark, Estonia, France, Germany, Greece, Hungary, Ireland, Italy, Lithuania, Luxembourg, Netherlands, Norway, Poland, Portugal, Serbia, Slovakia, Spain, Switzerland, Ukraine, and the United Kingdom. Albania, Malta, Moldova, North Macedonia, Romania, and Slovenia also have food banks in the development phases and are in partnership with FEBA (European Food Banks Federation, "Members").
50. European Food Banks Federation, "Our Mission, Impact, and Values."
51. European Food Banks Federation, "Our Story."

52. European Food Banks Federation, "Our Story."
53. European Food Banks Federation, "Our Mission, Impact, and Values," 1.
54. European Food Banks Federation, "Enlarge the Network."
55. European Food Banks Federation, "Our Mission, Impact, and Values."
56. Administrator at the European Food Banks Federation, interview with Daniel Warshawsky, January 28, 2021.
57. European Food Banks Federation, "European Food Banks Federation Annual Report 2021."
58. Administrator at the European Food Banks Federation, interview with Daniel Warshawsky, July 20, 2016.
59. Administrator at the European Food Banks Federation, interview with Daniel Warshawsky, July 20, 2016; administrator at the European Food Banks Federation, interview with Daniel Warshawsky, January 28, 2021.
60. Warshawsky, "Food Insecurity and the COVID Pandemic."
61. Administrator at the European Food Banks Federation, interview with Daniel Warshawsky, July 20, 2016.
62. Administrator at the European Food Banks Federation, interview with Daniel Warshawsky, July 20, 2016.
63. European Food Banks Federation, "Our Mission, Impact, and Values."
64. European Commission, *Redistribution of Surplus Food*; European Commission, *Recommendations for Action in Food Waste Prevention*.
65. Guthman, "Thinking Inside the Neoliberal Box."
66. Brenner and Theodore, "Cities and the Geographies of 'Actually Existing' Neoliberalism." United Nations, "68% of the World Population Projected to Live in Urban Areas."
67. Duncan, "The Food Security Challenge for Southern Africa"; Habib and Kotzé, "Civil Society, Governance and Development in an Era of Globalisation."
68. Salamon and Anheier, "In Search of the Non-profit Sector."
69. Eastwood and Lipton, "Pro-poor Growth and Pro-growth Poverty Reduction."
70. Parnell and Robinson, "Development and Urban Policy."
71. Brenner and Theodore, "Cities and the Geographies of 'Actually Existing' Neoliberalism."
72. United Nations, "68% of the World Population Projected to Live in Urban Areas."
73. Crush and Frayne, "Urban Food Insecurity and the New International Food Security Agenda"; Wiskerke, "Urban Food Systems."
74. Pieterse et al., "Consolidating Developmental Local Government."

75. Bebbington, Hickey, and Mitlin, "Can NGOs Make a Difference?"; Mohan and Stokke, "Participatory Development and Empowerment."
76. Seleoane, "Resource Flows in Poor Communities."
77. Comaroff and Comaroff, "Introduction."
78. Guthman, "Doing Justice to Bodies?"
79. Slocum, "Whiteness, Space, and Alternative Food Practice."
80. Shannon, "Food Deserts."
81. Mook, Murdock, and Gundersen, "Food Banking and Food Insecurity in High-Income Countries."
82. Garthwaite, *Hunger Pains*; Lambie-Mumford and Silvasti, "Introduction."
83. Lambie-Mumford, *Hungry Britain*; Williams et al., "Contested Space."
84. Administrator at the Ohio Association of Foodbanks, interview with Daniel Warshawsky, October 20, 2016.
85. Riches, *Food Bank Nations*.
86. Lambie-Mumford, "The Growth of Food Banks in Britain"; Loopstra and Tarasuk, "Food Bank Usage Is a Poor Indicator of Food Insecurity."
87. Riches and Silvasti, "Hunger in the Rich World"; Riches, *Food Bank Nations*.
88. Hebinck and Shackleton, "Livelihoods, Resources, and Land Reform"; Crush, Frayne, and Haysom, "Introduction to Urban Food Security in the Global South."
89. Spring et al., "Food Waste"; Stuart, *Waste*.
90. Damiani et al., "Quantifying Environmental Implications of Surplus Food Redistribution"; Garrone, Melacini, and Perego, "Opening the Black Box of Food Waste Reduction."
91. Mourad, "Recycling, Recovering and Preventing 'Food Waste.'"
92. Warshawsky, "New Power Relations Served Here"; Young, Salamon, and Grinsfelder, "Commercialization, Social Ventures, and For-Profit Competition."
93. Dickinson, *Feeding the Crisis*; May et al., "Food Banks and the Production of Scarcity."
94. De Souza, *Feeding the Other*.
95. Fisher, *Big Hunger*; Riches, *Food Bank Nations*.
96. Lohnes, "Regulating Surplus."
97. Henderson, "'Free' Food, the Local Production of Worth, and the Circuit of Decommodification."
98. Global Food Banking Network, *Waste Not, Want Not*.
99. Global FoodBanking Network, "The Food Bank Leadership Institute."
100. Henderson, "'Free' Food, the Local Production of Worth, and the Circuit

of Decommodification"; Riches, *Food Bank Nations*; Lindenbaum, "Countermovement, Neoliberal Platoon, or Re-gifting Depot?"
101. Fisher, *Big Hunger*.
102. Warshawsky, "Food Waste, Sustainability, and the Corporate Sector."
103. Global Food Banking Network, *Waste Not, Want Not*.
104. Fisher, *Big Hunger*; Riches, *Food Bank Nations*.
105. Lohnes, "Regulating Surplus."
106. Lohnes and Wilson, "Bailing Out the Food Banks?"; Warshawsky and Soma, "The Formal and Informal Governance of Urban Food Waste in Cities."
107. Busa and Garder, "Champions of the Movement or Fair-Weather Heroes?"
108. Fisher, *Big Hunger*.
109. Riches, *Food Bank Nations*.
110. Multiple methods were used to collect data on the organizational structure, mission, resources, and geography of key institutions in food systems. As the primary sources of data for this research, in-depth interviews were conducted utilizing a snowball method, in which one interviewee refers the researcher to another interviewee. Through the use of the triangulation method, individual and institutional perspectives were compared to multiple data sources and multiple methods, when possible, to ensure that one person or institution's point of view was not excessively cited or referenced in the text. For more information on these methods, see Creswell and Creswell, *Research Design*; Tashakkori and Teddlie, "The Past and Future of Mixed Methods Research."
111. In most cases, semistructured interviews were conducted during normal business hours; however, time differences and flexible schedules often necessitated meeting times outside this typical time frame. Although a list of questions often guided the conversation, most discussions were open ended. Typically, key interviews were recorded and transcribed with agreement from the interviewee. All interviews are cited in the same manner: interviewee role, institution, date. If the interviewee agreed to be identified, the interviewee is identified by name. However, most interviewees preferred to remain anonymous and be identified by their institutional role only. In some cases, organizations published their own interviews or public statements online and revealed the name of the person interviewed or behind the public statement. As multiple interviews were often completed on the same day, many interviews have the same date. Interviews were edited for grammar or writing clarity when necessary. When possible, volunteer work was conducted with food banks and their beneficiary agencies to allow for participant observation and to gather more nuanced

contextual information about the dynamics, motivations, and operational strategies and limitations of food banks and their member agencies. Volunteer work was conducted in small amounts of a few minutes or hours at a time. The results provided rich data on food banks and their member agencies. As noted, a range of methodological limitations, such as lack of data access, problems with data quality, and concerns pertaining to language, gender, class, race, and place of origin, limited the collection of high-quality, reliable, and representative data in some contexts. For more information on these methods, see Warshawsky, "Appendix A–F."

112. Sayer, "Problems of Explanation and the Aims of Social Science"; Warshawsky, "The Potential for Mixed Methods."

CHAPTER TWO

1. Katz, *The Undeserving Poor*.
2. Katz, *In the Shadow of the Poorhouse*.
3. Peck, *Workfare States*.
4. DeVerteuil, "Welfare Reform, Institutional Practices and Service Delivery Settings"; Wolch and DeVerteuil, "New Landscapes of Urban Poverty Management."
5. Food and Agriculture Organization, "The Right to Food around the Globe."
6. Riches, "The Right to Food."
7. Clapp and Fuchs, "Agrifood Corporations, Global Governance, and Sustainability."
8. Shannon, "Food Deserts."
9. Fisher, *Big Hunger*.
10. Aras and Crowther, "Corporate Sustainability Reporting?"
11. Brønn and Vidaver-Cohen, "Corporate Motives for Social Initiative?"
12. Warshawsky, "Food Waste, Sustainability, and the Corporate Sector."
13. Hoover, *Estimating Quantities and Types of Food Waste*; Warshawsky, "The Devolution of Urban Food Waste Governance."
14. Gunders, *Wasted*.
15. Evans, "Blaming the Consumer—Once Again."
16. Brito, "Barack Obama Surprises Food Bank Volunteers"; Trotter, "Looking Back at 40."
17. Greater Chicago Food Depository, "2022 Annual Report."
18. Greater Chicago Food Depository, "2022 Annual Report."
19. Greater Chicago Food Depository, "2022 Annual Report"; Greater Chicago Food Depository, "How We Distribute Food to Chicagoland Food Pantries."

20. Administrator at the Greater Chicago Food Depository, interview with Daniel Warshawsky, May 20, 2019.
21. Administrator at the Greater Chicago Food Depository, interview with Daniel Warshawsky, May 20, 2019.
22. Greater Chicago Food Depository, "2022 Annual Report."
23. Warshawsky, "New Power Relations Served Here."
24. Administrator at the Greater Chicago Food Depository, interview with Daniel Warshawsky, May 20, 2019.
25. Greater Chicago Food Depository, "Our Mission."
26. Administrator at the Greater Chicago Food Depository, interview with Daniel Warshawsky, May 20, 2019.
27. Maehr and Bouman, "Commentary."
28. Trotter, "Commentary."
29. Administrator at the Greater Chicago Food Depository, interview with Daniel Warshawsky, May 20, 2019.
30. Peter Nickeas, "Greater Chicago Food Depository Launches Coronavirus Crisis Grant Program."
31. DiGrino, "Interview with Kate Maehr of the Greater Chicago Food Depository"; Greater Chicago Food Depository, "COVID-19 Data Map"; Sanders, "Chicago Area Food Banks Continue to Serve Communities."
32. Greater Chicago Food Depository, "COVID-19 Data Map"; Rockett, "In Chicago-Area Food Deserts."
33. DiGrino, "Interview with Kate Maehr of the Greater Chicago Food Depository."
34. DiGrino, "Interview with Kate Maehr of the Greater Chicago Food Depository."
35. Freestore Foodbank, "About Freestore Foodbank"; Freestore Foodbank, "Fiscal Year 2020—FSFB Annual Report."
36. Freestore Foodbank, "Fiscal Year 2022 Impact Report."
37. Administrator at Freestore Foodbank, interview with Daniel Warshawsky, July 1, 2014.
38. Freestore Foodbank, "About Freestore Foodbank"; Freestore Foodbank, "Fiscal Year 2020—FSFB Annual Report."
39. Administrator at Freestore Foodbank, interview with Daniel Warshawsky, July 1, 2014; administrator at Ohio Association of Foodbanks, interview with Daniel Warshawsky, October 20, 2016; Ohio Association of Food Banks, "Annual Report."
40. Administrator at Freestore Foodbank, interview with Daniel Warshawsky, July 1, 2014.

41. Administrator at Freestore Foodbank, interview with Daniel Warshawsky, July 1, 2014.
42. Kroger Company, "News Release"; Kroger Company, "Zero Hunger/Zero Waste: Kroger's Plan."
43. Kroger Company, "Sharing Our Value."
44. Administrator at Freestore Foodbank, interview with Daniel Warshawsky, July 1, 2014.
45. Kroger Company, "News Release"; Kroger Company, Zero Hunger/Zero Waste: Kroger's Plan"; Kroger Company, "Zero Hunger/Zero Waste Foundation Report."
46. Jessica Adelman, as quoted in Kroger Company, "News Release."
47. Kroger Company, "Sharing Our Value."
48. Kroger Company, "Sharing Our Value."
49. Administrator at Kroger Corporation, interview with Daniel Warshawsky, October 18, 2013.
50. Kroger Company, "Sharing Our Value."
51. Administrator at Kroger Company, interview with Daniel Warshawsky, October 12, 2018.
52. Chief sustainability officer, Kroger Company, interview with Daniel Warshawsky, October 12, 2018.
53. Schweizer, "Why Kroger's Store Closures and Hazard Pay Reaction Are So Unsettling."
54. Coolidge and Coolidge, "Jesse Jackson Calls to Expand Kroger Boycott."
55. Aras and Crowther, "Corporate Sustainability Reporting"; Parr, *Hijacking Sustainability*.
56. Fisher, *Big Hunger*.
57. Poppendieck, *Sweet Charity*; Warshawsky, "New Power Relations Served Here."
58. Administrator at Cincinnati nonprofit organization, interview with Daniel Warshawsky, April 15, 2017.
59. Administrator at Cincinnati nonprofit organization, interview with Daniel Warshawsky, April 15, 2017.
60. Administrator at Cincinnati nonprofit organization, interview with Daniel Warshawsky, April 15, 2017.
61. Administrator at Kroger, interview with Daniel Warshawsky, July 1, 2014.
62. Freestore Foodbank, "Our Mission in Action," 1.
63. Artino, "Freestore Foodbank Rapidly Running Out of Supplies."
64. Administrator at Freestore Foodbank, interview with Daniel Warshawsky, January 15, 2021.

65. Administrator at Freestore Foodbank, interview with Daniel Warshawsky, January 15, 2021.
66. Reiber, "Freestore Foodbank in Dire Need of More Support."
67. Freestore Foodbank, "Fiscal Year 2020—FSFB Annual Report."
68. Administrator at Freestore Foodbank, interview with Daniel Warshawsky, January 15, 2021.
69. Administrator at Freestore Foodbank, interview with Daniel Warshawsky, January 15, 2021.
70. Kuhlman, "Cleveland, Cincinnati among Top 10 Poorest Big Cities."
71. Administrator at Freestore Foodbank, interview with Daniel Warshawsky, January 15, 2021.
72. Kroger Company, "The Kroger Company Zero Hunger/Zero Waste Foundation Launches Emergency COVID-19 Response Fund."
73. Wetterich, "Freestore Foodbank CEO Kurt Reiber Looks to Offer 'Hope in a Hungry World.'"
74. Kang, "Kroger Posts Stronger Sales, Profit Amid Coronavirus Pandemic."
75. Foodbank, "Basics."
76. Kronenberger, "Dayton Foodbank Ranked No. 2 in the Nation."
77. Post, "Daytonian of the Week"; *Dayton Daily News*, "Fighting Local Hunger a Never-Ending Effort."
78. Ohio Association of Food Banks, "Annual Report."
79. Foodbank, "The Foodbank Impact Statement."
80. Administrator at the Foodbank, interview with Daniel Warshawsky, September 15, 2016.
81. Foodbank, "The Foodbank Impact Statement."
82. Foodbank, "Annual Report."
83. Administrator at the Foodbank, interview with Daniel Warshawsky, September 15, 2016.
84. Foodbank, "The Foodbank Impact Statement FY2021."
85. Administrator at the Foodbank, interview with Daniel Warshawsky, September 15, 2016; Foodbank, "The Foodbank Impact Statement."
86. Foodbank, "The Foodbank Impact Statement."
87. Foodbank, "The Foodbank Impact Statement."
88. Foodbank, "Financial Statements and Supplementary Information."
89. Administrator at the Foodbank, interview with Daniel Warshawsky, September 15, 2016.
90. Friedhoff, Wial, and Wolman, "The Consequences of Metropolitan Manufacturing Decline."
91. Administrator at the Hall Hunger Initiative, interview with Daniel

Notes to Pages 48–53   143

Warshawsky, October 5, 2016; *Dayton Daily News*, "Fighting Local Hunger a Never-Ending Effort."
92. Food Research and Action Center, "How Hungry Is America?"
93. Cuy Castellanos et al., "Perspectives on the Development of a Local Food System."
94. *Dayton Daily News*, "Fighting Local Hunger a Never-Ending Effort."
95. Administrator at the Foodbank, interview with Daniel Warshawsky, September 15, 2016.
96. Administrator at nonprofit food advocacy organization, interview with Daniel Warshawsky, May 15, 2019.
97. Administrator at the Ohio Association of Foodbanks, interview with Daniel Warshawsky, October 20, 2016; administrator at the Foodbank, interview with Daniel Warshawsky, September 15, 2016.
98. Foodbank, "The Foodbank Impact Statement."
99. Meibers, "Coronavirus: Food Insecurity Has Doubled Locally."
100. Meibers, "Coronavirus: Foodbanks Could Serve 40 Percent of Ohioans"; Meibers, "Long Lines along Roadway to FoodBank."
101. Gallion and McIntosh, "Closing Out a Historic Fiscal Year at the Foodbank."
102. Kulish, "Food Banks Are Overrun."
103. McIntosh and Gallion, "COVID-19 Update," 1.
104. Administrator at the Foodbank, interview with Daniel Warshawsky, January 13, 2021.
105. McIntosh and Gallion, "COVID-19 Update," 1.
106. Administrator at the Foodbank, interview with Daniel Warshawsky, January 13, 2021.
107. Administrator at the Foodbank, interview with Daniel Warshawsky, January 13, 2021.
108. Perry, "Food Price Increases, More Need Hitting Local Foodbanks."
109. Wildow, "Dayton Foodbank Gets Step Closer to $2M Funding for Expansion."

CHAPTER THREE

1. Leket Israel, "About the Organization."
2. Levi, "Produce 'Rescue'"; Philip, Hod-Ovadia, and Troen, "A Technical and Policy Case Study of Large-Scale Rescue and Redistribution."
3. Leket Israel, "Food Waste and Rescue in Israel."
4. Administrator at Leket Israel, interview with Daniel Warshawsky, June 15, 2017.

5. Food Banking Regional Network, "FBRN 2013 Activity Report"; Food Banking Regional Network, "Current Food Banks."
6. Administrator at a global food advocacy organization, interview with Daniel Warshawsky, June 27, 2019.
7. Economic and Social Commission for Western Asia, *Changes in Public Expenditure on Social Protection in Arab Countries*.
8. Hayet, "Thirty-Six."
9. Halon, "Israelis Threw Away 2.5 Millions Tons of Food"; Leket Israel, "Food Waste and Rescue in Israel."
10. Global FoodBanking Network, "Israel: Combining Forces to Fight Food Insecurity"; Leket Israel, "History of Leket Israel."
11. Leket Israel, "Joseph Gitler Named One of 50 Most Influential Jews."
12. Administrator at Leket Israel, interview with Daniel Warshawsky, June 15, 2017.
13. Global FoodBanking Network, "Israel."
14. Levi, "Produce 'Rescue'"; Philip, Hod-Ovadia, and Troen, "A Technical and Policy Case Study of Large-Scale Rescue and Redistribution."
15. Administrator at Leket Israel, interview with Daniel Warshawsky, June 15, 2017.
16. Leket Israel, "About the Organization," 1.
17. Leket Israel, "Nutrition and Food Safety."
18. Lisa Moon, CEO of the Global FoodBanking Network, as quoted in Levi, "Produce 'Rescue,'" 1.
19. Leket Israel, "About Food Rescue"; Leket Israel, "About the Organization."
20. Leket Israel, "Financial Statements."
21. Administrator at Leket Israel, interview with Daniel Warshawsky, June 19, 2017.
22. Kroch, "Food Rescue."
23. Moses, "Israeli Food Prices 19 Percent Higher Than OECD Average"; Organisation for Economic Cooperation and Development, *OECD Economic Surveys*.
24. Leket Israel, "Daily Updates during the Corona Crisis."
25. Gomes-Hochberg, "Are Israelis Going Hungry?"; Jaffe-Hoffman and Benzaquen, "In the Wake of COVID Crisis."
26. Surkes, "National Food Bank Faces Rising Demand."
27. Administrator at Leket Israel, interview with Daniel Warshawsky, January 11, 2021.
28. Administrator at Leket Israel, interview with Daniel Warshawsky, January 11, 2021.

29. Administrator at Leket Israel, interview with Daniel Warshawsky, January 11, 2021.
30. Kroch, "Food Insecurity and the State Budget."
31. Gal and Madhala, "Israel's Social Welfare System."
32. Gal and Madhala, "Israel's Social Welfare System"; Peck, *Workfare States*.
33. Kashti, "Israel Must Take Food Insecurity Seriously"; Kroch, "Food Insecurity and the State Budget."
34. Administrator at Leket Israel, interview with Daniel Warshawsky, June 15, 2017.
35. Administrator at Leket Israel, interview with Daniel Warshawsky, June 15, 2017.
36. Leket Israel, "Law Passed to Promote Food Donations in Israel"; Deane, "Knesset Passes Food Donation Act."
37. Halon, "Israelis Threw Away 2.5 Millions Tons of Food."
38. Kroch, "Food Insecurity and the State Budget."
39. Food and Agriculture Organization, "The Right to Food around the Globe."
40. Administrator at Leket Israel, interview with Daniel Warshawsky, January 11, 2021.
41. Administrator at Leket Israel, interview with Daniel Warshawsky, January 11, 2021.
42. Administrator at Leket Israel, interview with Daniel Warshawsky, June 15, 2017.
43. FBRN's food banks in fourteen countries in Asia, with year founded: Saudi Arabia (three branches, 2011), Iraq (2011), Syria (2011), Lebanon (2012), Jordan (2012), Pakistan (2012), Bangladesh (2013), Palestine (2014), Bahrain (2015), United Arab Emirates (2017), Kuwait (2017), Yemen (2017), Afghanistan (2017), and Oman (2018). The FBRN's food banks in twenty-two countries in Africa, with year founded: Egypt (2006), Tunisia (2011), Sudan (2012), Mauritania (2012), Somalia (2015), Central African Republic (2015), Angola (2016), Cameroon (2016), Ghana (2016), Uganda (2016), Ivory Coast (2016), Malawi (2016), Sierra Leone (2017), Kenya (2017), Zambia (2017), Zimbabwe (2017), Mauritius (2017), Botswana (2017), Rwanda (2017), Benin (2018), Democratic Republic of the Congo (2018), and Ethiopia (2018). The FRBN also has one food bank in Europe: Albania (2018). As of 2021, ten additional food banks were in the development stages but not yet operational, including one in Asia (Nepal) and nine in Africa (South Sudan, Libya, Morocco, Chad, Mali, Guinea, Djibouti, Madagascar, and Liberia). Administrator at the Food Banking Regional Network, interview with

Daniel Warshawsky, February 5, 2021; Food Banking Regional Network, "Current Food Banks."
44. Egyptian Food Bank, "About Us."
45. Administrator at the Egyptian Food Bank, interview with Ummey Tabbassum, November 13, 2016.
46. Philanthropy Age, "Tackling Hunger in Egypt."
47. Philanthropy Age, "Tackling Hunger in Egypt."
48. Administrator at the Food Banking Regional Network, interview with Daniel Warshawsky, February 5, 2021.
49. Administrator at the Food Banking Regional Network, interview with Daniel Warshawsky, February 5, 2021.
50. Food Banking Regional Network, "Mission and Vision," 1.
51. Food Banking Regional Network, "Mission and Vision," 1.
52. Food Banking Regional Network, "Our Pillars to Fight Hunger"; administrator at the Food Banking Regional Network, interview with Daniel Warshawsky, February 5, 2021.
53. Food Banking Regional Network, "Key Performance Indicators"; administrator at the Food Banking Regional Network, interview with Ummey Tabbassum, November 29, 2016.
54. Administrator at the Food Banking Regional Network, interview with Daniel Warshawsky, February 5, 2021.
55. Philanthropy Age, "Tackling Hunger in Egypt," 2017.
56. Administrator at the Food Banking Regional Network, interview with Daniel Warshawsky, February 5, 2021; Food Banking Regional Network, "Food Banking Regional Network—Dubai Branch."
57. Administrator at the Food Banking Regional Network, interview with Daniel Warshawsky, February 5, 2021.
58. El Shohdi, "CEO Message," 1.
59. United Nations, "The Impact of COVID-19 on the Arab Region."
60. Woertz, "Whither the Self-Sufficiency Illusion?"; World Food Programme, *2020 Global Report on Food Crises*.
61. England and Terazono, "Pandemic Revives Gulf Fears over Food Security."
62. Jacobs, "The Ukraine Crisis Deepens Food Insecurity."
63. Zurayk, "Use Your Loaf."
64. Food and Agriculture Organization, "The Right to Food around the Globe."
65. Administrator at the Food Banking Regional Network, interview with Ummey Tabbassum, November 29, 2016.
66. Food and Agriculture Organization, "FAO and Egyptian Food Bank Launch 'Food Waste Awareness Campaign.'"

67. Administrator at the Food Banking Regional Network, interview with Ummey Tabbassum, November 29, 2016.
68. Administrator at a global food advocacy organization, interview with Daniel Warshawsky, June 27, 2019.
69. Philanthropy Age, "Tackling Hunger in Egypt."
70. Administrator at the Food Banking Regional Network, interview with Daniel Warshawsky, January 28, 2021.
71. Administrator at the Food Banking Regional Network, interview with Ummey Tabbassum, November 29, 2016.
72. United Nations Children's Fund, "Food Crisis Likely to Worsen in the Middle East and North Africa."
73. United Nations, "The Impact of COVID-19 on the Arab Region."
74. United Nations Children's Fund, "Food Crisis Likely to Worsen in the Middle East and North Africa."
75. United Nations, "The Impact of COVID-19 on the Arab Region."
76. Economic and Social Commission for Western Asia, *Changes in Public Expenditure on Social Protection in Arab Countries*.
77. Economist Intelligence Unit, *Democracy Index 2020*.
78. Administrator at the Food Banking Regional Network, interview with Daniel Warshawsky, January 28, 2021.

CHAPTER FOUR

1. Eurostat, "Expenditure on Social Protection Benefits."
2. European Commission, "Your Social Security Rights in Denmark"; European Commission, "Your Social Security Rights in Germany."
3. Andersen, Schoyen, and Hvinden, "Changing Scandinavian Welfare States"; Kessl, Lorenz, and Schoneville, "Social Exclusion and Food Assistance in Germany."
4. *Economist*, "The New Germans."
5. Amaro, "Germany Is Vastly Outspending Other Countries."
6. Berliner Tafel, "How an Idea Became a Movement"; Federal Association of German Food Banks, "History."
7. Administrator at the Federal Association of German Food Banks, interview with Daniel Warshawsky, June 30, 2016.
8. Gentilini, "Banking on Food."
9. Federal Association of German Food Banks, "Background Information."
10. European Food Banks Federation, "Members."
11. Federal Association of German Food Banks, "Background Information."
12. Federal Association of German Food Banks, "Annual Report, 2020."

13. Federal Association of German Food Banks, "Chalkboard Principles."
14. Federal Association of German Food Banks, "About Us."
15. Federal Association of German Food Banks, "Tafel Logistics."
16. Federal Association of German Food Banks, "ChalkboardPrinciples."
17. Administrator at the Federal Association of German Food Banks, interview with Daniel Warshawsky, June 30, 2016.
18. Food and Agriculture Organization, "The Right to Food around the Globe."
19. Eurostat, "Severe Material and Social Deprivation Rate."
20. Eurostat, "Living Conditions in Europe."
21. Federal Association of German Food Banks, "Annual Report, 2015"; Federal Association of German Food Banks, "Annual Report, 2018."
22. Kessl, Lorenz, and Schoneville, "Social Exclusion and Food Assistance in Germany"; Pfeiffer, Ritter, and Hirseland, "Hunger and Nutritional Poverty in Germany"; Simmet, Tinnemann, and Stroebele-Benschop, "The German Food Bank System and Its Users."
23. Shalal, "German Food Bank Draws Fire."
24. BBC News, "Chancellor Merkel Enters 'Germans Only' Food Bank Furore."
25. BBC News, "German Food Bank to Reopen Membership"; *Economist*, "The New Germans"; Schuetze, "German Food Bank Reopens Doors."
26. Administrator at the Federal Association of German Food Banks, interview with Daniel Warshawsky, June 30, 2016.
27. German Government, *National Strategy for Food Waste Reduction*.
28. Federal Association of German Food Banks, "Tafel Germany Calls for Law against Food Waste."
29. Kessl, Lorenz, and Schoneville, "Social Exclusion and Food Assistance in Germany."
30. Kessl, Lorenz, and Schoneville, "Social Exclusion and Food Assistance in Germany."
31. Administrator at the Federal Association of German Food Banks, interview with Daniel Warshawsky, June 30, 2016.
32. Federal Association of German Food Banks, "Coronavirus"; Kampf, "Close Hundreds of Boards."
33. Federal Association of German Food Banks, "Coronavirus," 1.
34. Amaro, "Germany Is Vastly Outspending Other Countries."
35. DW, "Germany Passes Coronavirus Aid Package."
36. Federal Association of German Food Banks, "Management Report from November 18, 2020"; Federal Association of German Food Banks, "Status Report of the Tafel Food Banks."

37. Federal Association of German Food Banks, "Together through the Crisis."
38. Federal Association of German Food Banks, "Management Report from November 18, 2020"; Federal Association of German Food Banks, "Status Report of the Tafel Food Banks."
39. Gram-Hanssen et al., *Food Redistribution in the Nordic Region.*
40. Eurostat, "Severe Material and Social Deprivation Rate."
41. European Food Banks Federation, "Members."
42. Food and Agriculture Organization, "The Right to Food around the Globe."
43. Administrator in the Danish Food Bank, interview with Daniel Warshawsky, August 11, 2016.
44. Hanssen et al., *Food Redistribution in the Nordic Region.*
45. Danish Food Bank, "Do You Want to Volunteer at the Food Bank?"
46. Danish Food Bank, "Do You Want to Volunteer at the Food Bank?"
47. Danish Food Bank, "Do You Want to Volunteer at the Food Bank?"
48. Danish Food Bank, "Annual Accounts for 2020."
49. Administrator in the Danish Food Bank, interview with Daniel Warshawsky, August, 11, 2016.
50. Danish Food Bank, "Annual Accounts for 2020."
51. Danish Food Bank, "Facts about FødevareBanken."
52. Danish Food Bank, "Facts about FødevareBanken"; Danish Food Bank, "We Are FødevareBanken"; Hanssen et al., *Food Redistribution in the Nordic Region.*
53. Administrator in the Danish Food Bank, interview with Daniel Warshawsky, August 11, 2016.
54. Administrator at the Danish Food Bank, interview with Daniel Warshawsky, August 11, 2016.
55. Andersen, Schoyen, and Hvinden, "Changing Scandinavian Welfare States."
56. Administrator in the Danish Food Bank, interview with Daniel Warshawsky, August 11, 2016.
57. Andersen, Schoyen, and Hvinden, "Changing Scandinavian Welfare States."
58. Administrator in the Danish Food Bank, interview with Daniel Warshawsky, August 11, 2016.
59. Halloran et al., "Addressing Food Waste Reduction in Denmark"; *Local*, "Danish Consumers Reduced Food Waste"; Stancu and Lähteenmäki, *Consumer Food Waste in Denmark.*
60. Danish Food Bank, "Socioeconomic Analysis of Food Bank's Activities."

150   Notes to Pages 74–80

61. Administrator in the Danish Food Bank, interview with Daniel Warshawsky, August 11, 2016; Hanssen et al., *Food Redistribution in the Nordic Region*.
62. Fisher, *Big Hunger*; Riches, *Food Bank Nations*.
63. Administrator in the Danish Food Bank, interview with Daniel Warshawsky, August 11, 2016.
64. Henderson, "'Free' Food, the Local Production of Worth."
65. Fisher, *Big Hunger*; Lohnes, "Regulating Surplus."
66. Administrator in the Danish Food Bank, interview with Daniel Warshawsky, August 11, 2016.
67. Danish Food Bank, "Facts about FødevareBanken."
68. Administrator in the Danish Food Bank, interview with Daniel Warshawsky, August 11, 2016.
69. Hanssen et al., *Food Redistribution in the Nordic Region*; Nordic Cooperation, "New Nordic Study."
70. European Food Banks Federation, "Members."
71. Administrator in the Danish Food Bank, interview with Daniel Warshawsky, January 17, 2021.
72. Administrator in the Danish Food Bank, interview with Daniel Warshawsky, January 17, 2021.
73. Thorsen and Christiansen, "The Food Bank and the Church Crusade," 1.

CHAPTER FIVE

1. Eurostat, "Expenditure on Social Protection Benefits."
2. Ascoli and Pavolini, "Introduction"; Agostini, Natali, and Sacchi, "The Europeanisation of the Italian Welfare State."
3. Eurostat, "Total Unemployment Rate."
4. Reuters, "Hungary Steps Up Anti-immigration Stance"; Hopkins, "Hungary's Ban on Homelessness."
5. *Budapest Business Journal*, "Hungary among EU Countries with Highest Poverty Rates"; Eurostat, "Expenditure on Social Protection Benefits"; Eurostat, "Severe Material Deprivation Rate."
6. Gumuchian, "'New Poor' in Italy Line Up for Free Food"; Jones, "Poverty in Italy at Worst for 12 Years."
7. Administrator at the European Food Bank Federation, interview with Daniel Warshawsky, July 20, 2016.
8. Administrator at the Italian Food Bank Network, interview with Daniel Warshawsky, June 12, 2017; Italian Food Bank Network, "Remembering Cavalier Fossati."
9. Gentilini, "Banking on Food."

Notes to Pages 80–82   151

10. Administrator at the Italian Food Bank Network, interview with Daniel Warshawsky, June 12, 2017.
11. European Food Banks Federation, "Our Mission, Impact, and Values."
12. Galli, Hebinck, and Carroll, "Addressing Food Poverty in Systems"; Rombach et al., "Comparing German and Italian Food Banks"; Rovati, "The Paradox of Scarcity in Abundance."
13. Food and Agriculture Organization, "The Right to Food around the Globe."
14. Italian Food Bank Network, "A Big Network to Support the Poorest."
15. Administrator at the Italian Food Bank Network, interview with Daniel Warshawsky, June 12, 2017; Italian Food Bank Network, "A Big Network to Support the Poorest."
16. Italian Food Bank Network, "National Day of Food Collection."
17. European Commission, *The Fund for European Aid to the Most Deprived (FEAD)*; European Commission, "Fund for European Aid to the Most Deprived (FEAD)."
18. European Commission, *The Fund for European Aid to the Most Deprived (FEAD)*.
19. Madama, *The Fund for European Aid to the Most Deprived*.
20. Italian Food Bank Network, *Social Balance*; Italian Food Bank Network, *A Big Network to Support the Poorest*.
21. Italian Food Bank Network, *Social Balance*; Italian Food Bank Network, "Management Report."
22. Ascoli and Pavolini, "Introduction"; Agostini, Natali, and Sacchi, "The Europeanisation of the Italian Welfare State."
23. Eurostat, "Expenditure on Social Protection Benefits."
24. Administrator in the Italian Food Bank Network, interview with Daniel Warshawsky, June 12, 2017.
25. European Commission, *The Fund for European Aid to the Most Deprived (FEAD)*; European Commission, "Fund for European Aid to the Most Deprived (FEAD)."
26. Watt, "Government under Fire for Rejecting European Union Food Bank Funding."
27. Caraher, "The European Union Food Distribution Programme for the Most Deprived Persons"; Madama, *The Fund for European Aid to the Most Deprived*.
28. Administrator at the Italian Food Bank Network, interview with Daniel Warshawsky, June 12, 2017.
29. BBC News, "Italy Adopts New Law to Slash Food Waste"; Bolton, "Italy Passes Law to Make Supermarkets Give Wasted Food to Charity."
30. Italian Food Bank Network, "The Key Points."

31. Administrator at the Italian Food Bank Network, interview with Daniel Warshawsky, June 12, 2017.
32. Eurostat, "Living Conditions in Europe."
33. Eurostat, "Total Unemployment Rate."
34. Eurostat, "Severe Material and Social Deprivation Rate."
35. Administrator at the Italian Food Bank Network, interview with Daniel Warshawsky, June 12, 2017.
36. Sage, "Italy's 'New Poor'"; Administrator in the Spanish Federation of Food Banks, interview with Daniel Warshawsky, February 12, 2021.
37. Chiesa, "The Alarm from the Food Bank."
38. Pinotti, "Coronavirus, Caritas Alarm"; *Rai News*, "Risk of Poverty, Instat."
39. Reuters, "Italy Approves New Stimulus Package."
40. Sage, "Italy's 'New Poor.'"
41. Amaro, "Germany Is Vastly Outspending Other Countries."
42. Stancati, "As the Coronavirus Lockdown Eases"; Villa, "Coronavirus and Nutrition."
43. Chiesa, "The Alarm from the Food Bank."
44. Italian Food Bank Network president Giovanni Bruno, as quoted in Pinotti, "Coronavirus, Caritas Alarm," 1.
45. Lucchini, "Banco Alimentare, Food Becomes Solidarity"; administrator at the Italian Food Bank Network, interview with Daniel Warshawsky, February 12, 2021.
46. Administrator at the Italian Food Bank Network, interview with Daniel Warshawsky, February 12, 2021.
47. Administrator at the Italian Food Bank Network, interview with Daniel Warshawsky, February 12, 2021; Italian Food Bank Network, *Social Balance*.
48. Administrator at the Italian Food Bank Network, interview with Daniel Warshawsky, February 12, 2021.
49. Hungarian Food Bank Association, "Who We Are."
50. Administrator at the Hungarian Food Bank Association, interview with Daniel Warshawsky, August 15, 2016.
51. European Food Banks Federation, "Our Team."
52. Administrator at the Hungarian Food Bank Association, interview with Daniel Warshawsky, August 15, 2016.
53. Food and Agriculture Organization, "The Right to Food around the Globe."
54. Hungarian Food Bank Association, "Who We Are."
55. Administrator at the Hungarian Food Bank Association, interview with Daniel Warshawsky, August 15, 2016.

56. Hungarian Food Bank Association, "Who We Are."
57. Hungarian Food Bank Association, "Who We Are."
58. Hungarian Food Bank Association, "Who We Are."
59. Administrator at the Hungarian Food Bank Association, interview with Daniel Warshawsky, August 15, 2016.
60. Administrator at the Hungarian Food Bank Association, interview with Daniel Warshawsky, August 15, 2016; BT/MTI, "Food Bank Association Saves 4 Million Kg Food in 2022."
61. Administrator at the Hungarian Food Bank Association, interview with Daniel Warshawsky, August 15, 2016.
62. Administrator at the Hungarian Food Bank Association, interview with Daniel Warshawsky, August 15, 2016.
63. Katz, *The Undeserving Poor*; de Souza, *Feeding the Other*.
64. Administrator at the Hungarian Food Bank Association, interview with Daniel Warshawsky, August 15, 2016.
65. Reuters, "Hungary Steps Up Anti-immigration Stance."
66. Kõre, "Hunger and Food Aid in Estonia"; Leskošek and Zidar, "Redistributing Waste Food to Reduce Poverty in Slovenia."
67. Administrator at the European Food Banks Federation, interview with Daniel Warshawsky, July 20, 2016.
68. Hopkins, "Hungary's Ban on Homelessness."
69. Administrator at the Hungarian Food Bank Association, interview with Daniel Warshawsky, August 15, 2016.
70. Amaro, "Germany Is Vastly Outspending Other Countries"; Dunai, "Hungary Prepares $30 Billion Coronavirus Package."
71. Lee, "EU Budget Blocked by Hungary and Poland."
72. Hungarian Food Bank Association, "Even in Emergency for the Needy"; Hungarian Food Bank Association, "Report on Last, Extraordinary Months."
73. Bech, Foda, and Roitman, *Drivers of Inflation*.
74. Fehér, "The Cost of Energy Crisis in Hungary."

CHAPTER SIX

1. Chen, "The Informal Economy."
2. Food and Agriculture Organization, "The State of Food Security and Nutrition in the World."
3. Organisation for Economic Cooperation and Development, *Society at a Glance*.
4. Department of Health, South Africa, *The South African National Health*

and Nutrition Examination Survey; Statistics South Africa, *Towards Measuring the Extent of Food Security in South Africa*.
5. Crush and Frayne, "Urban Food Insecurity and the New International Food Security Agenda"; Crush, Frayne, and Pendleton, "The Crisis of Food Insecurity in African Cities."
6. Department of Social Development, South Africa, "A Statistical Summary of Social Grants in South Africa"; Organisation for Economic Cooperation and Development, *Society at a Glance*.
7. Warshawsky, "The State and Urban Food Insecurity."
8. Food and Agriculture Organization, "The Right to Food around the Globe"; Athreya et al., *Report on the State of Food Insecurity in Urban India*; Gupta et al., "Coping Strategies Adopted by Households to Prevent Food Insecurity."
9. Dev and Sharma, *Food Security in India*; Narayanan, "Food Security in India."
10. Global Hunger Index, "Global Hunger Index Scores by 2022 GHI Rank."
11. India FoodBanking Network, "We Are Leading India's Fight against Hunger."
12. Global FoodBanking Network, "Global Leaders Alleviate Hunger"; Global FoodBanking Network, "India."
13. Global FoodBanking Network, "Exciting News about Food Banking in India."
14. Global FoodBanking Network, "Our Global Reach."
15. India FoodBanking Network, "About IFBN."
16. India FoodBanking Network, "About IFBN."
17. Administrator at India FoodBanking Network, interview with Daniel Warshawsky, January 23, 2019.
18. India FoodBanking Network, "About IFBN," 1.
19. India FoodBanking Network, "FoodBanking Solves Hunger Problem."
20. India FoodBanking Network, "About IFBN."
21. Administrator at India FoodBanking Network, interview with Daniel Warshawsky, January 23, 2019; administrator at Delhi Foodbanking Network, interview with Daniel Warshawsky, June 11, 2019; Global FoodBanking Network, "Exciting News about Food Banking in India."
22. Administrator at Delhi Foodbanking Network, interview with Daniel Warshawsky, June 11, 2019.
23. Administrator at the Global FoodBanking Network, interview with Daniel Warshawsky, June 27, 2019.
24. Administrator at the Global FoodBanking Network, interview with Daniel Warshawsky, June 27, 2019.

25. Administrator at the India FoodBanking Network, interview with Daniel Warshawsky, January 23, 2019.
26. Kikon, "Dirty Food, Racism and Casteism in India."
27. Sathyamala, "Meat-Eating in India."
28. Administrator at the India FoodBanking Network, interview with Daniel Warshawsky, January 23, 2019; administrator at the India FoodBanking Network, interview with Daniel Warshawsky, January 23, 2019.
29. Administrator at the India FoodBanking Network, interview with Daniel Warshawsky, January 23, 2019.
30. Administrator at the India FoodBanking Network, interview with Daniel Warshawsky, January 23, 2019.
31. Majumdar and Borbora, "Social Security System and the Informal Sector in India."
32. Chhibber and Soz, "India Is Becoming Welfare State before Developed State"; Duggirala and Kumar, "The Welfare State in India"; Kapur and Nangia, "Social Protection in India."
33. Department of Food and Public Distribution, Government of India, "National Food Security Act (NFSA)."
34. India FoodBanking Network, "GOI and State Governments"; India FoodBanking Network, "School Nutrition Program."
35. Chatterjee, "India's School Lunch Program May Be Imperfect"; Domínguez, "Fighting Hunger"; Shadbolt, "India Launches Ambitious Food Aid Program"; Kattumuri, *Food Security and the Targeted Public Distribution System*; United Nations, *Nutrition and Food Security*.
36. Administrator at the India FoodBanking Network, interview with Daniel Warshawsky, January 23, 2019; administrator at the Global FoodBanking Network, interview with Daniel Warshawsky, June 27, 2019.
37. Administrator at the India FoodBanking Network, interview with Daniel Warshawsky, January 23, 2019.
38. Ministry of Food Processing Industries, Government of India, "Wastage of Agricultural Produce"; Shrivastava, "India Grows More Food, Wastes More."
39. Administrator at the India FoodBanking Network, interview with Daniel Warshawsky, January 23, 2019.
40. Mishra and Rampal, "The COVID-19 Pandemic and Food Insecurity."
41. Summerton, "Implications of the COVID-19 Pandemic for Food Security."
42. Adhikari et al., "21 Days and Counting."
43. Abi-Habib and Yasir, "For India's Laborers, Coronavirus Lockdown Is an Order to Starve."
44. Mashal, Schmall, and Goldman, "Why Are Farmers Protesting in India?"

45. BBC News, "India's Poorest 'Fear Hunger May Kill Us before Coronavirus.'"
46. Wallen, "Hunger Plagues India—but There's No Shortage of Food."
47. Mishra and Rampal, "The COVID-19 Pandemic and Food Insecurity."
48. Summerton, "Implications of the COVID-19 Pandemic for Food Security."
49. International Commission of Jurists, "COVID-19 Pandemic in India."
50. Global FoodBanking Network, "Take Action by Nourishing Families Today!"
51. Global FoodBanking Network, "Take Action by Nourishing Families Today!"
52. Director of member food bank in the India Food Banking Network, as quoted in Global FoodBanking Network, "The Food Bank Organizations Reaching the Daily Wagers," 1.
53. Joburg Market, "Introduction."
54. Administrator at FoodForward South Africa, interview with Daniel Warshawsky, August 2, 2012.
55. Administrator at FoodForward South Africa, interview with Daniel Warshawsky, August 2, 2012.
56. Administrator at FoodForward South Africa, interview with Daniel Warshawsky, May 15, 2019.
57. Stakeholder at a CBO, interview with Daniel Warshawsky, May 13, 2009.
58. Crush and Frayne, "Urban Food Insecurity and the New International Food Security Agenda."
59. Mtintsilana et al., "Social Vulnerability and Its Association with Food Insecurity"; Statistics South Africa, *Towards Measuring the Extent of Food Security in South Africa*.
60. Warshawsky, "Civil Society and Urban Food Insecurity."
61. Frayne, "Pathways of Food."
62. Cousins, "What Is a 'Smallholder'?"
63. James, *Gaining Ground*?
64. Hebinck and Shackleton, "Livelihoods, Resources, and Land Reform."
65. Bond, *Elite Transition*; Drimie and Ruysenaar, "The Integrated Food Security Strategy of South Africa"; Mokone, "Handouts of Food Parcels to Be Probed"; Peet, "Ideology, Discourse, and the Geography of Hegemony."
66. Hendriks and McIntyre, "Between Markets and Masses."
67. McCain, "Want Not, Waste Not, Crop Is Food"; von Bormann, "Agri-food Systems."
68. Oelofse and Nahman, "Estimating the Magnitude of Food Waste"; Oelofse, Muswema, and Ramukhwatho, "Household Food Waste Disposal in South Africa."

69. Miraftab, "Neoliberalism and Casualization of Public Sector Services"; Mogale, "Developmental Local Government and Decentralised Service Delivery."
70. Republic of South Africa, "National Environmental Management Waste Act"; Republic of South Africa, "National Waste Management Strategy."
71. City of Johannesburg, *Integrated Waste Management Policy*.
72. Global FoodBanking Network, *Food*; Global FoodBanking Network, "Two Projects That Transformed Food Banking Globally."
73. FoodForward South Africa, "About Us"; FoodForward South Africa, "Repurpose the Surplus."
74. Global FoodBanking Network, "Two Projects That Transformed Food Banking Globally," 1.
75. FoodForward South Africa, "About Us"; FoodForward South Africa, "Annual Report, 2020/2021."
76. FoodForward South Africa, "Annual Report, 2020/2021"; FoodForward South Africa, "Our Work."
77. Administrator at FoodForward South Africa, interview with Daniel Warshawsky, May 15, 2019.
78. Hendriks and McIntyre, "Between Markets and Masses."
79. Riches and Silvasti, "Hunger in the Rich World."
80. FoodForward South Africa, as quoted in La Meyer, "Major Shifts in Poverty Highlighted by COVID-19," 1.
81. FoodForward South Africa, "Audited Annual Financial Statements."
82. Administrator at FoodForward South Africa, interview with Daniel Warshawsky, May 15, 2019.
83. Administrator at FoodForward South Africa, interview with Daniel Warshawsky, May 15, 2019.
84. FoodForward South Africa, "Audited Annual Financial Statements."
85. Hlati, "FoodFoward SA Pledges to Feed 1 Million People Daily."
86. La Meyer, "Initial Results."
87. Warshawsky, "Civil Society and Public-Private Partnership."
88. Administrator at FoodForward South Africa, interview with Daniel Warshawsky, May 15, 2019.
89. Administrator at FoodForward South Africa, interview with Daniel Warshawsky, May 15, 2019.
90. Patel and Steinhauser, "South Africa's Economy Shrinks 51%."
91. BBC News, "Coronavirus"; Devereux, Béné, and Hoddinott, "Conceptualising COVID-19's Impacts on Household Food Security."
92. FoodForward South Africa, "As Hardship Continues, Empathy Drives Our Social Agenda"; La Meyer, "COVID-19 Further Exposes the Fragility."

93. FoodForward South Africa, "Annual Report, 2020/2021"; FoodForward South Africa, "Repurpose the Surplus."
94. Bhorat and Köhler, "Lockdown Economics in South Africa."
95. Chutel, "South Africa's Big Coronavirus Aid Effort."
96. Arndt et al., "COVID-19 Lockdowns, Income Distribution, and Food Security."
97. La Meyer, "Food Poverty Is Emerging as a Significant Threat."
98. FoodForward South Africa, as quoted in La Meyer, "Food Poverty Is Emerging as a Significant Threat," 1.
99. Administrator at FoodForward South Africa, interview with Daniel Warshawsky, January 19, 2021.
100. FoodForward South Africa, "An Evaluation of Impact, 2019/2020."
101. Administrator at FoodForward South Africa, interview with Daniel Warshawsky, August 2, 2012.
102. Administrator at FoodForward South Africa, interview with Daniel Warshawsky, May 15, 2019.
103. Administrator at FoodForward South Africa, interview with Daniel Warshawsky, August 2, 2012; Doidge, "Statement by Minister of Public Works."
104. Warshawsky, "The State and Urban Food Insecurity"; Warshawsky, "Civil Society and Public-Private Partnership."
105. Administrator at FoodForward South Africa, interview with Daniel Warshawsky, May 15, 2019.
106. Administrator at a CBO, interview with Daniel Warshawsky, June 18, 2009.
107. Administrator at FoodForward South Africa, interview with Daniel Warshawsky, May 15, 2019.
108. Warshawsky, "FoodBank Johannesburg, State, and Civil Society Organisations."
109. Stakeholder at a CBO, interview with Daniel Warshawsky, May 13, 2009.
110. Statistics South Africa, *General Household Survey.*
111. Stakeholder at a CBO, interview with Daniel Warshawsky, June 18, 2009.
112. Administrator at FoodForward South Africa, interview with Daniel Warshawsky, August 2, 2012.
113. Administrator, FoodForward South Africa, interview with Daniel Warshawsky, May 15, 2019.
114. Administrator, FoodForward South Africa, interview with Daniel Warshawsky, August 2, 2013; administrator at FoodForward South Africa, interview with Daniel Warshawsky, May 15, 2019.

115. Administrator at FoodForward South Africa, interview with Daniel Warshawsky, May 15, 2019.
116. Administrator at FoodForward South Africa, interview with Daniel Warshawsky, August 2, 2012.
117. TechnoServe, *KZN Technical Assistance and Market Access Project (Tamap)*; TechnoServe, "About Us."
118. Department of Agriculture and Environmental Affairs, South Africa, "KwaZulu-Natal Farmers to Land a Lucrative Market"; Molewa, "Remarks by the Minister of Social Development."
119. Administrator at TechnoServe, interview with Daniel Warshawsky, July 20, 2012.
120. Administrator at TechnoServe, interview with Daniel Warshawsky, July 20, 2012.
121. Administrator at TechnoServe, interview with Daniel Warshawsky, July 20, 2012.
122. Stakeholder in Jozini, interview with Daniel Warshawsky, July 26, 2012.
123. Administrator at FoodForward South Africa, interview with Daniel Warshawsky, May 15, 2019.
124. Administrator at FoodForward South Africa, interview with Daniel Warshawsky, May 15, 2019.
125. Hendriks and McIntyre, "Between Markets and Masses."
126. Global FoodBanking Network, "Two Projects That Transformed Food Banking Globally."
127. Parnell and Robinson, "(Re)Theorizing Cities from the Global South"; Rakodi, "Introduction."

CONCLUSION

1. Kulish, "Food Banks Are Overrun."
2. European Food Banks Federation, "European Food Banks Federation Briefing"; European Food Banks Federation, "European Food Banks in a Post COVID-19 Europe"; European Food Banks Federation, "European Food Banks Today"; Global Food Banking Network, "Strengthening Food Donation Operations during COVID-19."
3. Warshawsky, "New Power Relations Served Here"; Lambie-Mumford and Silvasti, "Introduction."
4. Lohnes, "Regulating Surplus"; Poppendieck, *Sweet Charity*.
5. Gal and Madhala, "Israel's Social Welfare System."
6. Kashti, "Israel Must Take Food Insecurity Seriously."

7. Economic and Social Commission for Western Asia, *Changes in Public Expenditure on Social Protection*.
8. Kessl, Lorenz, and Schoneville, "Social Exclusion and Food Assistance in Germany."
9. Andersen, Schoyen, and Hvinden, "Changing Scandinavian Welfare States."
10. Ascoli and Pavolini, "Introduction"; Agostini, Natali, and Sacchi, "The Europeanisation of the Italian Welfare State."
11. Reuters, "Hungary Steps up Anti-immigration Stance."
12. Organisation for Economic Cooperation and Development, *Society at a Glance*.
13. Department of Social Development, South Africa, "A Statistical Summary of Social Grants in South Africa."
14. Clapp and Fuchs, "Agrifood Corporations, Global Governance, and Sustainability"; Riches and Silvasti, "Hunger in the Rich World."
15. Fisher, *Big Hunger*.
16. Henderson, "'Free' Food, the Local Production of Worth"; Riches, *Food Bank Nations*.
17. Lohnes, "Regulating Surplus."
18. Global FoodBanking Network, "About GFN."
19. Warshawsky, "Food Waste, Sustainability, and the Corporate Sector."
20. Fisher, *Big Hunger*.
21. Riches, "Canada Must Eliminate Food Banks."
22. Fisher, *Big Hunger*.
23. Fisher, *Big Hunger*; Lohnes, "Regulating Surplus."
24. De Souza, *Feeding the Other*; Dickinson, *Feeding the Crisis*.
25. Warshawsky, "Food Waste and the Growth of Food Banks."
26. De Armiño, "Erosion of Rights, Uncritical Solidarity and Food Banks in Spain."
27. DeParle, "Amid a Deadly Virus and Crippled Economy"; Organisation for Economic Cooperation and Development, "Supporting Livelihoods during the COVID-19 Crisis"; Riches, "The Right to Food"; Riol, *The Right to Food Guidelines*; Ziegler et al., *The Fight for the Right to Food*.
28. U.S. Department of Agriculture, "FNS Nutrition Programs."
29. Graddy-Lovelace and Diamond, "From Supply Management to Agricultural Subsidies."
30. Food and Agriculture Organization, "The Right to Food around the Globe."
31. Eurostat, "Expenditure on Social Protection Benefits."
32. Food and Agriculture Organization, "The Right to Food around the Globe."

33. Gal and Madhala, "Israel's Social Welfare System"; Economic and Social Commission for Western Asia, *Changes in Public Expenditure on Social Protection.*
34. United Nations, *Nutrition and Food Security.*
35. Warshawsky, "The State and Urban Food Insecurity."
36. Coleman-Jensen et al., *Household Food Security in the United States.*
37. Cooney and Shaefer, "Material Hardship and Mental Health" ; DeParle, "Vast Expansion in Aid."
38. Eurostat, "Severe Material and Social Deprivation Rate."
39. *Times of Israel*, "Despite Pandemic, Poverty Rate Dropped in 2020."
40. Mahler et al., "Updated Estimates of the Impact of COVID-19."
41. Statista, "Value of COVID-19 Fiscal Stimulus Packages."
42. Hoogeveen and Lopez-Acevedo, "Overview."
43. Masih, "In India, as the Virus Abates."
44. Hart et al., "The COVID-19 Pandemic Reveals an Unprecedented Rise in Hunger."
45. Anderson and Mayer, "Food Insecurity in Context."
46. Trauger, Claeys, and Desmarais, "Can the Revolution Be Institutionalized?"
47. Sampson et al., "Food Sovereignty and Rights-Based Approaches."
48. Food and Agriculture Organization, "The Right to Food around the Globe"; Ziegler et al., *The Fight for the Right to Food.*
49. United Nations, "Universal Declaration of Human Rights."
50. Food and Agriculture Organization, "The Right to Food around the Globe."
51. Riches, "The Right to Food."
52. Food and Agriculture Organization, "The Right to Food around the Globe."
53. Riol, *The Right to Food Guidelines*; Ziegler et al., *The Fight for the Right to Food*; Riches, "The Right to Food."
54. De Armiño, "Erosion of Rights, Uncritical Solidarity and Food Banks in Spain."
55. De Souza, *Feeding the Other*; Dickinson, *Feeding the Crisis.*
56. May et al., "Welfare Convergence, Bureaucracy, and Moral Distancing."
57. Frayne, "Pathways of Food."
58. Organisation for Economic Cooperation and Development, "Supporting Livelihoods during the COVID-19 Crisis" ; Swinnen and McDermott, "COVID 19."
59. Riches, "The Right to Food"; Riol, *The Right to Food Guidelines*; Ziegler et al., *The Fight for the Right to Food.*

BIBLIOGRAPHY

Abi-Habib, Maria. "Millions Had Risen Out of Poverty. Coronavirus Is Pulling Them Back." *New York Times*, April 30, 2020. https://www.nytimes.com/2020/04/30/world/asia/coronavirus-poverty-unemployment.html.

Abi-Habib, Maria, and Sameer Yasir. "For India's Laborers, Coronavirus Lockdown Is an Order to Starve." *New York Times*, March 30, 2020. https://www.nytimes.com/2020/03/30/world/asia/coronavirus-india-lockdown.html.

Adhikari, Anindita, Rajendran Narayanan, Sakina Dhorajiwala, and Seema Mundoli. "21 Days and Counting: COVID-19 Lockdown, Migrant Workers, and the Inadequacy of Welfare Measures in India." Stranded Workers Action Network, April 15, 2020. http://publications.azimpremjifoundation.org/2272/1/lockdown_and_distress_report_by_stranded_workers_action_network-2.pdf.

Agostini, Chiara, David Natali, and Stefano Sacchi. "The Europeanisation of the Italian Welfare State: Channels of Influence and Trends." In *The Italian Welfare State in a European Perspective: A Comparative Analysis*, edited by Ugo Ascoli and Emmanuele Pavolini, 259–282. Bristol: Bristol University Press, 2015.

Amaro, Silvia. "Germany Is Vastly Outspending Other Countries with Its Coronavirus Stimulus." CNBC, April 20, 2020. https://www.cnbc.com/2020/04/20/coronavirus-germany-vastly-outspends-others-in-stimulus.html.

Andersen, Jørgen Goul, Mi Ah Schoyen, and Bjørn Hvinden. "Changing Scandinavian Welfare States: Which Way Forward?" In *After Austerity: Welfare State Transformation in Europe after the Great Recession*, edited by Peter Taylor-Gooby, Benjamin Leruth, and Heejung Chung, 89–114. Oxford: Oxford University Press, 2017.

Anderson, Brett. "To Fight Waste and Hunger, Food Banks Start Cooking."

New York Times, May 14, 2020. https://www.nytimes.com/2020/05/14/dining/food-banks-free-meals-coronavirus.html.

Anderson, Molly D., and Tamar Mayer. "Food Insecurity in Context." In *Food Insecurity: A Matter of Justice, Sovereignty, and Survival*, edited by Tamar Mayer and Molly D. Anderson, 1–28. London: Routledge, 2021.

Aras, Güler, and David Crowther. "Corporate Sustainability Reporting: A Study in Disingenuity?" *Journal of Business Ethics* 87, no. 1 (2009): 279. https://doi.org/10.1007/s10551-008-9806-0.

Arndt, Channing, Rob Davies, Sherwin Gabriel, Laurence Harris, Konstantin Makrelov, Sherman Robinson, Stephanie Levy, Witness Simbanegavi, Dirk van Seventer, and Lillian Anderson. "COVID-19 Lockdowns, Income Distribution, and Food Security: An Analysis for South Africa." *Global Food Security* 26 (2020): 100410. https://doi.org/10.1016/j.gfs.2020.100410.

Artino, Lauren. "Freestore Foodbank Rapidly Running Out of Supplies." Fox 19 WXIX, April 14, 2020. https://www.fox19.com/2020/04/14/freestore-foodbank-rapidly-running-out-supplies/.

Ascoli, Ugo, and Emmanuele Pavolini. "Introduction." In *The Italian Welfare State in a European Perspective: A Comparative Analysis*, edited by Ugo Ascoli and Emmanuele Pavolini, 1–18. Bristol: Bristol University Press, 2015.

Athreya, V. B., R. Rukmani, R. V. Bhavani, G. Anuradha, and R. Gopinath. *Report on the State of Food Insecurity in Urban India*. Chennai, India: Swaminathan Research Foundation, 2010. http://www.networkideas.org/focus/feb2012/M_S_Swaminathan.pdf.

Atkinson, Sarah J. "Approaches and Actors in Urban Food Security in Developing Countries." *Habitat International* 19, no. 2 (1995): 151–163. https://doi.org/10.1016/0197-3975(94)00063-8.

Baker, Lauren, and Henk de Zeeuw. "Urban Food Policies and Programmes: An Overview." In *Cities and Agriculture: Developing Resilient Urban Food Systems*, edited by Henk de Zeeuw and Pay Drechsel, 44–73. London: Routledge, 2015.

BBC News. "Chancellor Merkel Enters 'Germans Only' Food Bank Furore." February 27, 2018. https://www.bbc.com/news/world-europe-43210596.

BBC News. "Coronavirus: South Africans in Massive Queues for Food Parcels." May 17, 2020. https://www.bbc.com/news/av/world-africa-52701571.

BBC News. "German Food Bank to Reopen Membership to Foreigners after Row." April 4, 2018. https://www.bbc.com/news/world-europe-43634109.

BBC News. "India's Poorest 'Fear Hunger May Kill Us before Coronavirus.'" March 25, 2020, https://www.bbc.com/news/world-asia-india-52002734.

BBC News. "Italy Adopts New Law to Slash Food Waste." August 3, 2016. https://www.bbc.com/news/world-europe-36965671.

Beall, Jo, Owen Crankshaw, and Susan Parnell. *Uniting a Divided City: Governance and Social Exclusion in Johannesburg*. London: Earthscan, 2002.
Beasley, David. "WFP Chief Warns of Hunger Pandemic as COVID-19 Spreads (Statement to UN Security Council)." World Food Programme, 2020. https://www.wfp.org/news/wfp-chief-warns-hunger-pandemic-covid-19-spreads-statement-un-security-council.
Bebbington, Anthony J., Samuel Hickey, and Diana C. Mitlin. "Can NGOs Make a Difference? The Challenge of Development Alternatives." In *Can NGOs Make a Difference?*, edited by Anthony J. Bebbington, Samuel Hickey, and Diana C. Mitlin, 3–37. New York: Zed, 2008.
Bech, Estefania Cohn, Karim Foda, and Agustin Roitman. *Drivers of Inflation: Hungary*. International Monetary Fund, February 2023. https://www.imf.org/en/Publications/selected-issues-papers/Issues/2023/02/27/Drivers-of-Inflation-Hungary-530224.
Berliner Tafel. "How an Idea Became a Movement." 2022. https://www.berliner-tafel.de/uber-uns/die-idee.
Bhorat, Haroon, and Tim Köhler. "Lockdown Economics in South Africa: Social Assistance and the Ramaphosa Stimulus Package." Brookings Institution, November 20, 2020. https://www.brookings.edu/blog/africa-in-focus/2020/11/20/lockdown-economics-in-south-africa-social-assistance-and-the-ramaphosa-stimulus-package/.
Bolton, Doug. "Italy Passes Law to Make Supermarkets Give Wasted Food to Charity." *Independent*, March 17, 2016. https://www.independent.co.uk/news/world/europe/italy-supermarkets-food-waste-law-charity-a6937001.html.
Bond, Patrick. *Elite Transition*. Sterling, VA: Pluto Press, 2000.
Brenner, Neil, and Nik Theodore. "Cities and the Geographies of 'Actually Existing' Neoliberalism." *Antipode* 34, no. 3 (2002): 349–379. https://doi.org/10.1111/1467-8330.00246.
Brito, Christopher. "Barack Obama Surprises Food Bank Volunteers Ahead of Thanksgiving." CBS News, November 21, 2018. https://www.cbsnews.com/news/barack-obama-thanksgiving-2018-volunteers-chicago-illinois-cook-county-food-depository/.
Brønn, Peggy Simcic, and Deborah Vidaver-Cohen. "Corporate Motives for Social Initiative: Legitimacy, Sustainability, or the Bottom Line?" *Journal of Business Ethics* 87, no. 1 (2009): 91–109. https://doi.org/10.1007/s10551-008-9795-z.
BT/MTI. "Food Bank Association Saves 4 Million Kg Food in 2022." *Budapest Times*, August 4, 2022. https://www.budapesttimes.hu/hungary/food-bank-association-saves-4-million-kg-food-in-2022/.

Budapest Business Journal. "Hungary among EU Countries with Highest Poverty Rates." April 25, 2018. https://bbj.hu/analysis/hungary-among-eu-countries-with-highest-poverty-rates_148538.

Busa, Julianne H., and Rebekah Garder. "Champions of the Movement or Fair-Weather Heroes? Individualization and the (A)politics of Local Food." *Antipode* 47, no. 2 (2015): 323–341. https://doi.org/10.1111/anti.12108.

Caraher, Martin. "The European Union Food Distribution Programme for the Most Deprived Persons of the Community, 1987–2013: From Agricultural Policy to Social Inclusion Policy?" *Health Policy* 119, no. 7 (2015): 932–940. https://doi.org/10.1016/j.healthpol.2015.05.001.

Caraher, Martin, and Alessio Cavicchi. "Old Crises on New Plates or Old Plates for New Crises? Food Banks and Food Insecurity." *British Food Journal* 116, no. 9 (2014): 1382–1391. https://doi.org/10.1108/BFJ-08-2014-0285.

Chatterjee, Rhitu. "India's School Lunch Program May Be Imperfect, but It Deserves Credit for Feeding Millions." *The World*, PRX, July 16, 2014. https://www.pri.org/stories/2014-07-16/indias-school-lunch-program-may-be-imperfect-it-deserves-credit-feeding-millions.

Chen, Martha Alter. "The Informal Economy: Definitions, Theories and Policies." WIEGO Working Paper Number 1, August 2012. https://www.wiego.org/sites/default/files/migrated/publications/files/Chen_WIEGO_WP1.pdf.

Chhibber, Ajay, and Salman Anees Soz. "India Is Becoming Welfare State before Developed State. But Even Welfare It Does Badly." *Print*, November 27, 2021. https://theprint.in/pageturner/excerpt/india-is-becoming-welfare-state-before-developed-state-but-even-welfare-it-does-badly/772397/.

Chiesa, Fausta. "The Alarm from the Food Bank: More and More People without Food, Autumn Will Be Critical." *Corriere Della Sera*, August 29, 2020. https://www.corriere.it/buone-notizie/20_agosto_29/allarme-banco-alimentare-sempre-piu-persone-senza-cibo-l-autunno-sara-critico-364c219c-e9df-11ea-80e5-bbd042ec2ced.shtml.

Chutel, Lynsey. "South Africa's Big Coronavirus Aid Effort Tainted by Corruption." *New York Times*, August 19, 2020. https://www.nytimes.com/2020/08/19/world/africa/coronavirus-south-africa-aid-corruption.html.

City of Johannesburg. *Integrated Waste Management Policy*, 2011. http://www.joburg-archive.co.za/2011/pdfs/iwm_policy2011.pdf.

Clapp, Jennifer. "Spoiled Milk, Rotten Vegetables and a Very Broken Food System." *New York Times*, May 8, 2020. https://www.nytimes.com/2020/05/08/opinion/coronavirus-global-food-supply.html.

Clapp, Jennifer, and Doris Fuchs. "Agrifood Corporations, Global Governance, and Sustainability: A Framework for Analysis." In *Corporate Power in Global*

Agrifood Governance, edited by Jennifer Clapp and Doris Fuchs, 1–25. Cambridge, MA: Massachusetts Institute of Technology Press, 2009.

Coleman-Jensen, Alisha, Matthew P. Rabbitt, Christian A. Gregory, and Anita Singh. *Household Food Security in the United States in 2020*. Economic Research Report Number 298. U.S. Department of Agriculture, September 2021. https://www.ers.usda.gov/webdocs/publications/102076/err-298.pdf.

Comaroff, John L., and Jean Comaroff. "Introduction." In *Civil Society and the Political Imagination in Africa,* edited by John L. Comaroff and Jean Comaroff, 1–43. Chicago: University of Chicago Press, 1999.

Coolidge, Alexander, and Sharon Coolidge. "Jesse Jackson Calls to Expand Kroger Boycott over Its Shuttering of Stores in Minority Neighborhoods." *Cincinnati Enquirer,* April 10, 2018. https://www.cincinnati.com/story/money/nation-now/2018/04/10/jesse-jackson-kroger-protest/502688002/.

Cooney, Patrick, and H. Luke Shaefer. "Material Hardship and Mental Health: Following the COVID-19 Relief Bill and American Rescue Plan Act." Poverty Solutions, University of Michigan, May 2021. https://sites.fordschool.umich.edu/poverty2021/files/2021/05/PovertySolutions-Hardship-After-COVID-19-Relief-Bill-PolicyBrief-r1.pdf.

Corkery, Michael, and David Yaffe-Bellany. "'We Had to Do Something': Trying to Prevent Massive Food Waste." *New York Times,* May 2, 2020. https://www.nytimes.com/2020/05/02/business/coronavirus-food-waste-destroyed.html.

Cousins, Ben. "What Is a 'Smallholder'? Class-Analytical Perspectives on Small-Scale Farming and Agrarian Reform in South Africa." In *Reforming Land and Resources Use in South Africa*, edited by Paul Hebinck and Charlie Shackleton, 86–111. New York: Routledge, 2011.

Cresswell, John W., and J. David Creswell. *Research Design: Qualitative, Quantitative, and Mixed Methods Approaches*. 5th ed. Thousand Oaks, CA: Sage, 2018.

Crush, Jonathan, Bruce Frayne, and Gareth Haysom. "Introduction to Urban Food Security in the Global South." In *Handbook on Urban Security in the Global South*, edited by Jonathan Crush, Bruce Frayne, and Gareth Haysom, 1–22. Northampton, MA: Edward Elgar, 2020.

Crush, Jonathan S., and Bruce G. Frayne. "Urban Food Insecurity and the New International Food Security Agenda." *Development Southern Africa* 28, no. 4 (2011): 527–544. https://doi.org/10.1080/0376835X.2011.605571.

Crush, Jonathan, Bruce Frayne, and Wade Pendleton. "The Crisis of Food Insecurity in African Cities." *Journal of Hunger and Environmental Nutrition* 7, no. 2–3 (2012): 271–292. https://doi.org/10.1080/19320248.2012.702448.

Cuy Castellanos, Diana, John C. Jones, Joanne Christaldi, and Katherine A.

Liutkus. "Perspectives on the Development of a Local Food System: The Case of Dayton, Ohio." *Agroecology and Sustainable Food Systems* 41, no. 2 (2017): 186–203. https://doi.org/10.1080/21683565.2016.1263893.

Dahir, Abdi Latif. "'Instead of Coronavirus, the Hunger Will Kill Us.' A Global Food Crisis Looms." *New York Times*, April 22, 2020. https://www.nytimes.com/2020/04/22/world/africa/coronavirus-hunger-crisis.html.

Damiani, Mattia, Tiziana Pastorello, Anna Carlesso, Stefania Tesser, and Elena Semenzin. "Quantifying Environmental Implications of Surplus Food Redistribution to Reduce Food Waste." *Journal of Cleaner Production* 289 (2021): 125813. https://doi.org/10.1016/j.jclepro.2021.125813.

Danish Food Bank. "Annual Accounts for 2020." 2020. https://foedevarebanken.dk/wp-content/uploads/Regnskab-til-web.pdf.

Danish Food Bank. "Do You Want to Volunteer at the Food Bank?" 2022. https://foedevarebanken.dk/.

Danish Food Bank. "Facts about FødevareBanken." 2022. https://foedevarebanken.dk/fakta/.

Danish Food Bank. "Socioeconomic Analysis of Food Bank's Activities." 2020. https://foedevarebanken.dk/wp-content/uploads/Samfundsoekonomisk-analyse-af-FoedevareBankens-aktiviteter-i-2021.pdf.

Dayton Daily News. "Fighting Local Hunger a Never-Ending Effort." April 9, 2016. https://www.daytondailynews.com/news/opinion/fighting-local-hunger-never-ending-effort/29OzHAgDQw9jXb6oXbAwNO/.

Deane, Yvette J. "Knesset Passes Food Donation Act to Minimize Liability in Food Donations." *Jerusalem Post*, October 22, 2018. https://www.jpost.com/Israel-News/Knesset-passes-Food-Donation-Act-to-minimize-liability-in-food-donations-570009.

de Armiño, Karlos Pérez. "Erosion of Rights, Uncritical Solidarity and Food Banks in Spain." In *First World Hunger Revisited*, 2nd ed., edited by Graham Riches and Tiina Silvasti, 131–145. New York: Palgrave Macmillan, 2014.

Del Casino, Vincent J., Jr. "Social Geography I: Food." *Progress in Human Geography* 39, no. 6 (2015): 800–808. https://doi.org/10.1177/0309132514562997.

DeParle, Jason. "Amid a Deadly Virus and Crippled Economy, One Form of Aid Has Proved Reliable: Food Stamps." *New York Times*, July 19, 2020. https://www.nytimes.com/2020/07/19/us/politics/coronavirus-food-stamps.html.

DeParle, Jason. "Vast Expansion in Aid Kept Food Insecurity from Growing Last Year." *New York Times*, September 8, 2021. https://www.nytimes.com/2021/09/08/us/politics/vast-expansion-aid-food-insecurity.html.

Department of Agriculture and Environmental Affairs, South Africa. "KwaZulu-Natal Farmers to Land a Lucrative Market through the Agri-FoodBank Partnership." South African Government, 2011. https://www.gov

.za/kwazulu-natal-farmers-land-lucrative-market-through-agri-foodbank-partnership.

Department of Food and Public Distribution, Government of India. "National Food Security Act (NFSA)." Ministry of Consumer Affairs, Food, and Public Distribution. Government of India, 2019. https://dfpd.gov.in/nfsa-act.htm.

Department of Health, South Africa. *The South African National Health and Nutrition Examination Survey*. 2014. https://www.hsrcpress.ac.za/books/south-african-national-health-and-nutrition-examination-survey.

Department of Social Development, South Africa. "A Statistical Summary of Social Grants in South Africa." Fact Sheet no. 12, December 31, 2022. https://www.sassa.gov.za/statistical-reports/Documents/FACT%20SHEET%20December%202022.pdf.

de Sousa, Agnieszka. "World Hunger Could Double as Coronavirus Disrupts Food Supplies." *Bloomberg*, April 9, 2020. https://www.bloomberg.com/news/articles/2020-04-09/world-hunger-could-double-as-coronavirus-disrupts-food-supplies.

de Souza, Rebecca T. *Feeding the Other: Whiteness, Privilege, and Neoliberal Stigma in Food Pantries*. Cambridge, MA: Massachusetts Institute of Technology Press, 2019.

Dev, S. Mahendra, and Alakh N. Sharma. *Food Security in India: Performance, Challenges and Policies*. Oxfam India Working Paper Series. New Delhi: Oxfam India, 2010. https://oxfamilibrary.openrepository.com/bitstream/handle/10546/346637/wp-food-security-india-performance-041010-en.pdf.

Devereux, Stephen, Christophe Béné, and John Hoddinott. "Conceptualising COVID-19's Impacts on Household Food Security." *Food Security* 12, no. 4 (2020): 769–772. https://doi.org/10.1007/s12571-020-01085-0.

DeVerteuil, Geoffrey. "Welfare Reform, Institutional Practices and Service Delivery Settings." *Urban Geography* 24, no. 6 (2003): 529–550. https://doi.org/10.2747/0272-3638.24.6.529.

Dickinson, Maggie. *Feeding the Crisis: Care and Abandonment in America's Food Safety Net*. Berkeley: University of California Press, 2019.

DiGrino, Mariah. "Interview with Kate Maehr of the Greater Chicago Food Depository." *Beyond the Curve*, podcast, DLA Piper, May 27, 2020. https://soundcloud.com/dla-piper/interview-with-kate-maehr-of-the-chicago-food-depository.

Doidge, Geoff. "Statement by Minister of Public Works, Geoff Doidge, MP on the Occasion of Social Protection and Community Development Cluster Media Briefing." Department of Public Works, South Africa, November 9, 2009. http://www.sanews.gov.za/south-africa/statement-minister-public-works-geoff-doidge-mp-occasion-social-protection-and.

Domínguez, Gabriel. "Fighting Hunger." *DW News*, August 6, 2013. https://www.dw.com/en/india-launches-vast-food-aid-program/a-16935690.

Drakakis-Smith, David. "Urban Food Distribution in Asia and Africa." *Geographical Journal*, no. 1 (1991): 51–61. https://doi.org/10.2307/635144.

Drimie, Scott, and Shaun Ruysenaar. "The Integrated Food Security Strategy of South Africa: An Institutional Analysis." *Agrekon* 49, no. 3 (2010): 316–337. https://doi.org/10.1080/03031853.2010.503377.

Duggirala, Aditya, and Rohit Kumar. "The Welfare State in India: From Segmented Approach to Systems Approach in Social Protection." *Indian Journal of Human Development* 15, no. 3 (2021): 547–556. https://doi.org/10.1177/09737030211062091.

Dunai, Marton. "Hungary Prepares $30 Billion Coronavirus Package to Jump-Start Economy." Reuters, April 4, 2020. https://www.reuters.com/article/us-health-coronavirus-hungary-economy/hungary-prepares-30-billion-coronavirus-package-to-jump-start-economy-idUSKBN21M0HP.

Duncan, Alex. "The Food Security Challenge for Southern Africa." *Food Policy* 23, no. 6 (1998): 459–475. https://doi.org/10.1016/S0306-9192(98)00055-4.

DW. "Germany Passes Coronavirus Aid Package." April 23, 2020. https://www.dw.com/en/germany-passes-coronavirus-aid-package-for-workers/a-53213509.

Eastwood, Robert, and Michael Lipton. "Pro-poor Growth and Pro-growth Poverty Reduction: Meaning, Evidence, and Policy Implications." *Asian Development Review* 18, no. 2 (2000): 22–58.

Economic and Social Commission for Western Asia. *Changes in Public Expenditure on Social Protection in Arab Countries.* United Nations, 2017. https://www.unescwa.org/sites/www.unescwa.org/files/page_attachments/changes-expenditure-social-protection-arab-countries.pdf.

Economic and Social Commission for Western Asia. "Mitigating the Impact of COVID-19: Poverty and Food Insecurity in the Arab Region." United Nations, 2020. https://www.unescwa.org/sites/www.unescwa.org/files/en_20-00119_covid-19_poverty.pdf.

Economist. "The New Germans: How Germany and the Germans Have Changed." April 12, 2018. https://www.economist.com/special-report/2018/04/12/how-germany-and-the-germans-have-changed.

Economist Intelligence Unit. *Democracy Index 2020: In Sickness and in Health?* Economist Intelligence, 2020. https://www.eiu.com/n/campaigns/democracy-index-2020/.

Egyptian Food Bank. "About Us." 2022. https://www.efb.eg/about-us.

El Shohdi, Moez. "CEO Message." Food Banking Regional Network, 2022. https://foodbankingregionalnetwork.com/en/about-fbrn/ceo-message-2.

England, Andrew, and Emiko Terazono. "Pandemic Revives Gulf Fears over

Food Security." *Financial Times*, August 5, 2020. https://www.ft.com/content/5ff72ce2-5947-497e-ac83-4aa4d008a73d.

EPA. "Putting Surplus Food to Good Use." U.S. Environmental Protection Agency, 2006. https://archive.epa.gov/wastes/conserve/tools/rogo/web/pdf/food-guide.pdf.

European Commission. *The Fund for European Aid to the Most Deprived (FEAD): Breaking the Vicious Circle of Poverty and Deprivation*. EU Directorate-General for Employment, Social Affairs and Inclusion, 2015. https://ec.europa.eu/social/BlobServlet?docId=14777&langId=en.

European Commission. "Fund for European Aid to the Most Deprived (FEAD)." EU Directorate-General for Employment, Social Affairs and Inclusion, 2022. https://ec.europa.eu/social/main.jsp?catId=1089#navItem-2.

European Commission. *Recommendations for Action in Food Waste Prevention Developed by the EU Platform on Food Losses and Food Waste*. 2019. https://food.ec.europa.eu/system/files/2021-05/fs_eu-actions_action_platform_key-rcmnd_en.pdf.

European Commission. *Redistribution of Surplus Food: Example of Practices in the Member States*. EU Platform on Food Losses and Food Waste, 2019. https://food.ec.europa.eu/system/files/2019-06/fw_eu-actions_food-donation_ms-practices-food-redis.pdf.

European Commission. "Your Social Security Rights in Denmark." 2021. https://ec.europa.eu/social/main.jsp?catId=1107&langId=en.

European Commission. "Your Social Security Rights in Germany." 2021. https://ec.europa.eu/social/main.jsp?catId=1111&langId=en.

European Food Banks Federation. "Enlarge the Network." 2022. https://www.eurofoodbank.org/foster-the-development-and-creation-of-food-banks/.

European Food Banks Federation. "European Food Banks Federation Annual Report 2021." 2022. https://www.eurofoodbank.org/wp-content/uploads/2022/12/1912_FEBA_2021_AR.pdf.

European Food Banks Federation. "European Food Banks Federation Briefing: Challenges and Urgent Needs of European Food Banks Due to COVID-19." April 15, 2020. https://lp.eurofoodbank.org/wpcontent/uploads/2020/04/Report_survey_FEBA_COVID19_FINAL.pdf.

European Food Banks Federation. "European Food Banks in a Post COVID-19 Europe." July 2020. https://lp.eurofoodbank.org/wp-content/uploads/2020/07/FEBA_Report_Survey_COVID_July2020.pdf.

European Food Banks Federation. "European Food Banks Today: Commitment, Creativity, and Openness to Change." September 2020. https://lp.eurofoodbank.org/wp-content/uploads/2020/09/FEBA_Report_Survey_COVID_Sept2020.pdf.

European Food Banks Federation. "Members." 2022. https://www.eurofood bank.org/find-our-members/.
European Food Banks Federation. "Our Mission, Impact, and Values." 2022. https://www.eurofoodbank.org/our-mission-impact-values/.
European Food Banks Federation. "Our Story." 2022. https://www.eurofood bank.org/our-story/.
European Food Banks Federation. "Our Team." 2022. https://www.eurofood bank.org/our-team/.
European Food Banks Federation. "Present Challenges and Urgent Needs of European Food Banks Due to COVID-19." April 2020. https://lp.eurofood bank.org/wp-content/uploads/2020/08/FEBA_Report_Survey_COVID _April2020.pdf.
European Union. "Directive 2008/1/EC of the European Parliament and of the Council of 15 January, 2008 Concerning Integrated Pollution Prevention and Control." 2008. https://www.eea.europa.eu/policy-documents/directive -2008-1-ec.
Eurostat. "Expenditure on Social Protection Benefits." 2019. https://ec.europa .eu/eurostat/databrowser/view/tps00098/default/table?lang=en.
Eurostat. "Living Conditions in Europe—Poverty and Social Exclusion." 2021. https://ec.europa.eu/eurostat/statistics-explained/index.php?title=Living _conditions_in_Europe_-_poverty_and_social_exclusion.
Eurostat. "Severe Material and Social Deprivation Rate." 2020. https://ec .europa.eu/eurostat/databrowser/view/tespm030/default/table?lang=en.
Eurostat. "Total Unemployment Rate." 2021. https://ec.europa.eu/eurostat /databrowser/view/tps00203/default/table?lang=en.
Evans, David. "Blaming the Consumer—Once Again: The Social and Material Contexts of Everyday Food Waste Practices in Some English Households." *Critical Public Health* 21, no. 4 (2011): 429–440. https://doi.org/10.1080/095815 96.2011.608797.
Federal Association of German Food Banks. "About Us." 2022. https://www .tafel.de/ueber-uns.
Federal Association of German Food Banks. "Annual Report, 2015." 2015. https://www.tafel.de/fileadmin/media/Publikationen/Jahresberichte/PDF /Jahresbericht_2015.pdf.
Federal Association of German Food Banks. "Annual Report, 2018." 2018. https://www.tafel.de/fileadmin/media/Publikationen/Jahresberichte/PDF /20190620_Tafel_Jahresbericht2018_Web.pdf.
Federal Association of German Food Banks. "Annual Report, 2020." 2020. https://www.tafel.de/fileadmin/media/Publikationen/Jahresberichte/PDF /Tafel_Deutschland_Jahresbericht_2020_DS.pdf.

Federal Association of German Food Banks. "Background Information: Facts and Figures, 2021." 2022. https://www.tafel.de/fileadmin/media/Presse/Hintergrundinformationen/2022-11-24_Zahlen_und_Fakten.pdf.

Federal Association of German Food Banks. "Chalkboard Principles." 2022. https://www.tafel.de/ueber-uns/unsere-werte/tafel-grundsaetze.

Federal Association of German Food Banks. "Coronavirus." 2022. https://www.tafel.de/fileadmin/media/Presse/Hintergrundinformationen/2022-04-29_TAFEL_Corona_Info.pdf.

Federal Association of German Food Banks. "History." 2022. https://www.tafel.de/ueber-uns/die-tafeln/geschichte/.

Federal Association of German Food Banks. "Management Report from November 18, 2020 of the Food Banks in Germany." November 18, 2020. https://www.tafel.de/fileadmin/media/Themen/Coronavirus/2020-11-20_Lagebericht_Tafel_Deutschland.pdf.

Federal Association of German Food Banks. "Overcoming the Crisis Together." 2021. https://www.tafel.de/fileadmin/media/Themen/Coronavirus/2020-12-04_Corona-Wirkungsbroschuere_DE_web.pdf.

Federal Association of German Food Banks. "Status Report of the Tafel Food Banks and Pantries in Germany." 2020. https://www.tafel.de/fileadmin/media/Themen/Coronavirus/2020-03-24_Report_Tafel_Germany.pdf.

Federal Association of German Food Banks. "Tafel Germany Calls for Law against Food Waste." February 5, 2022. https://www.tafel.de/presse/pressemitteilungen/pressemitteilungen-2022/tafel-deutschland-fordert-gesetz-gegen-lebensmittelverschwendung.

Federal Association of German Food Banks. "Tafel Logistics." 2022. https://www.tafel.de/ueber-uns/unsere-werte/logistik.

Federal Association of German Food Banks. "Together through the Crisis." 2021. https://www.tafel.de/fileadmin/media/Publikationen/Flyer_Broschuere/2021-02-24_Corona-Wirkungsbroschuere_Doppelseiten_web.pdf.

Feeding America. "About Feeding America." 2022. https://www.feedingamerica.org/about-us.

Feeding America. "Advocating for a Hunger-Free America." 2022. https://www.feedingamerica.org/take-action/advocate.

Feeding America. "Appropriations, Budget, and Taxes." 2022. https://www.feedingamerica.org/take-action/advocate/effects-of-federal-budget-on-hunger.

Feeding America. "Federal Food Assistance Programs." 2022. https://www.feedingamerica.org/take-action/advocate/federal-hunger-relief-programs.

Feeding America. "Feeding America Network Faces Soaring Demand, Plummeting Supply Due to COVID-19 Crisis." April 8, 2020. https://www.feedingamerica.org/about-us/press-room/soaring-demand-plummeting-supply.

Feeding America. "Leading the Movement to End Hunger." 2022. https://www.feedingamerica.org/our-work/our-approach/leading-the-fight.

Feeding America. "Our History." 2022. https://www.feedingamerica.org/about-us/our-history.

Feeding America. "Our Work." 2022. https://www.feedingamerica.org/our-work.

Feeding America. "2022 Annual Report." 2022. https://www.feedingamerica.org/sites/default/files/2022-12/FA_22ImpactReport_d9_FINAL.pdf.

Fehér, Boróka. "The Cost of Energy Crisis in Hungary: What Are the Impacts on Homelessness Service Providers?" *Homeless in Europe*, winter 2022, 13–16. https://www.feantsa.org/public/user/Magazine/Winter_Magazine_2022/FEA_008-22_magazine_winter_2022_v6.pdf.

Fisher, Andrew. *Big Hunger: The Unholy Alliance between Corporate America and Anti-hunger Groups*. Cambridge, MA: Massachusetts Institute of Technology Press, 2017.

Flanagan, Katie, Brian Lipinski, and Liz Goodwin. "SDG Target 12.3 on Food Loss and Waste: 2019 Progress Report." Champions 12.3, September 2019. https://champions123.org/sites/default/files/2020-09/champions-12-3-2019-progress-report.pdf.

Flanagan, Katie, Kai Robertson, and Craig Hanson. *Reducing Food Loss and Waste: Setting a Global Action Agenda*. World Resources Institute, 2019. https://files.wri.org/s3fs-public/reducing-food-loss-waste-global-action-agenda_1.pdf.

Food and Agriculture Organization. "COVID-19 Series/Identifying and Addressing the Threats against Food Recovery and Redistribution." 2020. http://www.fao.org/food-loss-reduction/news/detail/en/c/1271024/.

Food and Agriculture Organization. "FAO and Egyptian Food Bank Launch 'Food Waste Awareness Campaign.'" June 3, 2018. http://www.fao.org/neareast/news/view/en/c/1138984/.

Food and Agriculture Organization. "Food Security and Nutrition: Building a Global Narrative towards 2030." 2020. http://www.fao.org/3/ca9731en/ca9731en.pdf.

Food and Agriculture Organization. "Hunger and Food Insecurity." 2020. http://www.fao.org/hunger/en/.

Food and Agriculture Organization. "Impacts of COVID-19 on Food Security and Nutrition: Developing Effective Policy Responses to Address the Hunger and Malnutrition Pandemic." High Level Panel of Experts, United Nations, September 2020. http://www.fao.org/3/cb1000en/cb1000en.pdf.

Food and Agriculture Organization. "The Right to Food around the Globe." 2022. http://www.fao.org/right-to-food-around-the-globe/en.

Bibliography

Food and Agriculture Organization. "The State of Food Security and Nutrition in the World." 2021. https://www.fao.org/3/cb4474en/cb4474en.pdf.

Foodbank. "Basics: The Foodbank, Inc. 2021 Annual Report." 2021. https://thefoodbankdayton.org/wp-content/uploads/2022/03/FBAR20214WEB-1-compressed.pdf.

Foodbank. "Financial Statements and Supplementary Information." 2022. https://thefoodbankdayton.org/wp-content/uploads/2022/10/The-Foodbank-2022-Financial-Statement.pdf.

Foodbank. "The Foodbank Impact Statement." 2022. https://thefoodbankdayton.org/wp-content/uploads/2022/10/FY22-Tri-County-Impact-Statement.docx.

Foodbank. "The Foodbank Impact Statement FY2021." 2021. https://thefoodbankdayton.org/wp-content/uploads/2021/08/Fy2021-impact-statement-tri-county.docx.

Food Banking Regional Network. "Current Food Banks." 2022. https://foodbankingregionalnetwork.com/en/member/current-food-banks.

Food Banking Regional Network. "FBRN 2013 Activity Report (June 2013–April 2014)." 2014. https://foodbankingregionalnetwork.com/storage/posts/February2020/FBRN-Activity-Report-June-2013-April-2014.pdf.

Food Banking Regional Network. "Food Banking Regional Network—Dubai Branch: Financial Statements." December 31, 2015. https://foodbankingregionalnetwork.com/storage/posts/February2020/financial-Statment-Food-Banking-Regional-Network-2015.pdf.

Food Banking Regional Network. "Key Performance Indicators." 2022. https://foodbankingregionalnetwork.com/en/about-fbrn/key-performance-indicators.

Food Banking Regional Network. "Mission and Vision." 2022. https://foodbankingregionalnetwork.com/en/about-fbrn/missionvision.

Food Banking Regional Network. "Our Pillars to Fight Hunger." 2022. https://foodbankingregionalnetwork.com/en/our-pillars-to-fight-hunger.

Food Bank News. "Which Food Banks Are the Largest in America?" October 12, 2021. https://foodbanknews.org/which-food-banks-are-the-largest-in-america/.

FoodForward South Africa. "About Us." 2022. https://foodforwardsa.org/our-foodbanking-model/.

FoodForward South Africa. "Annual Report, 2020/2021." 2021. https://foodforwardsa.org/wp-content/uploads/2021/09/Annual-Report-2021.pdf.

FoodForward South Africa. "As Hardship Continues, Empathy Drives Our Social Agenda." February 2, 2021. https://foodforwardsa.org/news/as-hardship-continues-empathy-drives-our-social-agenda/.

FoodForward South Africa. "Audited Annual Financial Statements for the Year Ended 28 February 2021." 2021. https://foodforwardsa.org/wp-content/uploads/2022/04/FoodForward-SA-Annual-Financial-Statements-2021.pdf.

FoodForward South Africa. "An Evaluation of Impact, 2019/2020." 2020. https://foodforwardsa.org/wp-content/uploads/2021/03/FFSA-2020-Impact-Evaluation-Report_.pdf.

FoodForward South Africa. "Our Work." 2022. https://foodforwardsa.org/our-work/.

FoodForward South Africa. "Repurpose the Surplus." 2022. https://foodforwardsa.org/.

Food Research and Action Center. "How Hungry Is America? FRAC's National, State, and Local Index of Food Hardship, 2014." April 2015. http://www.frac.org/research/resource-library/hungry-america-fracs-national-state-local-index-food-hardship-april-2015.

Food Waste Reduction Alliance. "Messy but Worth It! Lessons Learned from Fighting Food Waste." 2020. http://foodwastealliance.org/wp-content/uploads/2020/04/FoodWaste_Final_small.pdf.

Forero, Juan. "In Developing World, Coronavirus Slams Workers in Informal Economy." *Wall Street Journal*, April 2, 2020. https://www.wsj.com/articles/in-developing-world-coronavirus-slams-workers-in-informal-economy-11585819801.

Frayne, Bruce G. "Pathways of Food: Mobility and Food Transfers in Southern African Cities." *International Development Planning Review* 32, no. 3–4 (2010): 291–310. https://doi.org/10.3828/idpr.2010.10.

Freestore Foodbank. "About Freestore Foodbank." 2022. https://freestorefoodbank.org/about-freestore-foodbank/.

Freestore Foodbank. "Fiscal Year 2020—FSFB Annual Report." 2020. https://freestorefoodbank.org/fiscal-year-2020-fsfb-annual-report/.

Freestore Foodbank. "Fiscal Year 2022 Impact Report." 2022. https://mediaserver.freestorefoodbank.org/wp-content/uploads/2022-Impact-Report_11-8-22-1.pdf.

Freestore Foodbank. "Our Mission in Action." 2021. https://freestorefoodbank.org/coronavirus-covid-19-updates-and-information/.

Friedhoff, Alec, Howard Wial, and Harold Wolman. "The Consequences of Metropolitan Manufacturing Decline: Testing Conventional Wisdom." Metropolitan Policy Program at Brookings, 2010. https://www.brookings.edu/wp-content/uploads/2016/06/1216_manufacturing_wial_friedhoff.pdf.

Gal, John, and Shavit Madhala. "Israel's Social Welfare System: An Overview." Taub Center for Social Policy Studies in Israel, December 2018. https://www.taubcenter.org.il/wp-content/uploads/2020/12/welfareoverview2018en.pdf.

Galli, Francesca, Aniek Hebinck, and Brídín Carroll. "Addressing Food Poverty in Systems: Governance of Food Assistance in Three European Countries." *Food Security* 10, no. 6 (2018): 1353–1370. https://doi.org/10.1007/s12571-018-0850-z.

Gallion, Emily, and Caitlyn McIntosh. "Closing Out a Historic Fiscal Year at the Foodbank." Foodbank, July 2020. https://thefoodbankdayton.org/2020/07/.

Garrett, James L., and Marie T. Ruel. "Are Determinants of Rural and Urban Food Security and Nutritional Status Different? Some Insights from Mozambique." *World Development* 27, no. 11 (1999): 1955–1975. https://doi.org/10.1016/S0305-750X(99)00091-1.

Garrone, Paola, Marco Melacini, and Alessandro Perego. "Opening the Black Box of Food Waste Reduction." *Food Policy* 46 (2014): 129–139. https://doi.org/10.1016/j.foodpol.2014.03.014.

Garthwaite, Kayleigh. *Hunger Pains: Life Inside Foodbank Britain*. Bristol: Policy Press, 2016.

Gentilini, Ugo. "Banking on Food: The State of Food Banks in High-Income Countries." *Institute of Development Studies Working Paper*, no. 415 (2013): 1–18. https://doi.org/10.1111/j.2040-0209.2013.00415.x.

German Government, Federal Ministry of Food and Agriculture. *National Strategy for Food Waste Reduction*. 2022. https://www.bmel.de/EN/topics/food-and-nutrition/food-waste/national-strategy-for-food-waste-reduction.html.

Global FoodBanking Network. "About GFN." 2022. https://www.foodbanking.org/about-gfn/.

Global FoodBanking Network. *Advancing the Sustainable Development Goals: A Roadmap to 2030*. 2020. https://www.foodbanking.org/resources/advancing-the-sdgs/.

Global FoodBanking Network. "The COVID-19 Pandemic Is Deepening the Hunger Crisis. Food Banks Can't Do It Alone." 2020. https://www.foodbanking.org/es/news/the-covid-19-pandemic-is-deepening-the-hunger-crisis-food-banks-cant-do-it-alone/.

Global FoodBanking Network. "Exciting News about Food Banking in India." November 22, 2017. https://www.foodbanking.org/exciting-news-about-food-banking-in-india/.

Global FoodBanking Network. "Financial Statements." 2022. https://archive.foodbanking.org/2022annualreport/.

Global FoodBanking Network. *Food*, winter 2006–2007.

Global FoodBanking Network. "The Food Bank Leadership Institute." 2020. https://www.foodbanking.org/food-banking-leadership-institute/.

Global FoodBanking Network. "The Food Bank Organizations Reaching the

Daily Wagers in India during COVID-19." April 29, 2020. https://www.food banking.org/food-bank-daily-wagers-covid/.

Global FoodBanking Network. "Food Banks Strive for the Gold Standard of Food Safety." July 7, 2022. https://www.foodbanking.org/blogs/food-banks-strive-for-the-gold-standard-of-food-safety/.

Global FoodBanking Network. "FY2022 Annual Report." 2022. https://www.foodbanking.org/2022annualreport/.

Global FoodBanking Network. "GFN Marks a Decade of Global Food Banking: As GFN Approaches Its 10-Year Anniversary, We Take a Look at How GFN Came to Be." August 24, 2015. https://www.foodbanking.org/gfn-marks-a-decade-of-global-food-banking-as-gfn-approaches-its-10-year-anniversary-we-take-a-look-at-how-gfn-came-to-be/.

Global FoodBanking Network. *The Global Food Donation Policy Atlas*. 2022. https://atlas.foodbanking.org/.

Global FoodBanking Network. "Global Leaders Alleviate Hunger: An Interview with Dr. Sam Pitroda." *Food* 4, no. 3 (2010): 13.

Global FoodBanking Network. "India: FoodBanking Planning Forum launched in NewDelhi." *Food* 4, no. 1 (2010): 6–7.

Global FoodBanking Network. "IRS Form 990." 2015. https://www.foodbanking.org/wp-content/uploads/2022/09/GFN-2015-Tax-Returns-Disclosure-Copy.pdf.

Global FoodBanking Network. "Israel: Combining Forces to Fight Food Insecurity." *Food* 4, no. 1 (2010): 4–5.

Global FoodBanking Network. "Israel." *Food* 5, no. 1 (2010): 14.

Global FoodBanking Network. "The Making of The Global FoodBanking Network: Major Milestones." 2015. https://www.foodbanking.org/the-making-of-the-global-foodbanking-network-major-milestones/.

Global FoodBanking Network. "Our Global Reach." 2022. https://www.foodbanking.org/global-reach/.

Global FoodBanking Network. "Reflections: Jeff Klein Answers 5 Questions about His Time at GFN." 2015. https://www.foodbanking.org/reflections-jeff-klein-answers-5-questions.

Global FoodBanking Network. "The State of Global Food Banking 2020." October 16, 2020. https://www.foodbanking.org/resources/the-state-of-global-food-banking-2020/.

Global FoodBanking Network. "Strengthening Food Donation Operations during COVID-19: Key Issues and Best Practices for Governments around the Globe." 2020. https://www.foodbanking.org/wp-content/uploads/2020/06/Global-Food-Donation-Policy-Atlas-COVID19-Issue-Brief.pdf.

Global FoodBanking Network. "Take Action by Nourishing Families Today!" December 28, 2020.
Global FoodBanking Network. "Training and Knowledge Sharing." 2022. https://www.foodbanking.org/advancing-food-banks/training-and-knowledge-sharing/.
Global FoodBanking Network. "Two Projects That Transformed Food Banking Globally." 2016. https://www.foodbanking.org/two-projects-that-transformed-food-banking-globally/.
Global FoodBanking Network. *Waste Not, Want Not: Towards Zero Hunger.* March 1, 2019. http://www.foodbanking.org/wp-content/uploads/2019/03/GFN_WasteNot.pdf.
Global Hunger Index. "Global Hunger Index Scores by 2022 GHI Rank." 2022. https://www.globalhungerindex.org/ranking.html.
Gomes-Hochberg, Cassandra. "Are Israelis Going Hungry?" *Jerusalem Post*, September 27, 2020. https://www.jpost.com/magazine/are-israelis-going-hungry-643405.
Graddy-Lovelace, Garrett, and Adam Diamond. "From Supply Management to Agricultural Subsidies—and Back Again? The US Farm Bill and Agrarian (In)Viability." *Journal of Rural Studies* 50 (2017): 70–83. https://doi.org/10.1016/j.jrurstud.2016.12.007.
Gram-Hanssen, Irmelin, Ole Jørgen Hanssen, Johan Hultén, Kirsi Silvennoinen, Mads Werge, Åsa Stenmarck, and Ane Kirstine Aare. *Food Redistribution in the Nordic Region. Phase II: Identification of Best Practice Models for Enhanced Food Redistribution.* Nordic Council of Ministers, 2016. http://norden.diva-portal.org/smash/record.jsf?dswid=5400&pid=diva2%3A902211.
Greater Chicago Food Depository. "COVID-19 Data Map." 2022. https://www.chicagosfoodbank.org/covid-19-data-map/.
Greater Chicago Food Depository. "How We Distribute Food to Chicagoland Food Pantries." 2022. https://www.chicagosfoodbank.org/about/how-w-help/.
Greater Chicago Food Depository. "Our Mission." 2022. https://annualreport.chicagosfoodbank.org/mission/.
Greater Chicago Food Depository. "2022 Annual Report." 2022. https://annualreport.chicagosfoodbank.org/wp-content/uploads/2018/10/100950-Greater-Chicago-Food-Depository-Annual-Report-0622-Final.pdf.
Gumuchian, Marie-Louise. "'New Poor' in Italy Line Up for Free Food." Reuters, October 29, 2008. https://www.reuters.com/article/us-financial-italy-poor/new-poor-in-italy-line-up-for-free-food-idUSTRE49S99520081029.
Gunders, Dana. *Wasted: How America Is Losing Up to 40 Percent of Its Food*

from Farm to Fork to Landfill. 2nd ed. New York: Natural Resources Defense Council, 2017. https://www.nrdc.org/sites/default/files/wasted-2017-report.pdf.

Gupta, Palak, Kalyani Singh, Veenu Seth, Sidharth Agarwal, and Pulkit Mathur. "Coping Strategies Adopted by Households to Prevent Food Insecurity in Urban Slums of Delhi, India." *Journal of Food Security* 3, no. 1 (2015): 6–10.

Gustavsson, Jenny, Christel Cederberg, Ulf Sonesson, Robert Van Otterdijk, and Alexandre Meybeck. "Global Food Losses and Food Waste." Rome: Food and Agriculture Organization of the United Nations, 2011. http://www.fao.org/docrep/014/mb060e/mb060e00.pdf.

Guthman, Julie. "Doing Justice to Bodies? Reflections on Food Justice, Race, and Biology." *Antipode* 46, no. 5 (2012), 1153–1171. https://doi.org/10.1111/j.1467-8330.2012.01017.x.

Guthman, Julie. "Thinking Inside the Neoliberal Box: The Micro-politics of Agro-Food Philanthropy." *Geoforum* 39, no. 3 (2008): 1241–1253. https://doi.org/10.1016/j.geoforum.2006.09.001.

Habib, Adam, and Hermien Kotzé. "Civil Society, Governance and Development in an Era of Globalisation: The South African Case." In *Governance in the New South Africa: The Challenges of Globalization*, edited by Guy Mhone and Omano Edigheji, 246–270. Cape Town: University of Cape Town Press, 2003.

Halloran, Afton, Jesper Clement, Niels Kornum, Camelia Bucatariu, and Jakob Magid. "Addressing Food Waste Reduction in Denmark." *Food Policy* 49, no. 1 (2014): 294–301. https://doi.org/10.1016/j.foodpol.2014.09.005.

Halon, Eytan. "Israelis Threw Away 2.5 Millions Tons of Food in 2018—Report." *Jerusalem Post*, March 5, 2019. https://www.jpost.com/Israel-News/Israelis-threw-away-25-million-tons-of-food-in-2018-Report-582487.

Hanssen, Ole Jørgen, Per Ekegren, Irmelin Gram-Hanssen, Pirjo Korpela, Nanna Langevad-Clifforth, Kristin Skov-Olsen, Kirsi Silvennoinen, Malin Stare, Åsa Stenmarck, and Erik Svanes. *Food Redistribution in the Nordic Region: Experiences and Results from a Pilot Study*. Nordic Council of Ministers, 2014. https://norden.diva-portal.org/smash/get/diva2:784307/FULLTEXT01.pdf.

Hart, Tim G. B., Yul Derek Davids, Stephen Rule, Precious Tirivanhu, and Samela Mtyingizane. "The COVID-19 Pandemic Reveals an Unprecedented Rise in Hunger: The South African Government Was Ill-Prepared to Meet the Challenge." *Scientific African* 16 (2022): e01169. https://doi.org/10.1016/j.sciaf.2022.e01169.

Hayet, Justin. "Thirty-Six: Leket's Joseph Gitler." *Times of Israel*, January 2, 2022. https://www.timesofisrael.com/spotlight/lekets-joseph-gitler/.

Hebinck, Paul, and Charlie Shackleton. "Livelihoods, Resources, and Land Reform." In *Reforming Land and Resource Use in South Africa*, edited by Paul Hebinck and Charlie Shackleton, 1–32. New York: Routledge, 2011.

Henderson, George. "'Free' Food, the Local Production of Worth, and the Circuit of Decommodification: A Value Theory of the Surplus." *Environment and Planning D* 22, no. 4 (2004): 485–512. https://doi.org/10.1068/d379.

Hendriks, Sheryl L., and Angela McIntyre. "Between Markets and Masses: Food Assistance and Food Banks in South Africa." In *First World Hunger Revisited*, 2nd ed., edited by Graham Riches and Tiina Silvasti, 117–130. New York: Palgrave Macmillan, 2014.

Hlati, Okuhle. "FoodFoward SA Pledges to Feed 1 Million People Daily in Five Years." *Cape Times*, April 26, 2019. https://www.iol.co.za/capetimes/news/foodforward-sa-pledges-to-feed-1-million-people-daily-in-five-years-21998837.

Hoogeveen, Johannes G., and Gladys Lopez-Acevedo. "Overview." In *Distributional Impacts of COVID-19 in the Middle East and North Africa Region*, edited by Johannes G. Hoogeveen and Gladys Lopez-Acevedo, 1–19. Washington, DC: World Bank Group, 2021. https://openknowledge.worldbank.org/bitstream/handle/10986/36618/9781464817762.pdf.

Hoover, Darby. *Estimating Quantities and Types of Food Waste at the City Level*. New York: Natural Resources Defense Council, 2017. https://www.nrdc.org/sites/default/files/food-waste-city-level-report.pdf.

Hopkins, Valerie. "Hungary's Ban on Homelessness Leaves Many People Vulnerable." *Financial Times*, November 23, 2018. https://www.ft.com/content/f8f0076e-e026-11e8-a6e5-792428919cee.

Huang, Ching-Hsu, Shih-Min Liu, and Nai-Yun Hsu. "Understanding Global Food Surplus and Food Waste to Tackle Economic and Environmental Sustainability." *Sustainability* 12, no. 7 (2020): 2892. https://doi.org/10.3390/su12072892.

Hungarian Food Bank Association. "Even in Emergency for the Needy—the Food Bank Distributed HUF 1.5 Billion Worth of Food in the Last 3 Months." April 8, 2020. https://www.elelmiszerbank.hu/hu/hirek/hireink/veszely helyzetben_is_a_nelkulozokert__-_15_milliard_forint_erteku_elelmiszert _osztott_az_elelmiszerbank_az_elmult_3_honapban_-.html.

Hungarian Food Bank Association. "Report on Last, Extraordinary Months March-April-May-June 2020." July 13, 2020. https://elelmiszerbank.hu/hu/hirek/hireink/beszamolo_2020_marcius-junius.html.

Hungarian Food Bank Association. "Who We Are." 2022. https://www.elel miszerbank.hu/en/about_us/who_we_are.html.

India FoodBanking Network. "About IFBN." 2022. https://www.indiafoodbank ing.org/about.

India FoodBanking Network. "FoodBanking Solves Hunger Problem." 2022. https://www.indiafoodbanking.org/foodbanking/.

India FoodBanking Network. "GOI and State Governments." 2022. https:// www.indiafoodbanking.org/central-state-governments/.

India FoodBanking Network. "School Nutrition Program." 2022. https://www .indiafoodbanking.org/school-nutrition-program/.

India FoodBanking Network. "We Are Leading India's Fight against Hunger." 2022. https://www.indiafoodbanking.org/about/.

International Commission of Jurists. "COVID-19 Pandemic in India: The Right to Food." June 2020. https://www.icj.org/wp-content/uploads/2020/06 /India-Right-to-Food-COVID19-Briefing-Paper-2020-ENG.pdf.

Italian Food Bank Network. "A Big Network to Support the Poorest." 2022. https://www.bancoalimentare.it/en/node/2.

Italian Food Bank Network. "The Key Points." 2022. https://www.bancoali mentare.it/en/node/4185.

Italian Food Bank Network. "Management Report." 2019. https://cdn2.bancoali mentare.it/sites/bancoalimentare.it/files/rendiconto2019_def.pdf.

Italian Food Bank Network. "National Day of Food Collection." 2022. https:// www.bancoalimentare.it/it/veneto/GNCA.

Italian Food Bank Network. "Remembering Cavalier Fossati." March 11, 2020. https://www.bancoalimentare.it/it/emiliaromagna/news/anniversario-fossati.

Italian Food Bank Network. *Social Balance*. 2021. https://cdn.bancoalimentare .it/sites/bancoalimentare.it/files/allegati/2022/06/bs_21.pdf.

Jacobs, Anna L. "The Ukraine Crisis Deepens Food Insecurity across the Middle East and Africa." Arab Gulf States Institute in Washington, April 11, 2022. https://agsiw.org/the-ukraine-crisis-deepens-food-insecurity-across-the -middle-east-and-africa/.

Jaffe-Hoffman, Maayan, and John Benzaquen. "In the Wake of COVID Crisis, Leket Israel Gives Food and Faith to Israel's Poor." *Jerusalem Post*, September 10, 2020. https://www.jpost.com/israel-news/in-the-wake-of-covid-crisis -leket-israel-gives-food-and-faith-to-israels-poor-641747.

James, Deborah. *Gaining Ground?* New York: Routledge, 2007.

Joburg Market. "Introduction." 2022. http://www.joburgmarket.co.za/aboutus _intoduction.php.

Jones, Gavin. "Poverty in Italy at Worst for 12 Years, New Government Vows Action." Reuters, June 26, 2018. https://www.reuters.com/article/us-italy

-politics-poverty/poverty-in-italy-at-worst-for-12-years-new-government-vows-action-idUSKBN1JM2GM.

Kampf, Lena. "Close Hundreds of Boards—Social Hardship Is Increasing." *Süddeutsche Zeitung*, April 2, 2020. https://www.sueddeutsche.de/wirtschaft/tafeln-corona-lebensmittel-1.4864489.

Kang, Jaewon. "Kroger Posts Stronger Sales, Profit Amid Coronavirus Pandemic." *Wall Street Journal*, June 18, 2020. https://www.wsj.com/articles/kroger-posts-stronger-sales-profits-amid-coronavirus-pandemic-11592482583.

Kapur, Devesh, and Prakirti Nangia. "Social Protection in India: A Welfare State Sans Public Goods?" *India Review* 14, no. 1 (2015): 73–90. https://doi.org/10.1080/14736489.2015.1001275.

Kashti, Or. "Israel Must Take Food Insecurity Seriously, Expert Panel Warns, Calling to Increase Aid." *Haaretz*, May 7, 2020. https://www.haaretz.com/israel-news/.premium-israel-must-take-food-insecurity-seriously-experts-warn-calling-to-increase-aid-1.8971885.

Kattumuri, Ruth. *Food Security and the Targeted Public Distribution System in India*. Asia Research Centre Working Paper 38. London: London School of Economics and Political Science, 2011.

Katz, Michael B. *In the Shadow of the Poorhouse*. New York: Basic Books, 1986.

Katz, Michael B. *The Undeserving Poor*. New York: Pantheon, 1989.

Kessl, Fabian, Stephan Lorenz, and Holger Schoneville. "Social Exclusion and Food Assistance in Germany." In *The Rise of Food Charity in Europe*, edited by Hannah Lambie-Mumford and Tiina Silvasti, 49–78. Bristol: Policy Press, 2020.

Kikon, Dolly. "Dirty Food, Racism and Casteism in India." *Ethnic and Racial Studies* 45, no. 2 (2022): 278–297. https://doi.org/10.1080/01419870.2021.1964558.

Kodras, Janet. "Restructuring the State: Devolution, Privatization, and the Geographic Redistribution of Power and Capacity in Governance." In *State Devolution in America*, edited by Lynn A. Staeheli, Janet E. Kodras, and Colin R. Flint, 79–96. Thousand Oaks, CA: Sage, 1997.

Kõre, Jüri. "Hunger and Food Aid in Estonia: A Local Authority and Family Obligation." In *First World Hunger Revisited*, 2nd ed., edited by Graham Riches and Tiina Silvasti, 57–71. New York: Palgrave Macmillan, 2014.

Kroch, Gidi. "Food Insecurity and the State Budget: Is the Right to Have Food Political?" *Jerusalem Post*, October 15, 2020. https://www.jpost.com/opinion/is-the-right-to-have-food-in-israel-political-645872.

Kroch, Gidi. "Food Rescue: An Answer to the Surge in the Economy." *Jerusalem Post*, December 22, 2018. https://www.jpost.com/Opinion/Food-rescue-An-answer-to-the-surge-in-the-economy-575135.

Kroger Company. "The Kroger Company Zero Hunger/Zero Waste Foundation Launches Emergency COVID-19 Response Fund." April 20, 2020. http://ir.kroger.com/CorporateProfile/press-releases/press-release/2020/The-Kroger-Co-Zero-Hunger--Zero-Waste-Foundation-Launches-Emergency-COVID-19-Response-Fund/default.aspx.

Kroger Company. "News Release: Kroger Announces Zero Hunger/Zero Waste Plan." September 19, 2017. https://www.thekrogerco.com/wp-content/uploads/2017/09/National-9-18-17-Kroger-Zero-Hunger-Zero-Waste-News-Release.pdf.

Kroger Company. "Sharing Our Value: 2021 Environmental, Social and Governance Report." 2021. https://www.thekrogerco.com/wp-content/uploads/2021/07/Kroger-2021-ESG-Report.pdf.

Kroger Company. *2020 Fact Book*. 2020. https://s1.q4cdn.com/137099145/files/doc_downloads/irw/fact_books/2020/KRO_FactBook2020_FINAL.pdf.

Kroger Company. "Zero Hunger/Zero Waste Foundation Report." 2021. https://www.thekrogerco.com/wp-content/uploads/2021/07/The-Kroger-Co.-Zero-Hunger-Zero-Waste-Foundation-Report-2021-Final.pdf.

Kroger Company. "Zero Hunger/Zero Waste: Kroger's Plan." 2017. https://www.thekrogerco.com/wp-content/uploads/2017/08/Kroger-ZeroHungerZeroWaste-Plan.pdf.

Kronenberger, Emily. "Dayton Foodbank Ranked No. 2 in the Nation." *Dayton Daily News*, November 19, 2018. https://www.daytondailynews.com/news/local/dayton-foodbank-ranked-the-nation/qMtxTRxOF9dNEk9dzOwMQM/.

Kuhlman, Mary Schuermann. "Cleveland, Cincinnati among Top 10 Poorest Big Cities." Public News Service, September 18, 2020. https://www.publicnewsservice.org/2020-09-18/poverty/cleveland-cincinnati-among-top-10-poorest-big-cities/a71506-1.

Kulish, Nicholas. "Food Banks Are Overrun, as Surging Hunger Meets Dwindling Supplies." *New York Times*, April 8, 2020. https://www.nytimes.com/2020/04/08/business/economy/coronavirus-food-banks.html.

Lambie-Mumford, Hannah. "The Growth of Food Banks in Britain and What They Mean for Social Policy." *Critical Social Policy* 39, no. 1 (2019): 3–22. https://doi.org/10.1177/0261018318765855.

Lambie-Mumford, Hannah. *Hungry Britain: The Rise of Food Charity*. Bristol: Policy Press, 2017.

Lambie-Mumford, Hannah, and Tiina Silvasti. "Introduction: Exploring the Growth of Food Charity across Europe." In *The Rise of Food Charity in Europe*, edited by Hannah Lambie-Mumford and Tiina Silvasti, 1–18. Bristol: Policy Press, 2020.

La Meyer, Julian. "COVID-19 Further Exposes the Fragility of Our Social Safety Net." FoodForward South Africa, April 6, 2020. https://foodforwardsa.org/news/covid-19-further-exposes-the-fragility-of-our-social-safety-net/.

La Meyer, Julian. "Food Poverty Is Emerging as a Significant Threat Alongside the COVID-19 Pandemic." *FoodForward South Africa*, June 5, 2020. https://foodforwardsa.org/news/food-poverty-is-emerging-as-a-significant-threat-alongside-the-covid-19-pandemic/.

La Meyer, Julian. "Initial Results: Year 1 of Our Five-Year Plan." *Food Forward South Africa*, March 6, 2020. https://foodforwardsa.org/news/initial-results-year-1-of-our-five-year-plan/.

La Meyer, Julian. "Major Shifts in Poverty Highlighted by COVID-19 Necessitate the Need for New Social Paradigms." FoodForward South Africa, 2020. https://foodforwardsa.org/news/major-shifts-in-poverty-highlighted-by-covid-19-necessitate-the-need-for-new-social-paradigms/.

Lee, Gavin. "EU Budget Blocked by Hungary and Poland over Rule of Law Issue." BCC News, November 16, 2020. https://www.bbc.com/news/world-europe-54964858.

Leket Israel. "About Food Rescue." 2022. https://www.leket.org/en/food-rescue/.

Leket Israel. "About the Organization." 2022. https://www.leket.org/en/about-leket/.

Leket Israel. "Daily Updates during the Corona Crisis." August 1, 2020. https://www.leket.org/en/crisis-update/.

Leket Israel. "Financial Statements." 2021. https://www.leket.org/wp-content/uploads/2021/08/Table-to-Table-Leket-Israel-2020-financial-statements.pdf.

Leket Israel. "Food Waste and Rescue in Israel: Report 2019." https://foodwastereport.leket.org/wp-content/uploads/2021/12/Leket-Report-2019-Eng_Digital.pdf.

Leket Israel. "History of Leket Israel." 2022. https://www.leket.org/en/leket-history/.

Leket Israel. "Joseph Gitler Named One of 50 Most Influential Jews." July 11, 2014. https://www.leket.org/en/joseph-gitler-named-one-of-50-most-influential-jews/.

Leket Israel. "Law Passed to Promote Food Donations in Israel." October 23, 2018. https://www.leket.org/en/law-passed-to-promote-food-donations-in-israel/.

Leket Israel. "Nutrition and Food Safety." 2022. https://www.leket.org/en/category/nutrition-food-safety-en/.

Leone, Kate. "Feeding America Statement on Able-Bodied Adults without Dependents Proposed Rule." Feeding America, December 20, 2018. https://www

.feedingamerica.org/about-us/press-room/feeding-america-statement-able-bodied-adults-without-dependents-proposed-rule.

Leone, Kate. "Feeding America Statement on Congress' Passage of CARES Act." Feeding America, March 27, 2020. https://www.feedingamerica.org/about-us/press-room/feeding-america-statement-passage-cares-act.

Leskošek, Vesna, and Romana Zidar. "Redistributing Waste Food to Reduce Poverty in Slovenia." In *The Rise of Food Charity in Europe*, edited by Hannah Lambie-Mumford and Tiina Silvasti, 135–164. Bristol: Policy Press, 2020.

Levi, Sarah. "Produce 'Rescue': Looking to Israeli Initiatives to Combat World Hunger." *Jerusalem Post*, September 5, 2017. https://www.jpost.com/Israel-News/Produce-rescue-Looking-to-Israeli-initiatives-to-combat-world-hunger-504233.

Lindenbaum, John. "Countermovement, Neoliberal Platoon, or Re-gifting Depot? Understanding Decommodification in US Food Banks." *Antipode* 48, no. 2 (2016): 375–392. https://doi.org/10.1111/anti.12192.

Lipinski, Brian, Craig Hanson, James Lomax, Lisa Kitinoja, Richard Waite, and Tim Searchinger. *Reducing Food Loss and Waste*. World Resources Institute, 2013. http://pdf.wri.org/reducing_food_loss_and_waste.pdf.

Local. "Danish Consumers Reduced Food Waste by 14,000 Tonnes in Six Years." April 18, 2018. https://www.thelocal.dk/20180418/danish-consumers-reduced-food-waste-by-14000-tonnes-in-6-years.

Lohnes, Joshua D. "Regulating Surplus: Charity and the Legal Geographies of Food Waste Enclosure." *Agriculture and Human Values* 38 (2021): 351–363. https://doi.org/10.1007/s10460-020-10150-5.

Lohnes, Joshua, and Bradley Wilson. "Bailing Out the Food Banks? Hunger Relief, Food Waste, and Crisis in Central Appalachia." *Environment and Planning A: Economy and Space* 50, no. 2 (2018): 350–369. https://doi.org/10.1177/0308518X17742154.

Loopstra, Rachel, and Valerie Tarasuk. "Food Bank Usage Is a Poor Indicator of Food Insecurity: Insights from Canada." *Social Policy and Society* 14, no. 3 (2015): 443–455. https://doi.org/10.1017/S1474746415000184.

Lougheed, Scott, and Charlotte Spring. "Conduits That Bite Back: Challenging the 'Win-Win' Solutions of Food Recalls and Redistribution." In *Routledge Handbook of Food Waste*, edited by Christian Reynolds, Tammara Soma, Charlotte Spring, and Jordon Lazell, 457–470. New York: Routledge, 2020.

Lucchini, Marco. "Banco Alimentare, Food Becomes Solidarity." Italian Food Bank Network, May 7, 2020. https://cdn3.bancoalimentare.it/sites/bancoalimentare.it/files/allegati/2020/05/il_sole_24_ore_supplemento_supplemento_4_20200506100000.pdf.

Madama, Ilaria. *The Fund for European Aid to the Most Deprived: A Contested and Contentious (but Successful) Reconciliation Pathway.* Working Paper 9. Milan: Department of Social and Political Sciences, University of Milan, 2016.

Maehr, Kate, and John Bouman. "Commentary: What If You Had to Feel Hunger Pangs?" *Chicago Tribune*, November 21, 2018. https://www.chicagotribune.com/opinion/commentary/ct-perspec-food-pantries-snap-food-stamps-public-charge-trump-food-assistance-1125-story.html.

Mahler, Daniel Gerszon, Nishant Yonzan, Christoph Lakner, R. Andres Castaneda Aguilar, and Haoyu Wu. "Updated Estimates of the Impact of COVID-19 on Global Poverty: Turning the Corner on the Pandemic in 2021?" *World Bank Blogs*, June 24, 2021. https://blogs.worldbank.org/opendata/updated-estimates-impact-covid-19-global-poverty-turning-corner-pandemic-2021.

Majumdar, Ashima, and Saundarjya Borbora. "Social Security System and the Informal Sector in India: A Review." *Economic and Political Weekly* 48, no. 42 (2013): 69–72.

Mashal, Mujib, Emily Schmall, and Russell Goldman. "Why Are Farmers Protesting in India?" *New York Times*, January 27, 2021. https://www.nytimes.com/2021/01/27/world/asia/india-farmer-protest.html.

Masih, Niha. "In India, as the Virus Abates, a Hunger Crisis Persists." *Washington Post*, December 6, 2021. https://www.washingtonpost.com/world/2021/12/06/india-hunger-coronavirus/.

May, Jon, Andrew Williams, Paul Cloke, and Liev Cherry. "Food Banks and the Production of Scarcity." *Transactions of the Institute of British Geographers* 45, no. 1 (2020): 208–222. https://doi.org/10.1111/tran.12340.

May, Jon, Andrew Williams, Paul Cloke, and Liev Cherry. "Welfare Convergence, Bureaucracy, and Moral Distancing at the Food Bank." *Antipode* 51, no. 4 (2019): 1251–1275. https://doi.org/10.1111/anti.12531.

McCain, Nicole. "Want Not, Waste Not, Crop Is Food." *News24*, July 5, 2018. https://www.news24.com/News24/want-not-waste-not-crop-is-food-20180704.

McIntosh, Caitlyn, and Emily Gallion. "COVID-19 Update: Continuing Our Relief Efforts in a Still-Uncertain Economy." Foodbank, May 2020. https://thefoodbankdayton.org/2020/05/.

Meibers, Bonnie. "Coronavirus: Food Insecurity Has Doubled Locally, across Ohio." *Dayton Daily News*, June 29, 2020. https://www.daytondailynews.com/news/local/coronavirus-food-insecurity-has-doubled-locally-across-ohio/cIXo5K5pzcIGbhKhF4lgmO/.

Meibers, Bonnie. "Coronavirus: Foodbanks Could Serve 40 Percent of Ohioans by Time Pandemic Ends." *Dayton Daily News*, April 10, 2020. https://www.daytondailynews.com/business/economy/coronavirus-foodbanks-could-serve-percent-ohioans-time-pandemic-ends/vwktGbiYlbUGuyaLGSepxN/.

Meibers, Bonnie. "Long Lines along Roadway to FoodBank." *Dayton Daily News*, March 26, 2020. https://www.daytondailynews.com/news/local/coronavirus-hundreds-line-foodbank-more-people-laid-off/KPVNuZuXio1usEGsYIJWbI/.

Ministry of Food Processing Industries, Government of India. "Wastage of Agricultural Produce." August 9, 2016. https://pib.gov.in/newsite/PrintRelease.aspx?relid=148566.

Miraftab, Faranak. "Neoliberalism and Casualization of Public Sector Services: The Case of Waste Collection Services in Cape Town, South Africa." *International Journal of Urban and Regional Research* 28, no. 4 (2004): 874–892. https://doi.org/10.1111/j.0309-1317.2004.00557.x.

Mishra, Khushbu, and Jeevant Rampal. "The COVID-19 Pandemic and Food Insecurity: A Viewpoint on India." *World Development* 135 (2020): 105068. https://doi.org/10.1016/j.worlddev.2020.105068.

Mogale, Thomas M. "Developmental Local Government and Decentralised Service Delivery in the Democratic South Africa." In *Governance in the New South Africa: The Challenges of Globalisation*, edited by Guy Mhone and Omano Edigheji, 1–15. Cape Town: University of Cape Town Press, 2003.

Mohan, Giles, and Kristian Stokke. "Participatory Development and Empowerment: The Dangers of Localism." *Third World Quarterly* 21, no. 2 (2000): 247–268. https://doi.org/10.1080/01436590050004346.

Mokone, Thabo. "Handouts of Food Parcels to Be Probed." *Sunday Times*, September 11, 2014. https://www.timeslive.co.za/news/south-africa/2014-09-11-handouts-of-food-parcels-to-be-probed/.

Molewa, Edna. "Remarks by the Minister of Social Development, Mrs. Edna Molewa on the Occasion of FoodBank South Africa Gala Dinner, Premier Hotel-Pretoria." Department of Social Development, South Africa, October 29, 2010. https://www.gov.za/remarks-minister-social-development-mrs-edna-molewa-occasion-foodbank-south-africa-gala-dinner.

Mook, Laurie, Alex Murdock, and Craig Gundersen. "Food Banking and Food Insecurity in High-Income Countries." *Voluntas: International Journal of Voluntary and Nonprofit Organizations* (2020): 1–8. https://doi.org/10.1007/s11266-020-00219-4.

Moragues-Faus, Ana, and Jane Battersby. "Urban Food Policies for a Sustainable and Just Future: Concepts and Tools for a Renewed Agenda." *Food Policy* 103 (2021): 102124. https://doi.org/10.1016/j.foodpol.2021.102124.

Moragues-Faus, Ana, and Kevin Morgan. "Reframing the Foodscape: The Emergent World of Urban Food Policy." *Environment and Planning A* 47, no. 7 (2015): 1558–1573. https://doi.org/10.1177/0308518X15595754.

Moses, Shany. "Israeli Food Prices 19 Percent Higher Than OECD Average." *Jerusalem Post*, April 3, 2018. https://www.jpost.com/israel-news/israeli-food-prices-19-percent-higher-than-oecd-average-547781.

Mourad, Marie. "Recycling, Recovering and Preventing 'Food Waste': Competing Solutions for Food Systems Sustainability in the United States and France." *Journal of Cleaner Production* 126 (2016): 461–477. https://doi.org/10.1016/j.jclepro.2016.03.084.

Mtintsilana, Asanda, Siphiwe Dlamini, Witness Mapanga, Ashleigh Craig, Justin Du Toi, Lisa J. Ware, and Shane A. Norris. "Social Vulnerability and Its Association with Food Insecurity in the South African Population: Findings from a National Survey." *Journal of Public Health Policy* 43 (2022): 575–592. https://doi.org/10.1057/s41271-022-00370-w.

Narayanan, Sudha. "Food Security in India: The Imperative and Its Challenges." *Asia and the Pacific Policy Studies* 2, no. 1 (2015): 197–209. https://doi.org/10.1002/app5.62.

National Council on Nonprofits. "Federal Law Protects Nonprofit Advocacy and Lobbying." 2022. https://www.councilofnonprofits.org/federal-law-protects-nonprofit-advocacy-lobbying.

Nickeas, Peter. "Greater Chicago Food Depository Launches Coronavirus Crisis Grant Program, Suspends Charges to Pantries for Food, Seeking Volunteers." *Chicago Tribune*, April 8, 2020. https://www.chicagotribune.com/news/ct-food-depository-20200408-rn77fqexdzctzjv4kbmfkqj22a-story.html.

Nordic Co-operation. "New Nordic Study: Food Banks Have a Big Unused Potential to Minimize Food Waste." February 6, 2015. https://www.norden.org/en/news/new-nordic-study-food-banks-have-big-unused-potential-minimize-food-waste.

O'Brien, Martin. *A Crisis of Waste? Understanding the Rubbish Society*. New York: Routledge, 2008.

Oelofse, Suzan, Aubrey Muswema, and Fhumulani Ramukhwatho. "Household Food Waste Disposal in South Africa: A Case Study of Johannesburg and Ekurhuleni." *South African Journal of Science* 114, no. 5–6 (2018): 1–8. http://dx.doi.org/10.17159/sajs.2018/20170284.

Oelofse, Suzan H. H., and Anton Nahman. "Estimating the Magnitude of Food

Waste Generated in South Africa." *Waste Management and Research* 31, no. 1 (2013): 80–86. https://doi.org/10.1177/0734242X12457117.

Ohio Association of Food Banks. "Annual Report 2021: Anything but Ordinary." 2021. https://ohiofoodbanks.org/site/assets/files/2677/sfy2021_annual_report.pdf.

Organisation for Economic Cooperation and Development. *OECD Economic Surveys: Israel*. September 2020. https://www.oecd.org/economy/surveys/Israel-2020-OECD-economic-survey-overview.pdf.

Organisation for Economic Cooperation and Development. *Society at a Glance: OECD Social Indicators*. 2019. https://www.oecd-ilibrary.org/sites/eo2ddoa9-en/index.html?itemId=/content/component/eo2ddoa9-en.

Organisation for Economic Cooperation and Development. "Supporting Livelihoods during the COVID-19 Crisis: Closing the Gaps in Safety Nets." May 20, 2020. https://www.oecd.org/coronavirus/policy-responses/supporting-livelihoods-during-the-covid-19-crisis-closing-the-gaps-in-safety-nets-17cbb92d/.

Parnell, Susan, and Jennifer Robinson. "Development and Urban Policy: Johannesburg's City Development Strategy." *Urban Studies* 43, no. 2 (2006): 337–355. https://doi.org/10.1080/00420980500406710.

Parnell, Susan, and Jennifer Robinson. "(Re)Theorizing Cities from the Global South: Looking Beyond Neoliberalism." *Urban Geography* 33, no. 4 (2012): 593–617. https://doi.org/10.2747/0272-3638.33.4.593.

Parr, Adrian. *Hijacking Sustainability*. Cambridge, MA: Massachusetts Institute of Technology Press, 2009.

Patel, Aaisha Dadi, and Gabriele Steinhauser. "South Africa's Economy Shrinks 51% as Lockdown Restrictions Hurt Businesses." *Wall Street Journal*, September 8, 2020. https://www.wsj.com/articles/south-africas-economy-shrinks-51-as-lockdown-restrictions-hurt-businesses-11599563965.

Peck, Jamie. *Workfare States*. New York: Guilford, 2001.

Peet, Richard. "Ideology, Discourse, and the Geography of Hegemony: From Socialist to Neoliberal Development in Postapartheid South Africa." *Antipode* 34, no. 1 (2002): 54–84. https://doi.org/10.1111/1467-8330.00226.

Perry, Parker. "Food Price Increases, More Need Hitting Local Foodbanks, Soup Kitchens." *Dayton Daily News*, May 17, 2022. https://www.daytondailynews.com/local/food-price-increases-more-need-hitting-local-foodbanks-soup-kitchens/AE6XWK5QKZBYBFKQ4E74I576RM/.

Pfeiffer, Sabine, Tobias Ritter, and Andreas Hirseland. "Hunger and Nutritional Poverty in Germany: Quantitative and Qualitative Empirical Insights." *Critical Public Health* 21, no. 4 (2011): 417–428. https://doi.org/10.1080/09581596.2011.619519.

Philanthropy Age. "Tackling Hunger in Egypt: The Egyptian Food Bank." Project Inspired, 2017. https://inspire.philanthropyage.org/media/pgrf5asj/project-inspired_efb_en.pdf.

Philip, Dana, Smadar Hod-Ovadia, and Aron M. Troen. 2017. "A Technical and Policy Case Study of Large-Scale Rescue and Redistribution of Perishable Foods by the 'Leket Israel' Food Bank." *Food and Nutrition Bulletin* 38, no. 2 (2017): 226–239. https://doi.org/10.1177/0379572117692440.

Pieterse, Edgar, Susan Parnell, Mark Swilling, and Mirjam van Donk. "Consolidating Developmental Local Government." In *Consolidating Developmental Local Government*, edited by Mirjam van Donk, Mark Swilling, Edgar Pieterse, and Susan Parnell, 1–23. Cape Town: University of Cape Town Press, 2008.

Pinotti, Ferruccio. "Coronavirus, Caritas Alarm: Boom of New Poor, 114% More People in Our Centers." *Corriere Della Sera*, April 24, 2020. https://www.corriere.it/cronache/20_aprile_24/coronavirus-allarme-caritas-boom-nuovi-poveri-nostri-centi-114percento-persone-piu-04865ac2-8627-11ea-9ac6-16666bda3d31.shtml#.

Poppendieck, Janet. "Food Assistance, Hunger, and the End of Welfare in the USA." In *First World Hunger Revisited*, 2nd ed., edited by Graham Riches and Tiina Silvasti, 176–190. New York: Palgrave Macmillan, 2014.

Poppendieck, Janet. *Sweet Charity*. New York: Viking, 1998.

Post, Connie. "Daytonian of the Week: Michelle Riley." *Dayton.com*, March 30, 2016. https://www.dayton.com/entertainment/personalities/daytonian-the-week-michelle-riley/iLMngxAEgzsOXWKW4wGoTM/.

Rai News. "Risk of Poverty, Instat: 16.4 Million Italians (27.3%) on the Edge of Social Exclusion." May 16, 2020. https://www.rainews.it/dl/rainews/articoli/rischio-poverta-esclusione-sociale-istat-italiani-805085c2-091e-443d-a84f-141e9e2d423e.html?refresh_ce.

Rakodi, Carole. "Introduction." In *The Urban Challenge in Africa*, edited by Carole Rakodi, 1–16. New York: United Nations, 1997.

Ramukhwatho, F. R., R. du Plessis, and S. Oelofse. "Household Food Wastage by Income Level: A Case Study of Five Areas in the City of Tshwane Metropolitan Municipality, Gauteng Province, South Africa." *Proceedings of the 23rd WasteCon Conference*, October 17–21, 2016, Emperors Palace, Johannesburg, South Africa, 57–64.

ReFED. *A Roadmap to Reduce U.S. Food Waste by 20 Percent*. 2016. https://www.refed.com/downloads/ReFED_Report_2016.pdf.

Reiber, Kurt. "Freestore Foodbank in Dire Need of More Support." *Cincinnati Enquirer*, April 17, 2020. https://www.cincinnati.com/story/opinion/2020/04/17/opinion-freestore-foodbank-dire-need-more-support/2987864001/.

Reiley, Laura. "Full Fields, Empty Fridges." *Washington Post*, April 23, 2020.

https://www.washingtonpost.com/business/2020/04/23/fixing-food-dumping-food-banks/.
Republic of South Africa. "National Environmental Management Waste Act." *Government Gazette* 525 (2009). https://www.gov.za/sites/default/files/gcis_document/201409/32000278.pdf.
Republic of South Africa. "National Waste Management Strategy." 2011. https://www.dffe.gov.za/sites/default/files/docs/nationalwaste_management_strategy.pdf.
Reuters. "Hungary Steps Up Anti-immigration Stance with Plans for NGO Tax." *Guardian*, June 19, 2018. https://www.theguardian.com/world/2018/jun/19/hungary-anti-immigration-plans-ngo-tax-orban-bill-criminalise-aid.
Reuters. "Italy Approves New Stimulus Package to Help COVID-Hit Business." October 27, 2020. https://www.reuters.com/article/health-coronavirus-italy-stimulus/italy-approves-new-stimulus-package-to-help-covid-hit-business-idUSR1N2E2016.
Riches, Graham. "Canada Must Eliminate Food Banks and Provide a Basic Income after COVID-19." *Conversation*, September 10, 2020. https://theconversation.com/canada-must-eliminate-food-banks-and-provide-a-basic-income-after-covid-19-144994.
Riches, Graham. *Food Bank Nations: Poverty, Corporate Charity and the Right to Food.* New York: Routledge, 2018.
Riches, Graham. "The Right to Food, Why US Ratification Matters." *Renewable Agriculture and Food Systems* 35, SI 4 (2020): 449–452. https://doi.org/10.1017/S1742170519000103.
Riches, Graham, and Tiina Silvasti. "Hunger in the Rich World: Food Aid and Right to Food Perspectives." In *First World Hunger Revisited*, 2nd ed., edited by Graham Riches and Tiina Silvasti, 1–14. New York: Palgrave Macmillan, 2014.
Riol, Katharine S. E. Cresswell. *The Right to Food Guidelines, Democracy and Citizen Participation: Country Case Studies.* London: Earthscan, 2016.
Rockett, Darcel. "In Chicago-Area Food Deserts, It's Getting Even Harder for Residents to Find Fresh, Healthy Groceries Because of the Coronavirus." *Chicago Tribune*, April 3, 2020. https://www.chicagotribune.com/coronavirus/ct-life-coronavirus-food-insecurity-tt-20200403-20200403-ytanbm6j75e2fhjitctqhgljay-story.html.
Rombach, Meike, Vera Bitsch, Eunkyung Kang, and Francesco Ricchieri. "Comparing German and Italian Food Banks: Actors' Knowledge on Food Insecurity and Their Perception of the Interaction with Food Bank Users." *British Food Journal* 120, no. 10 (2017): 2425–2438. https://doi.org/10.1108/BFJ-11-2017-0626.

Rovati, G. "The Paradox of Scarcity in Abundance: The Contribution of Food Banks against Poverty in Italy." In *Envisioning a Future without Food Waste and Food Poverty*, edited by Leire Escajedo San-Epifanio and Mertxe De Renobales Scheifler, 259–264. Wageningen, Netherlands: Wageningen Academic, 2015.

Roy, Ananya. *Poverty Capital*. New York: Routledge, 2010.

Russell, Helen. "How Did Denmark Become a Leader in the Food Waste Revolution?" *Guardian*, July 13, 2016. https://www.theguardian.com/environment/2016/jul/13/how-did-denmark-become-a-leader-in-the-food-waste-revolution.

Sage, Alexandria. "Italy's 'New Poor': The People Left Struggling to Eat in the Coronavirus Crisis." *Local*, 2020. https://www.thelocal.it/20200514/italys-new-poor-the-people-left-in-poverty-by-the-coronavirus-crisis.

Salamon, Lester M., and Helmut K. Anheier. "In Search of the Non-profit Sector. I: The Question of Definitions." *Voluntas: International Journal of Voluntary and Nonprofit Organizations* 3, no. 2 (1992): 125–151. https://doi.org/10.1007/BF01397770.

Sampson, Devon, Marcela Cely-Santos, Barbara Gemmill-Herren, Nicholas Babin, Annelie Bernhart, Rachel Bezner Kerr, Jennifer Blesh, Evan Bowness, Mackenzie Feldman, André Luis Gonçalves, Dana James, Tanya Kerssen, Susanna Klassen, Alexander Wezel, and Hannah Wittman. "Food Sovereignty and Rights-Based Approaches Strengthen Food Security and Nutrition across the Globe: A Systematic Review." *Frontiers in Sustainable Food Systems* (2021): 288. https://doi.org/10.3389/fsufs.2021.686492.

Sanders, Hosea. "Chicago Area Food Banks Continue to Serve Communities Record Numbers of People Seek Help Amid COVID-19 Pandemic." *ABC 7 News*, August 25, 2020. https://abc7chicago.com/chicago-food-bank-near-me-hungry-coronavirus/6388489/.

San-Epifanio, Leire Escajedo, and Mertxe De Renobales Scheifler, eds. *Envisioning a Future without Food Waste and Food Poverty: Societal Challenges*. Wageningen, Netherlands: Wageningen Academic, 2015.

Sathyamala, Christina. "Meat-Eating in India: Whose Food, Whose Politics, and Whose Rights?" *Policy Futures in Education* 17, no. 7 (2019): 878–891. https://doi.org/10.1177/1478210318780553.

Sayer, Andrew. "Problems of Explanation and the Aims of Social Science." In *Method in Social Science*, edited by Andrew Sayer, 232–257. New York: Routledge, 1992.

Schuetze, Christopher F. "German Food Bank Reopens Doors to New Foreign Applicants." *New York Times*, April 4, 2018. https://www.nytimes.com/2018/04/04/world/europe/germany-food-bank-foreigners.html.

Schweizer, Errol. "Why Kroger's Store Closures and Hazard Pay Reaction Are So Unsettling." *Forbes*, March 18, 2021. https://www.forbes.com/sites/errol schweizer/2021/03/18/krogers-hazard-pay-roulette/?sh=5bec75145348.

Seleoane, Mandla. "Resource Flows in Poor Communities: A Reflection on Four Case Studies." In *Giving and Solidarity*, edited by Adam Habib and Brij Maharaj, 121–158. Cape Town: Human Sciences Research, 2008.

Shadbolt, Peter. "India Launches Ambitious Food Aid Program to Feed Millions." CNN, July 4, 2013. https://www.cnn.com/2013/07/04/world/asia/india-food-program/index.html.

Shalal, Andrea. "German Food Bank Draws Fire over Move to Stop Accepting New Migrant Clients." Reuters, February 23, 2018. https://www.reuters.com/article/us-europe-migrants-germany-food-bank/german-food-bank-draws-fire-over-move-to-stop-accepting-new-migrant-clients-idUSKCN1G72D2.

Shannon, Jerry. "Food Deserts: Governing Obesity in the Neoliberal City." *Progress in Human Geography* 38, no. 2 (2014): 248–266. https://doi.org/10.1177/0309132513484378.

Shrivastava, Rahul. "India Grows More Food, Wastes More, While More Go Hungry." *India Today*, January 21, 2021. https://www.indiatoday.in/india/story/india-grows-more-food-wastes-more-while-more-go-hungry-1752107-2020-12-22.

Silvasti, Tiina, and Jouko Karjalainen. "Hunger in a Nordic Welfare State: Finland." In *First World Hunger Revisited*, 2nd ed., edited by Graham Riches and Tiina Silvasti, 72–86. New York: Palgrave Macmillan, 2014.

Simmet, Anja, Peter Tinnemann, and Nanette Stroebele-Benschop. "The German Food Bank System and Its Users—a Cross-Sectional Study." *International Journal of Environmental Research and Public Health* 15, no. 7 (2018): 1485–1502. https://doi.org/10.3390/ijerph15071485.

Slocum, Rachel. "Whiteness, Space, and Alternative Food Practice." *Geoforum* 38, no. 3 (2007): 520–533. https://doi.org/10.1016/j.geoforum.2006.10.006.

Sonnino, Roberta. "The New Geography of Food Security: Exploring the Potential of Urban Food Strategies." *Geographical Journal* 182, no. 2 (2016): 190–200. https://doi.org/10.1111/geoj.12129.

Spring, Charlotte, Tammara Soma, Jordon Lazell, and Christian Reynolds. "Food Waste: An Introduction to Contemporary Food Waste Studies." In *Routledge Handbook of Food Waste*, edited by Christian Reynolds, Tammara Soma, Charlotte Spring, and Jordon Lazell, 1–20. New York: Routledge, 2020.

Stancati, Margherita. "As the Coronavirus Lockdown Eases, Italy Confronts an Epidemic of Poverty." *Wall Street Journal*, May 21, 2020. https://www.wsj.com/articles/as-the-coronavirus-lockdown-eases-italy-confronts-an-epidemic-of-poverty-11590058801.

Stancu, Violeta, and Liisa Lähteenmäki. *Consumer Food Waste in Denmark*.

DCA Report No. 118, April 2018. Aarhus: Aarhus University. https://www.foedevarestyrelsen.dk/SiteCollectionDocuments/Foder-%20og%20foedeva resikkerhed/Madspild/Madspildsrapport.pdf.

Statista. "Value of COVID-19 Fiscal Stimulus Packages in G20 Countries as of May 2021, as a Share of GDP." 2021. https://www.statista.com/statistics/1107572/covid-19-value-g20-stimulus-packages-share-gdp/.

Statistics South Africa. *General Household Survey*. 2018. http://www.statssa.gov.za/publications/P0318/P03182018.pdf.

Statistics South Africa. *Towards Measuring the Extent of Food Security in South Africa*. 2019. http://www.statssa.gov.za/publications/03-00-14/03-00-142017.pdf.

Stop Wasting Food. "About Stop Wasting Food." 2018. https://stopwastingfood movement.org/.

Stuart, Tristram. *Waste: Uncovering the Global Food Scandal*. New York: Norton, 2009.

Summerton, Siân Alice. "Implications of the COVID-19 Pandemic for Food Security and Social Protection in India." *Indian Journal of Human Development* 14, no. 2 (2020). https://doi.org/10.1177/0973703020944585.

Surkes, Sue. "National Food Bank Faces Rising Demand for Meals, Plummeting Food Sources." *Times of Israel*, August 26, 2020. https://www.timesofisrael.com/national-food-bank-faces-rising-demand-for-meals-plummeting-food-sources/.

Swinnen, Johan, and John McDermott. "COVID 19: Assessing Impacts and Policy Responses for Food and Nutrition Security." In *COVID-19 and Global Food Security*, edited by Johan Swinnen and John McDermott, 8–14. Washington, DC: International Food Policy Research Institute, 2020.

Tarasuk, Valerie, and Joan M. Eakin. "Charitable Food Assistance as Symbolic Gesture: An Ethnographic Study of Food Banks in Ontario." *Social Science and Medicine* 56, no. 7 (2003): 1505–1515. https://doi.org/10.1016/s0277-9536(02)00152-1.

Tashakkori, Abbas, and Charles Teddlie. "The Past and Future of Mixed Methods Research: From Triangulation to Mixed Model Design." In *Handbook of Mixed Methods in Social and Behavioral Research*, edited by Abbas Tashakkori and Charles Teddlie, 671–701. Thousand Oaks, CA: Sage, 2003.

TechnoServe. "About Us." 2022. https://www.technoserve.org/about-us/.

TechnoServe. *KZN Technical Assistance and Market Access Project (Tamap): 1Qtr Report*. 2012.

Tefft, James, Marketa Jonasova, Fang Zhang, and Yixin Zhang. *Urban Food Systems Governance: Current Context and Future Opportunities*. Rome: Food and Agriculture Organization and World Bank, 2020. http://www.fao.org/3/cb1821en/cb1821en.pdf.

Teigiserova, Dominika Alexa, Lorie Hamelin, and Marianne Thomsen. "Towards

Transparent Valorization of Food Surplus, Waste and Loss: Clarifying Definitions, Food Waste Hierarchy, and Role in the Circular Economy." *Science of the Total Environment* 706 (2020): 136033. https://doi.org/10.1016/j.scitotenv.2019.136033.

Temple, Jeromey B., Sue Booth, and Christina M. Pollard. "Social Assistance Payments and Food Insecurity in Australia: Evidence from the Household Expenditure Survey." *International Journal of Environmental Research and Public Health* 16, no. 3 (2019): 455–469.

Thorsen, Karen-Inger, and Helle Christiansen. "The Food Bank and the Church Crusade: Charity Must Not Replace Welfare." *Altinget*, May 7, 2020. https://www.altinget.dk/social/artikel/foedevarebanken-og-kirkens-korshaer-velgoerenhed-maa-ikke-erstatte-velfaerd.

Times of Israel. "Despite Pandemic, Poverty Rate Dropped in 2020 Due to Government Aid—Report." December 29, 2021. https://www.timesofisrael.com/despite-pandemic-poverty-rate-dropped-in-2020-due-to-government-aid-report/.

Trauger, Amy, Priscilla Claeys, and Annette Aurélie Desmarais. "Can the Revolution Be Institutionalized?" In *Public Policies for Food Sovereignty: Social Movements and the State*, edited by Annette Aurélie Desmarais, Priscilla Claeys, and Amy Trauger. London: Routledge, 2017.

Trotter, Greg. "Commentary: Limiting SNAP Benefits Would Make Food Insecurity Worse, Not Better." *Chicago Tribune*, March 8, 2019. https://www.chicagotribune.com/opinion/commentary/ct-perspec-snap-food-insecurity-trump-work-requirement-0311-20190308-story.html.

Trotter, Greg. "Looking Back at 40: How the Food Depository Grew from Grassroots." Greater Chicago Food Depository, May 7, 2019. https://www.chicagosfoodbank.org/blog/looking-back-at-40-how-the-food-depository-grew-from-grassroots/.

United Nations. "The Impact of COVID-19 on the Arab Region: An Opportunity to Build Back Better." July 2020. https://www.un.org/sites/un2.un.org/files/sg_policy_brief_covid-19_and_arab_states_english_version_july_2020.pdf.

United Nations. *Nutrition and Food Security*, 2022. https://india.un.org/en/171969-nutrition-and-food-security/.

United Nations. "Policy Brief: The Impact of COVID-19 on Food Security and Nutrition." June 2020. https://unsdg.un.org/sites/default/files/2020-06/SG-Policy-Brief-on-COVID-Impact-on-Food-Security.pdf.

United Nations. "68% of the World Population Projected to Live in Urban Areas by 2050, Says UN." 2018. https://esa.un.org/unpd/wup/Publications/Files/WUP2018-PressRelease.pdf.

United Nations. *Sustainable Development Goal 2: Zero Hunger.* 2020. https://unstats.un.org/sdgs/report/2020/goal-02/.

United Nations. *Sustainable Development Goal 12: Responsible Consumption and Production.* 2020. https://www.un.org/sustainabledevelopment/sustainable-consumption-production/.

United Nations. "Universal Declaration of Human Rights." 2022. https://www.un.org/en/about-us/universal-declaration-of-human-rights.

United Nations Children's Fund. "Food Crisis Likely to Worsen in the Middle East and North Africa as COVID-19 Continues." May 27, 2020. https://www.unicef.org/mena/press-releases/food-crisis-likely-worsen-middle-east-and-north-africa-covid-19-continues.

United Nations Environment Programme. *UNEP Food Waste Index Report 2021.* March 4, 2021. https://www.unep.org/resources/report/unep-food-waste-index-report-2021.

U.S. Department of Agriculture. "FNS Nutrition Programs." 2022. https://www.fns.usda.gov/programs.

U.S. Department of Agriculture. "USDA Announces Coronavirus Food Assistance Program." April 17, 2020. https://www.usda.gov/media/press-releases/2020/04/17/usda-announces-coronavirus-food-assistance-program.

van Marrewijk, Marcel. "Concepts and Definitions of CSR and Corporate Sustainability: Between Agency and Communion." *Journal of Business Ethics* 44, no. 2–3 (2003): 95–105. https://doi.org/10.1023/A:1023331212247.

Villa, Stefania. "Coronavirus and Nutrition: Less Waste, More Cooking and Attention to Prices." *Altroconsumo*, April 23, 2020. https://www.altroconsumo.it/alimentazione/fare-la-spesa/news/coronavirus-cambiano-consumi-e-spesa#.

von Bormann, Tatjana. "Agri-food Systems: Facts and Futures. How South Africa Can Produce 50% More by 2050." World Wildlife Fund, 2019. https://www.wwf.org.za/our_research/publications/?27341/agri-food-systems-facts-and-futures.

Wallen, Joe. "Hunger Plagues India—but There's No Shortage of Food." *Telegraph*, October 28, 2022. https://www.telegraph.co.uk/global-health/climate-and-people/hunger-plagues-india-no-shortage-food/.

Wan, Gracelynn. "America's Top 100 Charities." *Forbes*, December 13, 2022. http://www.forbes.com/top-charities/.

Warshawsky, Daniel N. "Appendix A–F for Food Waste, Food Insecurity, and the Globalization of Food Banks." Geography Faculty Publications, CORE Scholar, Wright State University, 2023. https://corescholar.libraries.wright.edu/uag/52.

Warshawsky, Daniel N. "Civil Society and Public-Private Partnership: Case

Study of the Agri-FoodBank in South Africa." *Social and Cultural Geography* 17, no. 3 (2016): 423–443. https://doi.org/10.1080/14649365.2015.1077266.

Warshawsky, Daniel N. "Civil Society and Urban Food Insecurity: Analyzing the Roles of Local Food Organizations in Johannesburg." *Urban Geography* 35, no. 1 (2014): 109–132. https://doi.org/10.1080/02723638.2013.860753.

Warshawsky, Daniel N. "The Devolution of Urban Food Waste Governance: Case Study of Food Rescue in Los Angeles." *Cities* 49 (2015): 26–34. https://doi.org/10.1016/j.cities.2015.06.006.

Warshawsky, Daniel N. "Food Insecurity and the COVID Pandemic: Uneven Impacts for Food Bank Systems in Europe." *Agriculture and Human Values* 40 (2023): 725–743. https://doi.org/10.1007/s10460-022-10387-2.

Warshawsky, Daniel N. "Food Waste and the Growth of Food Banks in the Global South." In *Handbook on Urban Food Security in the Global South*, edited by Jonathan Crush, Bruce Frayne, and Gareth Haysom, 328–340. Northampton, MA: Edward Elgar, 2020.

Warshawsky, Daniel N. "Food Waste, Sustainability, and the Corporate Sector: Case Study of a U.S. Food Company." *Geographical Journal* 182, no. 4 (2016): 384–394. https://doi.org/10.1111/geoj.12156.

Warshawsky, Daniel N. "FoodBank Johannesburg, State, and Civil Society Organisations in Post-apartheid Johannesburg." *Journal of Southern African Studies* 37, no. 4 (2011): 809–829. https://doi.org/10.1080/03057070.2011.617947.

Warshawsky, Daniel N. "New Power Relations Served Here: The Growth of Food Banking in Chicago." *Geoforum* 41, no. 5 (2010): 763–775. https://doi.org/10.1016/j.geoforum.2010.04.008.

Warshawsky, Daniel N. "The Potential for Mixed Methods: Results from the Field in Urban South Africa." *Professional Geographer* 66, no. 1 (2014): 160–168. https://doi.org/10.1080/00330124.2013.768141.

Warshawsky, Daniel N. "The State and Urban Food Insecurity in Post-apartheid Johannesburg." In *Reducing Urban Poverty*, edited by Lauren E. Herzer, 46–68. Washington, DC: Woodrow Wilson International Center for Scholars, 2011.

Warshawsky, Daniel N., and Tammara Soma. "The Formal and Informal Governance of Urban Food Waste in Cities: Case Studies in the United States and Indonesia." In *The Handbook of Urban Food Governance*, edited by Ana Moragues-Faus, Jill K. Clark, Jane Battersby, and Anna Davies, 260–277. London: Routledge, 2022.

Watt, Nicholas. "Government under Fire for Rejecting European Union Food Bank Funding." *Guardian*, December 17, 2013. https://www.theguardian.com/society/2013/dec/17/government-under-fire-eu-funding-food-banks.

Wetterich, Chris. "Freestore Foodbank CEO Kurt Reiber Looks to Offer 'Hope in a Hungry World.'" *Cincinnati Business Courier*, September 4, 2020. https://

www.bizjournals.com/cincinnati/news/2020/09/04/reiber-helps-freestore-foodbank-offer-hope-in-a-h.html.

Wharton, Rachel. "Meet the Gleaners, Combing Farm Fields to Feed the Newly Hungry." *New York Times*, July 6, 2020. https://www.nytimes.com/2020/07/06/dining/gleaners-farm-food-waste.html.

Wildow, Samantha. "Dayton Foodbank Gets Step Closer to $2M Funding for Expansion." *Dayton Daily News*, July 14, 2022. https://www.daytondailynews.com/community/dayton-foodbank-gets-step-closer-to-2m-funding-for-expansion/HTSI3XZEJZHU5LLQBDXZDUVNTA/.

Williams, Andrew, Paul Cloke, Jon May, and Mark Goodwin. "Contested Space: The Contradictory Political Dynamics of Food Banking in the UK." *Environment and Planning A: Economy and Space* 48, no. 11 (2016): 2291–2316. https://doi.org/10.1177/0308518X16658292.

Wiskerke, Johannes S. C. "Urban Food Systems." In *Cities and Agriculture*, edited by Henk de Zeeuw and Pay Drechsel, 1–25. London: Routledge, 2015.

Woertz, Eckart. "Whither the Self-Sufficiency Illusion? Food Security in Arab Gulf States and the Impact of COVID-19." *Food Security* 12, no. 4 (2020): 757–760.

Wolch, Jennifer R. *The Shadow State: Government and Voluntary Sector in Transition*. New York: Foundation Center, 1990.

Wolch, Jennifer R., and Geoffrey DeVerteuil. "New Landscapes of Urban Poverty Management." In *TimeSpace*, edited by Jon May and Nigel Thrift, 149–168. London: Routledge, 2001.

World Food Programme. *2020 Global Report on Food Crises*. 2020. https://docs.wfp.org/api/documents/WFP-0000114546/download/.

Worley, William. "COVID-19 Threatens Decades of Progress on Global Poverty, Report Says." *Devex*, April 9, 2020. https://www.devex.com/news/covid-19-threatens-decades-of-progress-on-global-poverty-report-says-96965.

Yaffe-Bellany, David, and Michael Corkery. "Dumped Milk, Smashed Eggs, Plowed Vegetables: Food Waste of the Pandemic." *New York Times*, April 11, 2020. https://www.nytimes.com/2020/04/11/business/coronavirus-destroying-food.html.

Young, Dennis R., Lester M. Salamon, and Mary C. Grinsfelder. "Commercialization, Social Ventures, and For-Profit Competition." In *The State of Nonprofit America*, 2nd ed., edited by Lester M. Salamon, 423–446. Washington, DC: Brookings Institution Press, 2012.

Ziegler, Jean, Christophe Golay, Claire Mahon, and Sally-Anne Way. *The Fight for the Right to Food: Lessons Learned*. London: Palgrave Macmillan, 2011.

Zurayk, Rami. "Use Your Loaf: Why Food Prices Were Crucial in the Arab Spring." *Guardian*, July 16, 2011. https://www.theguardian.com/lifeandstyle/2011/jul/17/bread-food-arab-spring.

INDEX

agribusiness. *See* food system; global food system
Agri-FoodBank. *See under* Food-Forward South Africa
America's Second Harvest. *See* Feeding America

Banco Alimentare. *See* Italian Food Bank Network
beneficiary organization. *See* emergency food system; food bank
Brussels, Belgium, 21

Chicago, Illinois, USA, 13, 34–38. *See also* Greater Chicago Food Depository
Cincinnati, Ohio, USA, 10, 39–46. *See also* Freestore Foodbank
civil society, 3, 7, 9, 12, 17, 23–24, 122; definition, 23; state relations, 23–25. *See also* nonprofit sector
climate change. *See under* sustainability
collective solidarity, 125. *See also* human right to food
community-based organization. *See* nonprofit sector
consumers. *See under* local food system
coronavirus, 5–7, 46, 63–64, 71, 77, 83, 89, 98, 106
corporations. *See* food system; sustainability

Danish Food Bank, 65–66, 72–78, 118–119, 124; coronavirus, 77–78; funding, 73; geography, 72–73; government relations, 72–74, 76–78, 118–119; history, 72; impact, 75; mission, 73; structure, 73. *See also* Denmark
Dayton, Ohio, USA, 28, 34, 46–52. *See also* Foodbank (in Dayton)
Denmark, 65–66, 72–78, 118–119, 124; coronavirus, 77–78; political economy, 65–66; social context, 65–66, 72; state–civil society relations, 65–66, 73–74; welfare state, 65–66, 72–74. *See also* Danish Food Bank
Dubai, United Arab Emirates, 53. *See also* Food Banking Regional Network

economic recession, 10, 36, 80, 83, 87, 112, 118; 1970s and 1980s recession, 10, 118; 2007–2009 recession, 36, 80, 83, 87, 112. *See also* coronavirus

Egypt, 59–60, 62–63. *See also* Food Banking Regional Network

El Shohdi, Moez, 60–61. *See also* Food Banking Regional Network

emergency food system, 1, 3, 9–11, 49–50; definition, 3, 9–10; history, 9–11, 49–50; institutions, 1, 3, 12; structure, 12

European Food Banks Federation, 14–15, 19–23, 79–80, 85–86, 88–89; coronavirus, 21–22; funding, 21; geography, 15, 19; government relations, 22–23; history, 20; impact, 19; mission, 20; structure, 19–20. *See also* Danish Food Bank; Federal Association of German Food Banks; Hungarian Food Bank Association; Italian Food Bank Network

European Union, 2, 20–21, 72, 79, 81–83; food bank relations, 21; Food Recovery Hierarchy, 2; food waste initiatives, 2, 20; funding for food banks, 81–83; political support for food banks, 20–21, 81–83

farmers. *See under* local food system
farmers markets. *See under* local food system

Federal Association of German Food Banks, 65–72, 118, 120; coronavirus, 70–72; funding, 67; geography, 66–67; government relations, 65–66, 69–72; history, 66; impact, 67; mission, 67; refugees, 69; structure, 67–68. *See also* Germany

Feeding America, 9–13, 41, 50; coronavirus, 13; funding, 11; geography, 10–11; Good Samaritan Food Donation Act of 1996, 10; government relations, 11–13; history, 9–10; impact, 11; mission, 11; structure, 11–12. *See also* United States

FødevareBanken. *See* Danish Food Bank

food accessibility. *See* food insecurity
food affordability. *See* food insecurity
food aid. *See* emergency food system; welfare state

Food and Agriculture Organization (FAO). *See* United Nations

food bank, 3–7, 9–29, 122–125; Africa, 18, 91–92, 99–116; Asia, 18, 53–64, 91–99; Australia, 16, 18, 93; Canada, 20, 26, 93; coronavirus, 5–7, 12, 21–22; definition, 3–4; Denmark, 65–66, 72–78, 118–120; Egypt, 59–60, 62–63; Europe, 19–23, 70–90; food donation, 13–14; Germany, 65–72, 118–120; government relations, 11–13, 23–25, 118–119, 125–126; history, 3–4, 9–10; Hungary, 79–80, 85–90, 119–120; impact, 4–5; India, 91–99, 119, 121, 124, 126–127; Israel, 53–59, 120–121, 124, 126–127; Italy, 79–85, 119–120; locations, 4, 15; Mexico, 13; mission, 3–4; North America, 31–52; South Africa, 91–92, 99–116; South America, 13; structure, 11–12; United Arab Emirates, 53–54, 59–64, 118, 120; United Kingdom, 74, 77; United States, 31–52. *See also* Danish Food Bank; Federal Association of German Food Banks; Feeding America; Food Banking Regional Network; FoodForward South Africa; Hungarian Food Bank Association; India Food-

Banking Network; Italian Food
Bank Network; Leket Israel
Food Bank South Africa. *See* Food-
Forward South Africa
Food Banking Regional Network,
53–54, 59–64; coronavirus, 63–64;
funding, 61; geography, 61; government relations, 53, 64, 118; history, 59–60; impact, 60; mission,
60; structure, 60. *See also* Egypt;
United Arab Emirates
food charity. *See under* nonprofit
sector
food cost. *See under* food insecurity
food distribution. *See* emergency food
system; food bank
food donation. *See* emergency food
system; food bank
food industry. *See* food system; global
food system
food insecurity, 1–3, 5–7, 16, 25–26, 33,
41–42, 50–51, 77, 91–92, 96–100, 112,
115, 126–127; accessibility, 1–3, 50,
62, 64, 71, 93, 99–100, 102, 119, 125;
affordability, 2–4, 26, 56–57, 98–99,
118; causes, 1–3, 11, 26–27; data, 5,
26–27, 29; definition, 1–3, 26–27;
food cost, 2–4, 26, 56–57, 98–99, 118;
geography, 1–3; impact, 1–3, 5, 16,
26–27; nutrition, 2–3, 12, 18, 20, 27,
55, 97, 120, 125; rural, 1, 18, 26, 92–93,
99–100, 102, 112–115, 121, 126–127;
urban, 1, 3, 5, 17–18, 24–26, 42, 92,
99, 112, 123. *See also* hunger
food justice. *See* food sovereignty;
global food system; human right
to food
food loss, 2, 5–6, 17–18, 26, 97; causes,
2, 26; data, 2, 5, 26; definition, 5, 26
food pantry. *See* emergency food
system

Food Recovery Hierarchy. *See under*
United States Environmental Protection Agency
food retail. *See* local food system
food sovereignty, 127–128; definition,
127–128; geography, 127; history,
127
food supply chain. *See* food system;
global food system; local food
system
food surplus, 5, 26, 86, 123; causes, 5,
26, 123; data, 5; definition, 5, 26
food system, 2–3, 6, 25–29, 33, 93–94,
123–124; definition, 6, 25–27; geography, 1; institutions, 1–3, 25–27, 29;
rural, 1, 5, 126–127; structure, 25–27;
urban, 1, 3, 5, 17–18, 24–26, 42, 51,
99–100. *See also* global food system;
local food system
food waste, 2–5, 16–20, 23, 25–28, 33,
41–42, 70, 74, 77, 82, 86, 101, 122–124;
causes, 2–3, 5, 26–28; data, 5; definition, 5, 26, 33; geography, 2–4, 18;
impact, 2–5, 18, 122–124
Foodbank (in Dayton), 46–52; coronavirus, 51–52; funding, 48; geography, 47; government relations,
50–51; history, 46; impact, 47; mission, 48; structure, 48. *See also*
Dayton, Ohio, USA; United
States
FoodForward South Africa, 91–92,
99–116; Agri-FoodBank, 112–116;
coronavirus, 105–106; FoodShare,
102, 115, 122; funding, 104–105; geography, 102; government relations,
103–104, 106–107, 109–110, 113–116,
119; history, 101–102; impact, 106;
mission, 102; Rural Mobile Depot,
102, 115; Second Harvest, 102, 115;
structure, 102–103

Freestore Foodbank, 39–46; coronavirus, 44–46; funding, 39; geography, 39; government relations, 44–45; history, 39; impact, 39, 41; mission, 39, 41, 46; structure, 39–40. *See also* Cincinnati, Ohio, USA; United States

Gauteng, South Africa, 99, 107, 115. *See also* FoodForward South Africa

Germany, 65–72, 118, 120; coronavirus, 70–72; political economy, 65–66, 70–71; social context, 65, 67, 69–70; state–civil society relations, 65, 70–71; welfare state, 65, 70–71, 118. *See also* Federal Association of German Food Banks

Gitler, Joseph, 54. *See also* Leket Israel

global food system, 2, 26–27, 123; financial speculation, 2; social inequality, 26, 28, 120, 129. *See also* food system; local food system

Global FoodBanking Network, 13–19, 54, 93, 102, 105; coronavirus, 6; the Food Bank Leadership Institute, 16; funding, 13, 15; geography, 4, 14–15, 18; *The Global Food Donation Policy Atlas*, 16; government relations, 16; history, 13; impact, 14; mission, 17–18; structure, 15; *Waste Not, Want Not: Towards Zero Hunger*, 17. *See also* Chicago, Illinois, USA

governance. *See under* neoliberalism

Greater Chicago Food Depository, 34–38; coronavirus, 38; funding, 36; geography, 34–25; government relations, 34, 36, 37; history, 34; impact, 34; mission, 37; structure, 34. *See also* Chicago, Illinois, USA; United States

grocery stores. *See under* local food system

human right to food, 125, 127–129; definition, 26, 127–128; history, 127–128; international law, 32, 58, 62, 69, 72, 80, 86, 92, 100, 115, 124, 125, 128. *See also* International Covenant on Economic, Social and Cultural Rights

Hungarian Food Bank Association, 85–90; coronavirus, 89; funding, 89; geography, 87; government relations, 87–90; history, 85–86; impact, 86–87; mission, 86; structure, 87

Hungary, 79–80, 85–90, 119; coronavirus, 89; political economy, 79–80, 87–89; social context, 79–80, 119; state–civil society relations, 79–80, 87–89, 119; welfare state, 79–80, 87–89, 119. *See also* Hungarian Food Bank Association

hunger, 1–2, 7, 41–42, 51, 91, 93, 96–99, 126, 128; causes, 1–2, 11, 26–27; data, 5, 26–27, 29; definition, 1–2, 26–27; geography, 1–2; impact, 1–2, 5, 16, 26–27; malnutrition, 2, 12, 18, 20, 27, 55, 91, 93, 96–99, 120, 125; rural, 1, 18, 26, 92–93, 99–100, 102, 112–115, 121, 126–127; urban, 1, 3, 5, 17–18, 24–26, 42, 92, 99, 112, 123. *See also* food insecurity

income. *See under* poverty

India, 91–99, 119, 121, 124, 126–127; coronavirus, 97–99; political economy, 97–98; social context, 91–92, 94, 97–98; state–civil society relations, 95–98; welfare state, 95–98. *See also* India FoodBanking Network

India FoodBanking Network, 91–99, 119, 121, 124, 126–127; coronavirus, 97–99; funding, 94–95; geography, 93; government relations, 79–80, 87–89, 119; history, 92–93; impact, 93; mission, 93; structure, 93. *See also* India
informal food vendors. *See under* local food system
International Covenant on Economic, Social and Cultural Rights, 32, 58, 62, 69, 72, 80, 86, 92, 100, 128
Israel, 53–59, 118–121, 124, 126–127; coronavirus, 56–59; political economy, 56–59, 118, 126; social context, 56–59; state–civil society relations, 56–59, 118, 126; welfare state, 56–59, 118, 126. *See also* Leket Israel
Italian Food Bank Network, 79–85; coronavirus, 83–85; funding, 81–82; geography, 81; government relations, 81–84; history, 80; impact, 81; mission, 81; structure, 81. *See also* Italy
Italy, 79–85, 119–120, 124; coronavirus, 83–85; political economy, 81, 82–83; social context, 79, 82–83; state–civil society relations, 79, 119–120, 124; welfare state, 79, 82–83, 85, 119–120, 124. *See also* Italian Food Bank Network

Johannesburg, South Africa, 99, 101, 107, 109–111. *See also* FoodForward South Africa

Kroger, 39–44, 46
KwaZulu-Natal, South Africa, 112–115. *See also* FoodForward South Africa

Leket Israel, 53–59; coronavirus, 56–59; funding, 56; geography, 55; government relations, 56–59; history, 54; impact, 56; mission, 54, 55, 57; structure, 55. *See also* Israel
local food system, 1–3, 5–6, 25–29, 33, 37–38, 93–94, 121–129; consumers, 2, 33, 42, 84; definition, 1, 6, 25–27; farmers, 1, 12, 27, 33, 48, 73, 96–97, 111, 113–114; farmers markets, 1, 17–18, 33, 42–44, 50–52, 67; geography, 1; grocery stores, 1, 10; informal food vendors, 1, 29, 62, 97–100, 113; institutions, 1–3, 25–27, 29; restaurants, 1, 6, 12, 33, 97; small shops, 1; structure, 25–27; supermarkets, 1, 12, 67, 76, 87; urban, 1, 3, 5, 17–18, 24–26, 42, 51, 99–100. *See also* food system; global food system

Maehr, Kate, 34, 37–38. *See also* Greater Chicago Food Depository
Magyar Élelmiszerbank Egyesület. *See* Hungarian Food Bank Association
minimum wage campaigns. *See* poverty

neoliberalism, 23–25, 74, 100–101, 118, 127; causes, 23; definition, 23–25; governance, 23, 100; history, 23; impact, 23–25
nongovernmental organization. *See* nonprofit sector
nonprofit sector, 3, 13, 23, 32, 43, 51, 82, 84, 92, 99; accountability, 24, 27, 125; advocacy, 11, 13, 27, 37, 50–51, 58, 76, 118, 123; civil society, 3, 7, 9, 12, 17, 23–24, 122; community-based organization, 107, 109, 111, 122;

nonprofit sector (*continued*)
definition, 10, 13, 23; food charity, 26–27, 29, 123; history, 23, 32; lobbying, 13; nongovernmental organization, 4, 10, 24, 86, 101; voluntary sector, 10, 23, 31
nutrition. *See under* food insecurity

Orbán, Viktor, 79. *See also* Hungary
Organisation for Economic Co-operation and Development, 32, 56, 64, 91, 128

Paris, France, 20–21. *See also* European Food Banks Federation
Phoenix, Arizona, USA, 9–10. *See also* Feeding America
Pitroda, Sam, 92. *See also* India FoodBanking Network
Poppendieck, Janet, 25–26, 43
poverty, 3–5, 7, 24–28, 53, 56–58, 61, 64, 69–70, 79, 81, 83, 86, 115, 126–127; causes, 3, 24, 26; deserving and underserving poor, 31, 88; income, 1, 3, 25–26; minimum wage campaigns, 13; regulation of poor, 27; rural, 1, 18, 26, 92–93, 99–100, 102, 112–115, 121, 126–127; stigma, 27, 124, 128; unemployment, 1, 3, 51, 56–57, 77, 79–80, 83, 98, 106, 119, 127; urban, 1, 3, 5, 17–18, 24–26, 42, 99–100, 112, 123

Reiber, Kurt, 39, 44. *See also* Freestore Foodbank
restaurants. *See under* local food system
Riches, Graham, 26, 28–29, 103, 128
Riley, Michelle, 47. *See also* Foodbank (in Dayton)

safety net. *See* welfare state
small shops. *See* local food system
social inequality. *See under* global food system
soup kitchen. *See* emergency food system
South Africa, 24, 91–92, 99–116; coronavirus, 105–106; political economy, 99–101; social context, 91–92, 99–101; state–civil society relations, 103–104, 106–107, 109–110, 113–116, 119; welfare state, 91–92, 103–104, 106–107, 109–110, 113–116, 119. *See also* FoodForward South Africa
St. Mary's Food Bank, 10. *See also* Feeding America
state, 10–13, 23–28, 31–33, 125–126; accountability, 125; austerity, 23, 79, 82; definition, 10, 23–28; Denmark, 65–66, 72–74; Germany, 65, 70–71, 118; Hungary, 79–80, 87–89, 119; India, 95–98; Israel, 56–59, 118, 126; Italy, 79, 82–83, 85, 119–120, 124; South Africa, 91–92, 103–104, 106–107, 109–110, 113–116, 119; United States, 10–13, 26, 31–33, 125–126. *See also* welfare state
supermarkets. *See under* local food system
sustainability, 3, 9, 17, 32–33, 42, 120; climate change, 4; corporate social investment, 27, 93; definition, 9, 17, 32–33; green philanthropy, 42; triple bottom line, 4, 9, 17. *See also* global food system; United Nations

Tafel Deutschland. *See* Federal Association of German Food Banks

unemployment. *See under* poverty
United Arab Emirates, 61–62, 64. *See also* FoodBanking Regional Network
United Nations, 2, 18, 128; Food and Agriculture Organization, 1, 5, 91; Sustainable Development Goals, 2, 18
United States, 10–13, 25–26, 31–33, 125–126; coronavirus, 13; political economy, 25–26; social context, 31–33; state–civil society relations, 10–13, 26, 31–33, 125–126; welfare state, 10–13, 26, 31–33, 125–126. *See also* Feeding America; United States Department of Agriculture; United States Environmental Protection Agency; United States presidential administrations
United States Department of Agriculture, 10, 48; Commodity Supplemental Program, 12–13; Emergency Food Assistance Program, 10, 12, 13, 48; Farm Bill, 12, 125; Supplemental Nutrition Assistance Program, 12, 125

United States Environmental Protection Agency, 2, 33; Food Recovery Hierarchy, 2, 33, 42
United States presidential administrations, 10, 13, 32, 34; Carter, 32; Clinton, 10; Obama, 34; Reagan, 10; Trump, 13

van Hengel, John, 9–10. *See also* Feeding America
voluntary sector. *See* nonprofit sector

welfare state, 10–13, 23–28, 31–33, 125–126; austerity, 23, 79, 82; definition, 10, 23–28; Denmark, 65–66, 72–74; Germany, 65, 70–71, 118; Hungary, 79–80, 87–89, 119; India, 95–98; Israel, 56–59, 118, 126; Italy, 79, 82–83, 85, 119–120, 124; restructuring, 10; South Africa, 91–92, 103–104, 106–107, 109–110, 113–116, 119; United States, 10–13, 26, 31–33, 125–126. *See also* state